# MODERN COMPARATIVE EDUCATION

# MODERN COMPARATIVE EDUCATION

*[Strictly According to the UGC Syllabus for B.Ed. Course]*

*By*

**Mohammad Abbas Khan**

**ANMOL PUBLICATIONS PVT. LTD.**

**NEW DELHI - 110 002 (INDIA)**

ANMOL PUBLICATIONS PVT. LTD.
*H.O.:* 4374/4B, Ansari Road, Darya Ganj,
New Delhi-110 002 (India)
Ph.: 23278000, 23261597
*B.O.:* No. 1015, Ist Main Road, BSK IIIrd Stage
IIIrd Phase, IIIrd Block
Bangalore - 560 085 (India)
Visit us at: www.anmolpublications.com

*Modern Comparative Education*



First Published, 2004
**Reprint, 2007**



PRINTED IN INDIA

Printed at Mehra Offset Press, Delhi.

# Contents

## Part–Three : Education in France



## Part–Four : Education in U.S.A.



## Part-Five : Education in Russia

## Part–Six : Education in India

# Preface

Education is a vast discipline and Teachers' Training is a vital part of it. The responsibilities of the educationists and educators are focused on the task of providing better training to the future teachers for their better learning and proper development. Needless to say that this responsibility can only be exercised, if the trainers are equipped with the required knowledge of the subject concerned. That's why it becomes essential for making adequate provisions for each course to the student-teachers or teacher trainees. The present series is designed for providing a solid workable base for all course-papers. It has been prepared strictly according to the syllabus of the B.Ed class, prescribed by the UGC for different universities.

No doubt, there are so many other books on the subject, available in the market, written by worthy authors. However, every writer has his or her own style and way of presentation. The present work also has its own features and characteristics.

In preparation of this series of texts, the editor had to refer to the works of other authors and information sources. The editor feels a deep sense of gratitude for incorporating their ideas in the text. Hopefully, this series would serve as a 'ready to refer' tool for all teachers, teacher-students and others.

**—Editor**

# PART–ONE

# BASIC ISSUES

# 1

# Introduction

In this space age the various countries of the world are interdependent on each other. The activities and movements of one country have their impact on another. Indeed the countries of the world were never so near to each other before. The war started in one corner of the world has its inevitable influence immediately on other ones, as if fire broken at one place is likely to engulf the whole surrounding area. Famine, earthquake, epidemics, drought and flood if found in one country, they have their impact on other neighbouring lands. Thus the entire world has become interwoven today. Similarly, we find that the educational systems or ideas of one country influence the education of other countries. Because of this feature, our attention is drawn towards the study of educational systems of various countries. This study reveals that there are certain factors of these educational systems which are common everywhere. Simultaneously, there are some such factors which appear to be quite different. In the study of contemporary or comparative educational systems we find these commonness and differences.

**Basic Issues**

Marco-Antoine Jullien de Paris started the study of comparative education in 1817 A.D. He has opined that the analysis of the commonness and differences found in the educational systems of various countries are very important. Antoine Jullien wanted to bring the discipline of education in the category of science. He did not like that the educational system of a particular country should be restricted to the narrow educational ideas of the rulers concerned. Therefore, he wanted to tabulate the basic elements of the educational system for drawing out some principles and conclusions. Jullien believed that certain principles and definite rules might be deduced from such a tabulated analysis. In this tabulated analysis, due care was not paid to the political, economic, religious and social conditions of the country concerned. But these have their inevitable impact on its education. Therefore, at that time it was not considered whether the social, political, economic and religious conditions of the country were comparable to the some of the country whose educational system had to be followed. In this phase of development of comparative education, the names of Victor Cousin of France, Horace Mann and Henry Berneg of U. S. A., Mathew Arnold of U. K., Sarminto of Argentina and Tolstoy of Russia may be especially mentioned. These persons and their followers believed that for the development of education of any country, the study of educational systems of other countries was necessary. Therefore, the study of comparative education was begun especially with a view to strengthen the educational system of one's own country.

The Second Phase of the Development of Comparative Education. In the first phase of the development of comparative education we have seen that such factors as social and economic etc. which influenced education of a land were not studied. At the same time, it was also not seen if the basic characteristics of the educational system of a country were followed by another country or not. Thus the particular factors and potentialities were not at all taken into consideration. But in the second phase of the study of comparative education all these factors were carefully studied. In other words, it was noted whether foreign educational system, if followed by another country, would be conductive to its circumstances or not. In this connection, the potentialities of a particular characteristic were also assessed. Thus the prevailing tendency of blind imitation was abandoned.

Sir Michael Sadler of U. K. is regarded as the father of the second phase of comparative education. He published an essay in 1907 in which he emphasised the point that education of a country is also related with its social environment. Thus according to Sadler the social environment of the country cannot be ignored in the study of its educational system. Some other leading educationists supported this contention of Sadler. Amongst these supporters the names of Issac Kandel and Robert Ulich of U. S. A., Friendrich Schneider of Germany and Joseph Lauwerys and Nicholas Hans of U. K. are worthy of mention. All of these persons have emphasised the point that the relationship between the social environment and the educational system of a country should be studied simulataneously.

The Third Phase of the Development of Comparative Education. This phase starts from 1950. Bereday, George, Z. F. has called this phase as 'the period of analysis'. Because of the progress of science special emphasis was laid on the process of analysis in the study of all subject... As a result, analytical study was also emphasised in the study of comparative education. In methods, before accepting the educational system of one country for another, the economic, political, social and religious characteristics of each country (that is, of the country whose educational system has to be accepted and of the country for which this system has to be adopted) have to be analytically studied in order to ascertain to what extent the educational system to be adopted is favourable or otherwise. Thus the related factors of education are particularly studied. It may be noted that in comparative education only commonness and differences are not studied, but the favourableness or unfavourableness of the same are also assessed in the context of social, political, economic, religious and cultural conditions of the country concerned. This discussion about the second and third phases of development of comparative education clarified that there is only a difference of form in the two phases.

In the third phase we try to reach a conclusion by systematising the various factors and characteristics of the educational system, whereas in the second phase this systematisation was not done.

The writings of Robert Ulich, Friendrich Schneider and Issac Kandel have contributed immensely to the development of the third phase of comparative education. These writers contend that a comparative study of educational systems of various countries will help us to understand the identicalness of the social, political, economic and religious problems of these countries and thus we shall come to know the common human aspirations. Thus the feeling of unity of the world will be strengthened.

**Aims and Objectives**

We have said earlier that the study of comparative education was begun by Marco-Antoine Jullien of France. According to Jullien, the purpose of study of educational systems of various countries is to effect reforms in one's own national educational system. But now the scope of comparative education has been widened. Now we study educational systems of various countries for understanding their educational problems with a view to find out solutions of our own educational problems. In this process of understanding educational problems of others for finding out solutions of our own educational problems, we also study the philosophical background of the country concerned, because the educational system is always influenced by the philosophical points of view of the people concerned. When we try to find out solutions of our educational problems on the basis of educational problems of other countries then it means that there are some such bases of education which are universal. When we think of the philosophical background, then it implies that in comparative education we have to study the philosophical background in an un-prejudiced manner. We have already remarked above that the educational system of a country is always influenced by its social, political, economic and religious conditions.

Therefore, the purpose of comparative education is to study these conditions also, because without this study we shall not understand the factors that affect the educational system of a place. In fact, by understanding these problems, we shall be able to find out their solutions.

Another purpose of comparative education is to study those differences which make the educational system of one place different from that of another place. In the study of these differences the causes that generate them are also studied. Simultaneouly, the purpose of comparative education is also to study those social, political and economic situations which have created these differences.

The above account should not lead one to construe that the purpose of comparative education is only to study the inherent differences of various educational systems. In fact, under this purpose the implication is also to discover those general principles around which the development of educational system of a country goes on. Thus within the differences comparative education point out to the uniformity of general principles. Thus by drawing our attention to certain common principles and aims inherent in various educational systems, comparative education places our feeling of oneness of the world on a firmer ground.

Another purpose of comparative education is to understand those causes which make the educational system of one place progressive and that of another backward. The kind of rule in the country causes progressiveness or backwardness. In fact; the educational administration and control is strictly according to the prevailing rule in the country. For example, in Switzerland, U. S. A., Japan and Canada the administration is combined with local autonomy and decentralized control. As a result, in the educational administration of these countries, this feature is quite evident. Thus the administrative setup and political philosophy of country determine the nature of its educational administration and Control. Hence there appears to be a close relationship between the administrative setup and the existing educational system of a country. Needless to add that the purpose of comparative education is to study all these elements very minutely.

**The Evaluation**

We have already stated in the beginning of this chapter that in comparative education, an analytical approach is always present. In this context we have also to note that a synthesis is also emphasised in it's study. In the synthetic approach it is seen to what extent the social structure, political philosophy and educational philosophy have influenced the educational system of a country. In comparative education we keep in view the totality of all the situations and factors involved. Now both the formal and informal agencies of education working in a land are studied. In other words, in comparative education, now sociological bases are emphasised. In other words, social process, social control, social organisation and social change of a country are carefully studied in comparative education, because it is believed that its educational system cannot be understood without understanding these phenomena. Evidently, the scope of comparative education has become quite comprehensive and inclusive now.

The foregoing account leads us to conclude that in comparative education we try to study the national systems of education. By understanding these we come to know about various social systems. It has been truly remarked that 'education is the mirror of the society'. In the study of national systems of education, we have to study the commonnesses and differences found in the educational systems of other lands, because a country is influenced by the social phenomena going on in the neighbouring countries. The educational system of one country influences education in another. Thus, in comparative education we have to employ both national and international outlook.

The study of comparative education acquaints one with similarities and differences. The Beginning of Comparative Education begun by Antoine Jullien of France. He emphasised the analytical approach in the study of similar and dissimilar elements. During the twentieth century foreign travellers presented their accounts of various systems of education. They pointed to the role of education in social and economic prosperity.

***Development of Comparative Education.*** The First Phase-The ideas of Antoine Jullien. The characteristics of educational system of a country may be adopted by another country. At first a tendency of blind imitation. The study of comparative education with a view to study one's own educational system.

The Second Phase-Study of the social, political and economic conditions of the country whose characteristics of educational system have to be adopted. No blind imitation.

The Third Phase-The period of analysis. Favourableness or unfavourableness of a particular element to be determined on the basis of analysis of economic, social, political and religious conditions of the country concerned. Knowledge of common human aspirations. The feeling of oneness of the world strengthened.

***Meaning and Purpose.*** To effect reforms in one's own system of education by the study of systems of foreign lands. Knowledge of educational problems and their solutions. Philosophical, social, economic, political and religious backgrounds have to be studied. The study of differences and their causative factors. The study of those common principles on the basis of which the educational system of a land grows. Oneness of common principles. The study of causes of progressiveness and backwardness of education of a country. In the context of totality of all elements the study of educational system of a country. To study the formal and informal agencies of education, Sociological bases emphasised. The study of both national and international points of view.

# 2

# Development of Education

In the educational systems of various countries of the world we have herein discussed, certain general trends that may be easily perceived. In this section of the book we propose to hint very briefly at these trends for obvious reasons. It is needless to add that these general trends may be also accepted as some specific areas of educational research of great value in the field of Comparative Education. Quite indeed, a discussion of the techniques of research in these areas would have been very interesting and fruitful. But doing this will amount to a big diversion from our major theme of General Trends. Hence this is not possible. For these techniques a student must depend upon some independent book dealing with techniques of various types of researches.

In this chapter we propose to refer to the general trends in respect to the following areas alone:

1. Pre-primary Education,
2. Primary Education,

3. Secondary Education,
4. Teacher and Student,
5. Educational Administration and Discipline,
6. School Building and Finances,
7. Research,
8. Practical Literacy,
9. The Need of Change in the Very Concept of Education,
10. Democratisation of Education,
11. The Problem of Developing Efficiency in the Educational System,
12. The Problem of Education not being Consistent with the Realities of Life,
13. Women Education, and
14. University Education.

**The Significance**

Upto the 18th century it was thought that in educating young children, the parents were quite competent to deal with the related problems and difficulties. But as a result of industrial revolution when both the parents (*i.e.,* father and mother), had to be out at some job for earning their livelihood, it was considered necessary to do the needful for education of young ones while their parents were at some jobs. This idea was further strengthened when it became imperative for both the parents to accept some jobs in some factory because of ever-growing complexities of life demanding more and more money as a result of Industrial Revolution. In due course the Chief Executive of each factory was legally required to organise pre-primary education near his factory for the benefits of young children of mothers while they were at some job in the factory. Simultaneously, some private organizations, too opened nursery and infant schools for giving pre-primary education to young children of working mothers. Gradually, social demand became the basis of running pre-primary educational schools. In this field, Pestalozzi, Froebel and Maria Montessori did pioneering work. As a result, Kindergarten and nursery schools were opened in many parts of the world. In due course, sending of young children to some Kindergatten or nursery schools became a status symbols for many parents. Population explosion and compulsiveness of some working mothers led to the mushroom growth and expansion of pre-primary schools all over the world. Now in most of the countries of the world arrangements have been made to run training schools for preparing teachers for pre-primary schools, that is, Kindergarten and Nursery and Montessori schools. However, it will have to be admitted that now a days most of the pre-primary educational institutions are run on commercial basis. The tacit desires of parents to save themselves from the responsibility of teaching their own young ones the three Rs has led to the huge expansion of pre-primary schools like shops in several corners of each urban locality.

**Educational Levels**

Untill now in many countries it has not yet been possible to make primary education compulsory and free for children between 11 or 12 years of age. Here it is not necessary to draw the attention of readers to the problem and difficulties of primary education in the various countries, as the same has already been done in the various relevant chapters herein earlier. Nonetheless, at least this much once again be repeated that paucity of necessary funds, non-availability of trained teachers, poor and inadequate buildings, hilly areas and jungles through which the children have to go to schools in absence of proper roads and laid-out pathways, and rivers etc. are great hurdles in the expansion of primary education. The government of the day in each country has not been able to do the needful towards minimising the difficulties of primary school teachers and children.

The status of secondary education all over the world appears to be shaking in the sense that its very concept appears to be in transforming process. As a result, some practical difficulties in its relation to its reorganization of its various wings appears to be quite natural. Therefore a student of comparative education finds the scope of secondary education much wider than that of any other stage of education. Because of its particular social, financing cultural and historical backgrounds the nature of secondary education has become different from another educational stage in any country. But when we look at the universalness of human tendencies we happen to find some common trends in the secondary education of all the countries. Onwards we shall be discussing these common trends.

***Five Main Tendencies.*** The folliowing five main tendencies are found in secondary education all over the world:

(a) Unprecedented expansion of secondary education in each country.

(b) An effort to effect a co-ordination between primary and secondary education.

(c) Unification of vocational and cultural elements in the curriculum of secondary education.

(d) The need of a flexible curriculum.

(e) The problem of over-loaded curriculum.

Now we shall understand onwards the nature of these five main tendencies in secondary education.

***Unprecedented Expansion of Secondary Education.*** It is true that population explosion has also led to the unprecedented expansion of secondary education, but this explosion alone is not the only cause of expansion of secondary education. In fact, this expansion is also due to the expansion of primary education after the 2nd World War (1939-1945). After the 2nd World War new primary schools have been opened at several places in each country. This feature led to an expansion of secondary education in order to accommodate the graduates of the primary schools due to pressure of social demands projected by parents. Even then it has been very hard for parents to get their wards admitted to secondary schools, which are not so many as needed. This difficulty still exists.

***Towards a Comprehensive Co-ordination between Secondary and Primary Education.*** Huge expansion of secondary education created a tendency to co-ordinate it with primary education. Up to the 19th century primary education was regarded as complete in itself, because it was thought that after completing it, a person was able to take up some vocational occupation successfully. In a way, secondary education was also regarded as complete in itself, but at the same time it was also thought that after completing it, a person might think to proceed further for higher education. After completing his education in a primary school, an individual had to face hard difficulties in obtaining admission in some secondary school. From the 20th century onwards the idea gained ground that education should be considered a continuous process and it is wrong to demarcate it as separate units like primary and secondary. Today in each country the duration of compulsory education is being enlarged and it is thought that at least each individual should receive education upto the secondary stage and it is after this stage that an individual has to decide whether he will pursue his studies further or enter some vocation. In some well developed western countries education upto secondary stage has been made compulsory and free and in some even fooding and lodging has been made free for students at the secondary level of education along with full facilities for transport and stationaries. At some places, vocational courses have also been introduced in secondary schools and in some, number of subjects to be taught has been increased. Because of this unique feature at many places guidance services have been organized for guiding students to choose curricular courses in consonance with their likings and abilities.

***Integration of Cultural and Vocational Elements with Curriculum.*** Now in the curriculum of secondary education modern literature, modern science, commerce and some other technical subjects are also being introduced. These new subjects are being given a place in the curriculum because of modern industrialization. As a protest against the new development in education, some educationists have vehemently argued that upto the secondary stage an individual should be given general education with the sole purpose of enabling him to take his own decision for developing some technical (or vocational) skill.

***The Need of a Flexible Curriculum.*** In many countries the idea has gained ground that the curriculum of secondary education should be so flexible and comprehensive that a student may be able to choose subjects according to his own liking. Therefore, now the curriculum in some countries is being forged to suit the individual, national and local requirements. An attempt is also being made that the curriculum should be so designed as to promote physical, mental, emotional and moral development of a student. Now at the primary stage the emphasis is on 'learning by doing' and at the secondary level the emphasis has to be on 'learning by production'. It has been thought that this type of innovation in the curriculum will ultimately help in releasing out the problem of unemployment. Russia and many African countries are adjusting their curricular offerings in secondary schools for meeting the social aspirations of the rural people. The curriculum in Hungary has been so formulated as to prevent physical and mental fatique. In France, co-curricular activities have been so arranged as to encourage students to participate in sports, games and physical training. In order to fulfil this objective in Belgium some schools have been organised near coastal areas and hilly surroundings.

***The Problem of Over-loaded Curriculum.*** From the middle of the 20th century the problem of over-loaded curriculum has led to much mental exercise in many countries. The overloaded curriculum is troubling each and every student a great deal. This feature has resulted into assigning huge home-work to a student each day. The student carries a big load of books on his back or be has it hanging down, pressing down his shoulders. A child of 7 or 8 years of age has to carry to school every day a number of books and note-books; indeed, it is a pitiable sight to look at children going to school with such a big load which they cannot easily carry without being bent down making their whole structure defective. This position persists upto class 12 in many countries except in U. S. A. where in the curriculum has been diversified into different groups. As a result, in U.S. A. the students have been made free to choose subjects according to their own specific interests. Since they have not to carry big loads of book on their backs. Quite opposite to this situation in many other countries the conviction of people still persists that the children must be taught some intellectual subjects. This feature bring great pressure on children in schools. Happily, now parents also have started feeling the bad impact of over-loaded curriculum resulting into compelling students to carry big load of reading materials to school every day. Consequently, leaders in the field of education have also advocate for introducing some suitable changes in the curriculum and teaching technique in order to minimize the load of books on students.

The problem of over-loaded curriculum is almost of identical nature in all the countries of the world. In some countries children are required to study a number of subjects, thus making the curriculum over-loaded. In some countries the compulsiveness of studying one extra foreign language makes the curriculum over-loaded. This feature is found in India and in some other lands of Asia and Africa. In some lands along with the study of mother-tongue the children are required to study a number of regional languages. This position prevails in India and in some other countries wherein the people emphasize the study of different mother-tongues along with other common subjects. Thus making the curriculum over-loaded.

In order the curtail the size of the over-loaded curriculum, some educationists have advised to give some place in the curriculum to objective portions of knowledge. During the 2nd

World War period (1939- 1945), in the schools of some European countries some basic elements alone were included in the curriculum of science and mathematics. This procedure proved to be a great success in the sense that the students could grasp the basic elements of these subjects and could proceed further very swiftly.

The Audio-Visual Aids and new text-books have proved to be helpful in leading students to grasp the essentials of science and mathematics. The concept of core curriculum also emphasizes the basic elements of general subjects to be grouped together. In this context teaching of general sciences and social studies may be cited as an example. For examples, the basic elements of botany, zoology, geology, chemistry, physics and nature studies may be grouped together as one subject, and history, geography, civics, economics and sociology may be merged into one group as a single subject of school study. Towards the achievement of this end new text-book have also been produce at many places. During the fifth and sixth decades of the 20th century the above types of informations were successfully implemented. But these innovations were almost discarded after the 7th decade of the 20th century. As a result, separate subjects as before have again been put into operation leading to an unbearable over-loaded curriculum in several countries of the World. In order to lighten the pressure of over-loaded curriculum, it has been suggested that the system of external examination should be supplemented by internal evaluation by teachers. But this idea, too, has not succeeded in curtailing the size of the over-loaded curriculum, and the study of various subjects in secondary schools that has come into vogue again. This situation is existing in several countries of the world.

**Student and Teacher**

In the entire educational process the teacher has to play a very important role. The student desires to obtain practical knowledge and skill in order to be successful in life. It falls upon the teacher to perform his sacred duties to fulfil all the legitimate demands of the student. In each country this expectation of the student and duty of the teacher have been recognised. Through the invention of some teaching machines and programmed learning techniques a sense of change has been felt in the field of teaching and teacher-education programmes in some countries. Short time refresher courses for the benefit of teachers-in-service have also been started in order to acquaint the teacher with the latest developments in educational technology. In under-developed countries refresher courses are more popular. Short term training programmes have also been started for preparing certain persons to teach children in remote rural areas where generally teachers do not like to go to teach because of non-availability of necessary living facilities that they want. The prospective teachers are guided in such a way that in the actual practice of teaching they regard children as the central point of attention, in other words the teachers are told that they are to guide children to acquire the necessary tools and skills of knowledge. This means that the attention of teachers should be more on guiding children and less on teaching some particular subjects. This basic thought-current is followed in each and every country.

**Organisational Setup**

Adequacy of educational administration and good discipline go all way to make any educational system well founded. In each developing country certain vested interests and inherent indiscipline in the concerned workers, teachers and students have vitiated the entire educational atmosphere so much so that the very foundation of education appears to be not shaking. As a result, the parents are being fleeced through shylock-like charge of heavy tuition fees and also through exploiting the employed teachers by keeping them extremely busy due to heavy teaching load and too many co-curricular activities which are being organised by managers and principals in order to obtain outside publicity. There are now very few government officers who are particularly appointed to look after the prevailing educational administration with a view to make to it what it should be. Red-tapism often comes in the way of some innovation to be introduced. This results into spoiling whole proposition before it is put into operation. Happily, now in each country, educational administration is being decentralized in order to make it more alert, efficient, vigilent, meaningful and really effective. The UNESCO has also tried to train some persons for efficiently, handling the problem of educational administration in some country. But so far, no success worth the name has been achieved in this respect. Almost in all the countries it is not realised that the co-operation of parents, teachers, students and all related with any area of educational endeavour is very necessary to make educational administration healthy and effective. If this objective is achieved the frictions of indiscipline disturbing the educational process will be gradually wiped off. This success will also achieve the, objective of relating education with realities of life situations. In Yugoslavia some attempts of this nature has been made with remarkable outcomes.

Now in many countries it is being realized that as long as indifferent mechanism exist there can not be efficient educational administration and good discipline. Therefore, now in place of inspection, the term supervision is being used, because the term inspection implies a sense of power, whereas supervision may stand for sympathy, co-operation, and advice with feeling of identical fraternity. In order to achieve this objective in some countries, training of supervisors has also been started.

In order to run a school a suitable building is one of its first requisites. But in many, developed and developing countries tents, open sky, tree shades, rented buildings of very old shattered houses are being used for running primary and secondary schools. The author was amazed to look at this pitiable condition of some schools even in U. S. A. which is supposed to be the richest and very well equipped country in the world. Needless to remark that no school can ever fulfil its obligations in such a terrible condition. Such a poor situation of schools exists even in Germany, France and U. K. as well. For a good school buildings money is necessary. But in matters relating to adequate financial assistance for education government of each country bluntly says, that there is no extra money to be given for educational purposes. In India and in many European, Arab, Asian and African countries schools are being held in shift system. When there is no adequate funds for buildings how can libraries and various types of laboratories and sports and games equipments be arrange? In order to understand and explain the necessity of adequate finance for education, now a new subject of study has been forged. This new subject is named as Economics of Education. Therefore, students of education in universities are now required to study this particular subject as well. In this connection leading educationists have argued that money spent on education should be considered as 'Investment'. This idea is bound to usher in a new era in the field of education.

**Research in Progress**

Almost in all the countries in the field of educational research, in place of traditional practice, now greater emphasis is placed on carrying applied and experimental research. So a tendency has creeped in for frowning at philosophical, historical and survey types of researches. Now in the field of educational research greater emphasis is on functional research which principally is aimed at bringing in reforms and modifications in educational structures and procedures, so now only institutional, problematic and reform oriented researches are being encouraged in various countries. This wave may be easily felt in the research in comaparative education.

**Common Education**

Each country wants to wipe off illiteracy from its boundary completely. But U. K., U. S. A., Germany, France and Russia along with some other countries have not yet succeeded in this enterprise to a remarkable degree. The real cause of this failure has been the short duration of the literacy drive and it is not being functional (or practical) in real life-situations. Therefore, educationists have advised that literacy drive should be related with the process of production. By doing this the adults will be able to pick up the required rudiments for experessing themselves more fluently. In this connection the specific vocations of the adults should be kept in view.

**Question of Attitude**

The above mentioned points in various connections had led to a change in the very concept of the meaning of the term 'Education'. The scientific and technological inventions have ushered in many changes in the existing social values. The upheaval in values has resulted into a change in the very concept of education and it appears that this change will always be in the process of transformation or modification in consonance with the specific change in social values.

During the 2nd World War (1939-1945) the so-called civilized nations practised such attrocities on human multitudes that the very humanity was put to shame. Even the shame itself was put to shame. So much so that no writer can pendown the same explicitly. In fact all the shameful activities during the 2nd World War period clearly indicated the failure of the entire educational systems of those countries whose soldiers could think of perpetuating barbarous activities. Evidently, their educational system made the concerned armies devoid of all human values which preachers of all religions have stood for since ages. Upto that time educational system was working in the light of material prosperities and the related intellectual excellencies. This situation has led to a change in the very conception of education with a view to bring in human virtues again into human life.

Those who look at education as an investment have a blurred vision and can think only of mundane affairs. They are practically blind to real human virtue which have sustained human civilization so far. This situation resulted into fulfilling only selfish ends. In fact, only that education is meaningful which also takes into account the development of moral and spiritual values along with striving for material prosperities. That educational system which cares for universal brotherhood, tolerance and peace to all can ensure lasting happiness to all. Therefore, in the ideals of education, the necessary modifications are necessary in this sacred direction.

Today almost all countries are striving towards obtaining scientific and technological excellencies. As a result, we find now that in our social structure which appears to be pathological in the sense that, that the past human virtue and delicate feelings are thrown to winds. Now we find that the very relationship, between parents and children, husband and wife, brother and brother, teacher and student the employee and employer, politicians and the public, the shopkeeper and the customer, home and school, government and the concerned people has been revolutionzed. Radio, T. V., Newspapers and magazines and books have also added fuel to the fire of ailing social structure. This kind of cancerious situations has called upon all the noble minded people to do the needful towards bringing in the necessary changes in the very conception of education in the interest of motivating the people towards imbibing the real social, moral and spiritual values of life. Unless the needed efforts are made in this direction, the ills as referred to above can never be removed.

**Popular Process**

Imperialist powers, naturally in order to protect their own interests, kept the general public under their domination deprived of eduction. For example, during the British rule in India for about 175 years the effects in the area of education never meant expansion of education in the interest of the general public. The major attention was only to produce some office clerks through education for helping the administrative routine work. The end of the 2nd World War in 1945 ushered in a new era in many part of the world and many countries in Asia, Africa and other continents were able to establish their own governments, which naturally began to strive for expanding education in their lands. It is true that during the last 57 years enough success has not been achieved, but the fact remains that a consciousness has grown everywhere to democratize education through expansion of mass education. Population explosion has further accelerated the speed of spreading education amongst all young, adults and old, as far as possible within the limits of their meagre financial resources. However, the consciousness has dearly come up to make education available to all, because education alone can help one to understand his right, and duties, so everywhere an attempt has been made to make education popular, meaningful and as cheap as possible. As a result, the number of students in schools, colleges and universities of all countries are ever-increasing. Thus an attempt has been made everywhere to democratize education.

## Enhancement of Capability

Earlier we have already remarked that education everywhere is becoming costlier and costlier day by day. Because of the rising number of students at each stage of education it is impossible to pay proper attention to the quality of education. One of the reasons of this situation may be lack of efficiency in the current educational system. In order to make education meaningful, we have to bring in efficiency in it. In this connection we will have to enlist the co-operation of all the related people in our endeavour.

## Practical Application

The purpose of education is to promote the whole development of an individual. We have drifted far away from this ideal because today education is not at all related to realities of life. The current education has never developed an individual properly nor has it fulfilled the expectations of the society. The gulf between society and education is getting wider and wider day by day. The individual today is not self-reliant. It is not being adequately benefited from education that he is receiving. There appears to be a wave of vocationalization of education. Many people believe that education should be such as to provide job to each educated person. They think that education should be production-oriented and not to make a job available to each individual. They further believe that if through education an individual is able to produce some useful thing, this will benefit him and the society also. Today many countries are planning their education keeping in view the above points. With the consent of its people Albania has introduced revolutionary changes in the curriculum and its educational administration. Rumania has enacted many laws in order to introduce many changes in its educational system. China, Spain, Brazil and Yugoslavia have made several surveys in order to make education suitable to their people. In India and France education is being related to social and economic life of the people.

Japan, Thialand and Turkey have organised such central units which will propose changes in order to improve the prevailing educational systems in their respective lands. In Sweden and Spain some such educational researches have been conducted on the basis of which educational reform will be introduced.

**Education for Girls**

These days women are steering hard towards equal participationship in social, political and financial aspect of life along with men. From the social point of view this is a happy sign. In the Indian parliament in 1997 the various affairs of life participation of women along with men has been supported quite vehemently. In this support 33 per cent share was alloted to women. In India, like other countries, boys and girls have been granted equal rights to receive education. But at some educational centre boys outnumber girls and in some even girls do the same. At some places number of girls is less and it may be due to economic and social barriers. However, it will have to be admitted that especially in India the position of girls is considered as inferior in domestic affairs and in marriage relationship. But now the women are awakened enough and they cannot be subdued as before. Due to some social causes the girls in India have to stop their educational career much earlier than boys. However, the status of women in technological and scientific and other spheres has been regarded as almost equal the same as in all the countries of the world. Now a woman may be as efficient in any field of activity as a man may be. But because of their special physical status, than they have to be behind men in some areas.

**Higher Education**

Universities in all the countries are facing great financial crisis. The prevailing indiscipline in University students and unsympathetic relationship between the University and government of the day does not speak well of university position. Each university everywhere is ailing with the problems of curriculum organization, students' indiscipline, acute financial condition, bad conditions of hostels, ill-equipped libraries and laboratories.

Importance of Pre-primary Education is ever increasing. Almost in all countries, nursery, Kindergarten and Montessori school are found. Sending their young ones in some such a school has become a status symbol with many parents.

***Primary Education***-In many countries inadequate provision. In India there are very few in rural areas.

***Seconadary Education***-The position is not good. Differences in people about its conception and structures. The five tendencies in secondary education are: (1) unprecedented expansion, (2) The wave of co-ordination between primary and secondary education, (3) Inclusion of elements of culture and vocation, (4) Inclusion of vocational subjects in the curriculum, (5) The need of a flexible curriculum, over-loaded curriculum, Core curriculum, Use of machines as educational devices.

***Teacher and Student-Training of In-service Teachers:*** Preparing teachers for rural areas.

***Educational Administration and Indiscipline***-Due to ineffective administration. Decentralization of administration, Supervision in place of inspection.

***Inadequate Research***-Emphasis on applied and experimental research.

***Functional Literacy***-The work in hand to be related with literacy.

***Change in the Very Conception*** of ***Education***-Due to changes in social values.

***Democratisation of Education***-To make education available to all.

***More Efficiency in Educational System***-Very necessary.

***Women Education***-Identical participation in various vocations of life along with men-folk.

***University Education***-Ailing with various problems.

## QUESTIONS

1. Discuss the nature of universal tendency towards the expansion of pre-primary education.
2. Throw light on the main tendencies in secondary education today.
3. In what way should the curriculum of secondary education be modified and why ?
4. Why has been there a change in the very conception of education ?
5. Discuss any three general trends in comparative education.

# 3

# Effective Elements

Now, we should understand those factors which influence the educational system of a country. There are always pre-existing some such factors, which mould the nature of education of a country. In a way, these factors are independent of social situations. Such factors are generally known as natural. Under this natural group, we may include geographical, racial, economic and linguistic factors. Below we shall understand these factors.

**Importance of the Subject**

The geographical position of a country is bound to influence its culture, civilization and education. Geographical situations of various countries are different. Therefore, their cultures, civilization, social structures and educational systems are also varying from other's. Similarly, there are inevitable differences between the cultures of cold and warm countries. Educational system is always influenced by the social structure of the place. In an agricultural country especial emphasis is naturally laid on agricultural education. The country which is rich in various types of minerals, iron, coal and other materials requiring establishment of industries has an educational system in which technical education is emphasised and the curriculum is loaded with industrial subjects. In cold countries long leave is given during winter and in warm countries long vacation is given during summer. Thus the educational structure is inevitably influenced by its geographical nature.

### Significance of Language

An individual since birth gets a certain language as a heritage, because he has to learn the language of his particular society. The culture and civilization of a place is closely associated with its language in many respects. It is true that the culture and civilization symbolise many other things as well, but the role of language in its growth cannot be ignored.

Language has a especial place in the educational system of a country. We know that country has a strong national character in which the mother tongue is the medium of instruction. Quite contrary to this a foreign language as the medium of instruction weakens the national character of the land. There are many other factors that influence the, development of national character, but the particular contribution of language in it cannot be denied. Those problems of education of a place that are related with cultural aspects can be understood on the basis of linguistic factors.

### Generational Impact

Each country is inhabitated by various races. These races influence its educational system. Of these races there might be some people who regard themselves superior to other races in their country and they try to have an upper hand in all administrative affairs. If they succeed in this attempt, they want to introduce a particular kind of educational system, which may help in the perpetuation of their so-called superiority. For example, in Africa, the French and British people established their colonies. They considered themselves superior to the native people who were dark in complexion. So the French and the British thought that they were destined to rule over them. Because of this feeling, for the French and British Colonies special types of educational systems were introduced. Evidently, in these educational systems, the racial factors determined the pattern of education. The example of India is also quite pertinent here. The English people established their empire in India and in order to strengthen it, they introduced a particular kind of educational system. They made English as the medium of instruction and propogated the idea that the British culture and civilization was superior to the Indian one. Accordingly, they introduced a curriculum and an educational system. As a result, decline began. Thus, it is quite evident that racial factor is of great importance in the development of an education system. Needless to remark that in the study of comparative education, the racial factor is of great importance.

**Financial Aspects**

There is a close relationship between the economic condition and education of a place. According to the economic condition, the aim of education and curriculum in a country are determined. The faith of the nation in a particular economic setup is natually promoted in the citizens. For example, in the former U. S. S. R. all the property and wealth were regarded as of the State. So there even from the primary stage the idea is developed in children that all the property belongs to the State and they have to protect it. The situation in U. S. A. and U. K. is entirely different. In these countries the claim of the individual over property is duly recognised, therefore, in the development of education due attention is paid in these countries on the right of the individual. That is why the public schools of these countries are actually not meant for the general people but for a selected few of a certain class. Thus the economic factor is quite effective and in the study of comparative education, it has to be particularly noted.

Under the natural category of factors we have mentioned above some such factors that also influence education. The philosophical, religious and moral background of place also influence education. In a way, these three factors may be considered as spiritual. Below we shall understand these factors.

Philosophy of life of a country influences its education. Philosophy influences life. So its effect on education is inevitable. We may quote the example of ancient Greece here. Socrates, Plato and Aristotle of Greece based its educational system on particular philosophy of life and advised that the whole administration of the country should be left in the hands of philosophers. We find that the educational system of the former U. S. S. R. was governed by the Marxist philosophy. In ancient India education was coloured with the Vedic philosophy of life. During the Buddhist days the educational system in Vihars and Maths was patterned on the Buddhist philosophy. On the Vedic philosophy as propounded by Swami Dayanand Saraswati are founded many such colleges and schools in Northern India which emphasise the incorporation of main elements of the ancient Gurukuls. Similarly, there are some educational institutions in India based on Aurobindo's philosophy of life. Today there are some people in India who emphasise the need of running education according to the Sarvodaya philosophical factor is quite important for education. So it should be given due importance in comparative education.

**Religious Aspects**

Religion occupies a special position in the life of an individual. We know that many have sacrificed their lives on the alter of religion. We find many such examples in European history. In the Sikhs of India we find such examples. In a religious country the majority of the population is conservative and it strictly adheres to its old traditions and ways of living. Therefore in the organisation of any educational system we have to pay due attention on the religious beliefs of the people. In an industrially developed country, the impact of science weakens the old traditions and superstitions.

Accordingly, a new social structure is developed there. Education has a main hand in this development. Contrary to this in an agricultural country, the people are generally more conservative and look at any change with suspicion and want to preserve their religious beliefs. Accordingly, an educational system is evolved. So it becomes necessary to honour and protect the basic religious beliefs of the people. Thus religous factor is quite effective and its importance cannot be overlooked in comparative education. It is very useful to note how educational systems of various places are influenced by religious belief.

**Moral Aspects**

Some countries emphasise religious ideals and some attach more importance to moral behaviours. In a democratic setup, the moral behaviour of an individual is considered very important, because moral behaviour is the very soul of a democratic system. Democracy can remain safe only when each citizen shows moral behaviour. In a country which has a democratic goverment, moral development of citizens is especially stressed in its aims of education. Educational systems of Japan, Switzerland and U. K. are good examples of this espectial stress. Thus moral factor is quite important for education and due importance has to be attached to its study in comparative education.

Now we shall understand below some such factors which are, in a way, results of development of science in modern times. The effect of these factors on education starts from the last phase of the medieval period and start of the modern era. Humanism, socialism, nationalism and democratic factors may be regarded as the main ones in this context.

**Human Aspects**

Towards the close of the medieval period of European history a spirit of humanism swept over the continent. This spirit wanted to free man from blind beliefs and superstitions and make his life more scientific in order that his personality might be fully developed. Consequently, undue religious pressure on man was regarded as harmful for his free development. Humanism keeps the human welfare above everything else. This tendency begins mainly from the start of Renaissance. It was because of this tendency that in due course the relationship between the Church and State became controversial and both of them separated themselves from each other. During the sixteenth and seventeenth centuries some educationists tried to incorporate such elements in their systems of education which clearly show the impact of humanistic trends. By emphasising that education should be based on senses, Comenius showed his humanistic tendencies. Humanistic factor influenced the French system of education during the seventeenth century and in due course education was separated there from the influence of Church and the state owned the responsibility or education. In Germany, new methods of education were evolved under the influence of humanism. In U. K. under its influence a new curriculum was developed. In various countries such educational institutions were established in which an attempt was made to impact knowledge of geography, mathematics and science in a manner which may be of practical utility in life. At this time an attempt was also made to effect a harmony between philosophy and science. In U. S. A. Thomson Jefferson and Thomson Paine supported the incorporation of humanistic outlook in the educational system of the country. From the third decade of the twentieth century John Dewey advocated the incorporation, of humanistic elements in education in a very strong manner.

Today the impact of humanism on education is quite apparent. Now the idea of human welfare is kept at the top in any scheme of education, now only that curriculum and method of teaching are considered appropriate which promote the full development of human personality. Thus, we find that the factor of humanism has influenced education almost everywhere. So the study of this factor cannot be over-emphasised in comparative education.

**Social Aspects**

Today the impact of socialism is quite visible on various aspects of our life. Seeds of socialism may be preceived in Platos ideas. Plato attached more importance to the state and relegated the individual in the background. According to Plato, the development of children and their education should be under the strict supervision of the state. In due course education of Greece was very much influenced by these ideas. Sir Thomas Moore of U. K. in his famous book *'Utopia'* advocated the socialististic principles on the basis of Platonic ideas. According to him it is the responsibility of state to spread universal education. Education should be such as 'to acquaint the individual with art, literature and the laws of the state and to enable him to perform his duties as an efficient citizen. More emphasis on manual labour and science should be adequately included in education'.

Rousseau also advocates the socialistic philosophy. He stands for universal education under the supervision of an ideal state. Coudorcet may also be mentioned in this context. Coudorcet places the idea of identical education for all citizens. Many educators of U. K. and France have supported the educational views of Rousseau and Coudorcet. In this context the names of Saint Simon (1760-1825), Robet Owen (1771-1858), Charles Fourier (1772-1837), Etienne Cabet (1786-1856) and Louis Blahc (1811-1882) are worthy of mention. The current form of socialism is generally found in the writings of Karl Marx (1818-83). Karl Marx made Hegel's materialism the basis of his thought process. According to Karl Marx the economic system (*i.e.*, feudalism, capitalism or socialism) builds up the social, political and spiritual process of a country. According to socialism the function of education is to develop the means of production for the welfare of the state. This socialistic approach to education was found in U. S. S. R., Poland, Rumania, East Germany, Yugoslavia and Hungary. Evidently, factor of socialism has influenced modern education in many countries immensely; so in comparative education we shall have to study its impact.

**Importance of Nation**

For developing unity in a country, the feeling of nationalism is developed through education. After 1947, in the independent

India, this spirit is quite evident. Many religions, castes and languages in India are prone to weaken the national solidarity. Similarly regionalism may also weaken the national unity. But in spite of all these unfavourable factors, an attempt is made in India to emphasise the social, cultural and political unity of the country in order to strengthen the feeling of nationalism. Consequently, in the aims of education and curriculum these points are stressed. But in education the national spirit may be appropriate only when it is combined with the feeling of internationalism. In absence of the feeling of internationalism, the citizens might be misled by blind patriotism and may ignore the inadequacies of their own nation and they may regard their country as the best in the world. This feeling will lead his country to decline as Hitler's Germany went down the stream during the Second World War due to over-emphasis on blind nationalism. It is a different thing that Germany has again come up in the category of advanced countries within two decades. Needless to remark that the factor of nationalism influences education immensely and it must be adequately studied in comparative education.

**Political Aspects**

Two main types may be mentioned regarding a democratic setup. In one type political setup is emphasised and in another social. In the first type come U. S. A., U. K., India, France and Japan etc. and in the other come the former U. S. S. R. and the other socialistic countries. The study of the educational systems of these two types of democracies will reveal how in each of them an attempt is made to develop the democratic spirit. Each country has setup its own educational structure in strict adherence of its own views and beliefs about democracy. Variations in these views and beliefs have created differences in their educational systems. In aims of education, organisation of schools and curriculum's the particular democratic belief is quite evident. In the study of comparative education this factor of democracy will have to be kept in view.

***Geographical Factor.*** The geography of a certain place differs from that of another. So the culture and modes of living also differ. Cultures and modes of living, influence education. Therefore geographical factor is quite effective.

***Linguistic Factor.*** Language has a special place in education. When mother tongue is the medium of education, a strong feeling of nationalism is developed. Educational problems related with cultural aspects may be understood on the basis of linguistic factor.

***Racial Factor.*** The races that consider themselves superior develop a type of educational system which promotes the rule of the so-called superior. For example, in Africa the French and the British people evolved a system of education for perpetuating their rule over the native Negroes. The educational system of India of the British rule is also an example of this type.

***Economic Factor.*** According to the economic condition the aim, curriculum and programme of education are determined. The belief regarding economic setup is promoted in the citizens through education. For example, in the former U. S. S. R. the faith in the socialistic economy was promoted in citizens through education. For this purpose education was regarded as the chief means.

***Philosophical Factor.*** The philosophy of life of the country influences education. For example, in the former U. S. S. R. the educational system was based on the philosophy of socialism. Many similar examples may be cited.

***Religious Factor.*** A special place of religion in life. In the organisation of the educational system the religious beliefs of the people will have to be honoured.

***Moral Factor.*** Moral aims of education especially emphasised in a democratic setup. Hence moral factor important.

***Factor of Humanism.*** Human welfare is above everything else. In education of all the countries in modern times human welfare is attached greatest importance. Hence factor of humanism is very important.

***Factor of Socialism.*** Many countries of the world today are leading socialistic pattern of life. Hence this philosophy of life has influenced their educational systems.

***Factor of Nationalism.*** The feeling of nationalism is developed through education. So the aims of education and curriculum are determined for promoting the spirit of nationalism.

***Factor of Democracy.*** Democratic views are widely spread in the world today. These views have influenced education in all countries.

## QUESTIONS

1. Describe the importance of any three factors of comparative education.
2. Explain the impact of geographical factor on education.
3. Explain the place of racial factor in education.
4. What do you understand by philosophical, religious and moral factors of education?
5. How has the factor of humanism influenced education?

# 4

# Different Approaches

We have briefly dealt with the nature, development, meaning and purpose of comparative education. Now we shall understand its methods of study. There is a close relationship between the development and methods of study of comparative education. This relationship will be clear from the following discussion. Descriptive, quantitative historical, sociological, analytical and synthetical methods are generally used for the study of comparative education.

## Descriptive Approach

Descriptive method was employed for comparative education during the nineteenth century, because then the chief purpose was to imitate the good points of the educational system of another country. For finding out the good points it was naturally necessary that the educational system of the country concerned should be well described. Under this prevailing method some educationists visited some foreign lands and presented descriptive accounts of their educational system. In this context the name of John Griscom of U. S. A. is worthy of mention. During 1818-19 John Griscom toured over some European countries and published a book entitled *'A Year In Europe'* which contained descriptions of the educational systems of Great Britain, Holland, Italy, Switzerland and France. An attempt was made to incorporate in the American system of education the salient features as highlighted in this unique production. In the same manner Victor Cousin of France published a report on the educational system of Russia in 1831. In addition to French, this report was published in English also. Many of the points listed in this book about the Russian education were followed by France and Great Britain for making their educational systems more adequate. Victor Cousin did not compare the Russian system with his French or any other system. Therefore his report could be understood either by understanding one's own system of education or of any other country. Evidently, during the nineteenth century only that person could fruitfully make the study of comparative education who knew his own national system thoroughly well. Needless to add that it is true even this day.

In the development of descriptive method Horace Mann (1796-1859) of U. S. A. and Matthew Arnold (1822-1888) of Great Britain have done praiseworthy work. Horce Mann during his six month travel in Europe studied the educational systems of Germany, Ireland, Great Britain, France and Holland and published his report in 1843. Horace Mann in his account described the chief characteristics of the educational systems of these countries and also indicated the features that might be adopted by others. Thus while using the descriptive method Horace Mann made an evaluation also of the basic features and highlighted their utility. As a result, after Horace Mann other writers of comparative education also described the basic features of the educational systems and pointed towards their utility.

Matthew Arnold made a study of the educational systems of France and Germany. He published his report on France in 1859 and on Germany in 1865. He described the basic features of the educational systems of these countries but also drew our attention to those elements which made one system different from that of another. Sir Michale Sadler and Paul Munroe followed Sir Arnold's method of study. Thus the study of comparative education become more well organised.

Michale Sadler emphasised the point that in the study of comparative education we might understand those factors which influenced the education of a place. Simultaneously, Michale Sadler also made the point that in the study of comparative education we may also understand those points which are indicative of its progress or decline. Further, he said that comparative education was helpful in the development of one's national system of education. By all these he stressed the point that the study of comparative education is useful.

Henry Bernard published 31 volumes of the American Journal of Education during the period 1856 and 1881. In these volumes he described the educational systems of the various states of U. S. A. and also of some other foreign countries. Through these efforts he placed before us standard facts pertaining to education. In the process of describing educational system of a certain place, he explained its historical background also.

The above account indicates that the descriptive method organised the study of comparative education. We have to keep in mind that the various methods of comparative education may appear to be different, but they are very closely related, because the theme of all of them is the same.

## Statistical Approach

In the foregoing pages we have already remarked that in comparative education we also try to find out the similarities inherent in the various systems of education. Therefore some persons are of the view that in comparative education we should employ statistical method, because through this we shall come to know about the progress and decline of education of a certain country. In this method various kinds of data regarding the educational system are collected. For example, the data regarding the number of students at a certain level, the number of successful students and those who failed, the number of teachers and other workers in the school, the money spent per year on various items-such as salary of teachers and expenditure on purchase of books and office and laboratory equipments and school buildings and furnitures are collected regarding some stage of education of a country. Then the same are compared with the corresponding data of another country. This procedure comes within the statistical method. This kind of statistical anlaysis may reveal the nature of progress or decline of education of the place concerned.

But the difficulty of the statistical method is to obtain reliable data. Generally due care is not taken in the collection of data. Another difficulty is that of different types of terms used in the educational systems of various countries. The dissimilarities in terms render the statistical analysis extremely difficult. As a result, the utility of the statistical method becomes doubtful. Another difficulty to be noted about the statistical method is that through this method we are not able to ascertain those special characteristics of educational systems which are resultants of the social, political, economic and religious conditions of the land concerned. This difficulty limits the utility of the statistical method.

**Historical Approach**

In the descriptive method we have seen that only current features of the educational system are studied and we do not study the causative factors responsible for these features. But in the historical method we also study the causative factors of modern educational problems. Thus through this method we come to understand those factors which have led to the present structure of education. Needless to add that this knowledge will help us to eliminate the undesirable features and to strengthen further the desirable ones. For example, let us suppose that the percentage of women literacy in a country is very poor. This poor percentage informs us about the present position. But for the improvement of this poor percentage, this information alone is not helpful. At the same time, we should also know the causes that have been responsible for this poor percentage. We shall also concentrate our attention on the education of those countries in which also the percentage of women education is similarly poor and we shall also try to understand the cause of the same. Thus through a comparative study we shall try to understand to what extent the causes of the poor percentage in the various countries are the same. Thus we may take up those steps which may raise the percentage of women education.

It will be wrong to think that in the historical method we concentrate our attention only on the past in order to understand the present well. In fact, in this process our aim is to build up the future also. In other words, through historical method we try to discover those features which may help us to build a stronger future position. In the historical method we study all those geographical, social, racial, political, religious, economic, linguistic and national factors which influence the national system of education of a country. Nicholas Hans, Schneider and Kandel have attached especial importance to this method.

The above discussion clarifies the utility of the historical method. But we should also be careful about its limitations. The greatest difficulty in this method is that the authenticity of the historical data on which this method is based may be doubtful, because in the collection of data the necessary precautions are not observed and many data are false. Therefore the conclusions based on doubtful data may not be very useful. So we should remember that the historical data regarding education of most of the countries are not authentic. More intensive investigations are necessary for making them reliable. This situation limits the utility of historical method.

Another difficulty in the historical method is that generally the historian is not impartial in his descriptions. The historian may conceal the undesirable and unfavourable points about his own country and may keep only the good points on the surface. In the same manner a foreign historian describes events with a prejudices anlge. In both the situations the factors are hidden. Therefore through the historical method we may err in reaching a right conclusion. Another difficulty of the historical method is that it over emphasises the past features more than any thing else. Consequently, through this method, a balanced study of comparative education is not possible.

## Sociological Approach

In the sociological method the educational problems are studied in a social context. This method is based on the belief that the educational system of a land is inevitably influenced by its social, cultural, economic, political and religious situations. In other words, we may say that the educational problem stands on its own, because it is inter-woven with the social, political and other relevant conditions of the place. Therefore, for understanding it we shall have to understand the structure and the problems of the society concerned. Thus an educational problem may be called a social problem. Evidently, there is an integral relationship between the various educational problems and the society concerned. This means that one is provocative to another. The sociological method does not emphasise only the causative factors of the past, but also clarifies the importance of the study of the responsible social and cultural aspects as the same have their impacts on the existing structure of education. In this context it is quite appropriate to remark that when the education of a certain place is not according to the prevailing social conditions and the aspirations of the people, then it becomes an impediment in progress. For example, we may say that during the British rule in India there was no harmony between the educational system and social aspirations of the people. Therefore in those days education was not helpful in the development of the country, because the purpose of the imperialists was just to produce such workers through the educational system who could be helpful in running the administrative machinery. So the national leaders conceived of a new pattern of national education and established new centres of education in the form of Vidyapeeths at various places, Jamia Milia at Delhi and Visva Bharati at Bolpur (near Calcutta) in order to produce youths with the required national character.

Here a limitation of the sociological method may be pointed out. It is contended by some educationists that this method ignores those things which are related with individual contributions. History is a testimony to the fact that in every country there are always some such persons who contributed to the development of new traditions in place of old ones. Therefore the sociological method must not ignore these individual contributions which are, in fact the part and parcel of the social situation.

**Analytical Approach**

Analytical method has been evolved because of the limitations of the sociological method. Above we have remarked many a time that there is an integral relationship between the education and the social, political and economic situations of a place. Because of this relationship the comparative study was considered necessary. No comparative study is possible without analysis, because it is through analysis that the various elements are separated for a comparative study. Analytical method may be successful only when the social and educational organisations are duly compared. For this comparison the following four things are necessary:

***Collection of Educational Material:*** For the success of the analytical method all the educational informations and materials are collected through the descriptive and statistical methods. Then their analysis may be possible.

***Explanation of the Social, Political, Economic and Historical Elements:*** The elements chosen for analysis are explained from the social, political, economic and historical points of view in order that the similarities and differences in the educational systems of various countries may be understood.

***Determination of the Basis:*** After analysing the similarities and differences the same are compared on certain bases (criteria). To determine these criteria of bases is the third aspect of the analytical method. Under these bases political philosophy of the land, its aims of education and control of education are explained. In the context of these bases we will perceive the similarities and dissimilarities between the systems of various countries. As an example, we may say that there are many dissimilarities in the educational system of U. S. A. and the former U. S. S. R. because of the differences in their political philosophies.

***Exposition and Conclusion:*** On the basis of the above three aspects we explain the collected materials. In this process of explanation we draw comparisons and try to reach some conclusion.

The above discussion clarifies that the analytical method of comparative education is very useful. But there appears to be a defect in this method that in the process of analysis the investigator misses the perspective of the whole. Just as the whole world is knit together in spite of different types of countries, similarly in spite of varying differences in the various systems of education in the world, there are some similarities. The idea of these similarities is likely to be ignored. Therefore in comparative education the method of synthesis has been evolved which we shall understand below.

## Synthetic Approach

In the study of comparative education "the idea of the unity of the world" is attached special importance. The synthetic method supports this point of view. In this method the problems of education are studied from the point of view of the world as a whole. This method has been advocated by Edmund King in his famous book entitled *'World Perspective in Education'*. The welfare of the entire world is implied in its outlook. In the synthetic method when we study the differences in the various educational systems, we perceive some universal principles because there is much similarity in the needs and aspirations of the entire humanity. The U. N. O. has contributed immensely in the development of the feeling of this similarity. The synthetic method has not yet been fully developed. It is still in its early stage. It is just possible that in future this method may be further developed.

***Descriptive Method.*** The aim of incorporating good points. Descriptions by foreign travellers. Attention on the utility of the characteristics. Attention on national characteristics. The explanation of the historical background.

***Statistical Method*** Quantitative or Statistical method to collect data about educational systems. Then to draw comparison between them. Difficulty in collecting authentic data. Difference in the term used in various countries. Hence statistical analysis difficult. Limited utility.

***Historical Method.*** The study of the causes of the current educational problems. The aim of building a future. Reliability of the historical data is doubtful, because due precaution is not observed in the collection of data. Hence the utility of historical method limited. A balanced study of comparative education not possible because of over emphasis on the past.

***Sociological Method.*** The study of educational problems in the social context. An educational problem is a social problem. The two are interrelated.

***The Analytical Method.*** Analysing various educational elements separately. To collect educational data. Explanation of social, political, economic and historical elements, to determine bases of comparison and to reach a conclusion. The idea of unity missing in this method.

***Synthetic Method.*** The whole world perspective. To perceive similarities in dissimilarities.

## QUESTIONS

1. Explain the descriptive method in the study of comparative education.

2. What are the merits and demerits of the historical method of comparative education?

3. Discuss the comparative value of analytical and synthetic methods of comparative education.

4. What is the sociological method of comparative education ?

# 5

# Perception of National Education

A close relationship between nationalism and national system of education is there. No system of education can be regarded national unless it is imbued with national elements adequately. In comparative education it is necessary to understand those elements which make a system national. Below we shall understand some such elements.

## Significance of Culture

A system of education is called national when through it an attempt is made to generate love in the people for the great cultural heritage that its great ancestors have left and an endeavour is also made to promote that heritage in their style of life. In the context of culture, three aims of education are emphasised-(1) to preserve the ancient culture (2) to acquaint the coming generations with one's own culture, and (3) to contribute to the development of one's own culture. Needless to remark that in any national system of education the ideal of promoting cultural consciousness must be made active.

## Fundamental Values

In every culture, there are certain values which are independent of time and place. In other words, these values are permanent and are not subject to change due to time and place. Some religious and cultural faiths may be mentioned in the group of these values. For example faith in the existence of God, love for truth, belief in non-violence and universal brotherhood and love for justice are inseparable elements of many cultures of the world. These values are continued in the same form since centuries. Besides these, in each culture there are some such elements which are always influenced by time and place. For example, we may cite certain elements of Indian culture which have always been influenced by forces of history. It is a matter of our living memory that after the Second World War (1939-45) there have been many perceptible changes in many values of our life. In fact, this is true for almost all the countries of the world. For example, in our country, the joint family is shaken, the previous respect for elders in behaviour of younger generation appears to be disappearing, the students now do not show that sense of respect for their teachers which the latter group enjoyed about 30 years ago. The teachers, too, are now more interested in getting their emoluments and facilities increased than in doing their teaching job well. The teacher who is now dutiful is ridiculed. The guardians too, do not show previous respect to teachers. Similarly, the relationship between the parents and their children, between sisters and brothers and between other members of the joint family system is under heavy strain. Now, we are on the way of leaving off many old traditions and have begun to adopt in their place more liberal attitudes. In this way time and place transform many of our values.

But it has to be noted that other great cultures of the world too, have certain values which have been before us eternally. We have already referred to these eternal values. But in India these values have been ignored in the educational systems developed by the foreign rulers in the medieval and modern periods of history. There are clear evidences of this neglect during the Muslim and British rules in the country. Documents available pertaining to the

British rule clearly indicate that the British rulers wanted to ignore the Indian culture and they aimed to colour the Indian youth in European culture and civilization for the relisation of this objective, they promoted a particular kind of educational system. Consequently, some educated youths began to lose love for their own Indian culture. This inevitably happens when education is evolved by foreign rulers on the basis of their own foreign culture. That is why, the system of education developed in India by foreign rulers led the people to forget the beauties of their own culture.

It is necessary to generate a love for one's own culture through the system of education, because it strengthens the spirit of nationalism. For making the country prosperous and strong it is necessary that the blood of nationalism is running through the veins of all the people of the land. Ofcourse this nationalism should not be blind. True nationalism is that which helps the citizens to recognise the inadequacies and adequacies of the nation and to strive hard to make up the inadequacies in order that the nation may become stronger and stronger day by day. In every country, there are people of various races, sects, religions and vested interests. Because of the lack of national spirit these people very often ignore the national interests. In a country the minority group is suspicious of the majority group and they regard their own interest above the national interest. In a certain sense this may be true of some people of the majority group also. Our Indian constitution guarantees protection of all religions, sects and class. But only this much is not enough for the protection of the culture of the land. In fact, it is necessary to create a love for Indian culture in every citizen no matter whatever religion he follows and no matter to whatever caste and group he belongs. The national system of education should meet this need, otherwise it cannot be regarded as national.

In the context of a cultural basis the Indian system of education, today appears to be defective and inadequate. In our existing system of education we do not find those things which may lead a Hindu to regard himself an Indian first and a Hindu afterwards, a Muslim to regard himself an Indian first and a

Muslim afterwards and a Christian to regard himself an Indian first and a Christian afterwards and likewise any citizen belonging to any faith or group. In fact, so far we have not succeeded in moulding our educational system in such a manner as to let every citizen feel proud of being an Indian, in the same manner as every Britisher is proud of being British. So far we have succeeded in letting the old system of education developed during the British rule continue as before. So far we have failed in giving an Indian cultural basis to our education. There is no doubt that we have now begun to think in this direction. It is just possible that some positive steps may be taken in future in this direction.

The history of education of such countries as France, Great Britain, U. S. A., the former U. S. S. R. and Japan indicates that the people of these countries have great faith in their traditions. Consequently, especial care is taken in the educational systems of these countries to protect these traditions. In fact, in many respects in the national system of education of these countries the basis of cultural consciousness is quite evident.

By introducing in the curriculum certain common religious beliefs, ideas and social and human values, an attempt may be made at the national level to let the citizen belonging to various religions and communities feel a sense of unity. Thus the educational system of the country will get a cultural basis. In the absence of this basis no system of education can be called national. It must be noted here that in order to generate cultural consciousness the sub-cultures must be well protected. The sub-cultures are just branches of the same general culture. So their protection makes their followers faithful to the general culture and they think that the various sub-cultures are just branches of the main culture. Education will be most helpful in realising this aim. When education will fulfil this objective, then our culture will be basis of education and this type of education will be called as national. This type of national education will be helpful in solving many of our national problems.

Only that system of education is national which strengthens the feeling of national unity in the country. This feeling is necessary, because in almost every country, there are people of different religions, sects, castes and communities. India and U.S.A. may be cited as examples in this context. In India there are people of various religions and communities speaking different languages. In U. S. A. there are people of different European origins and they have some different sub-cultures. In the former U.S.S. R. there were people speaking different languages. In this situation it is necessary that people feel the bond of one national unity forgetting their varying regional loyalties and affiliations. Education will be very helpful for this purpose. The curriculum should be so devised that the spirit of national unity is strengthened. The leaders of the country should be very careful about it. In every country there are some political parties with narrow and sectarian outlook. During the freedom struggle days in India, the political faction of the Muslim League became instrumental in getting the country partitioned in 1947 when the Britishers decided to grant independence. The British policy was also such as to obstruct the growth of a national feeling in the country. The papers and documents left by Lord Macaulay and other British politicians indicate that the British Government in India did not want to promote national feeling in Indians and they wanted to perpetuate their rule by making Indian European in views, thinking and mode of behaviour.

As a result, for long a lack of national feeling in the educational system of the country continued. After the achievement of independence in 1947 we have been trying to develop a national feeling in our countrymen. But still we are far behind our goal. The Education Commission of 1964-66 had been only a chain in our efforts to promote national feeling through education in our country.

In Great Britain, the Education Act of 1944 was passed for further strengthening a national feeling in the country. This was done because it was considered necessary to promote a feeling of unity between the three parts of the country-England, Wales and Scotland.

The history of U. S. A. is an eloquent testimony to the fact that there education was used as a means for promoting a national feeling. People of many European origins with their varying languages and loyalties settled down in U. S. A. during the sixteenth century and later. So in order to make the country strong these people had to be knit together in one national unity. W. T. Harris, Henry Bernard and Horace Mann, to mention a few of the American educationists, strove hard in promoting a national feeling in the country through education.

We know how Adolf Hittler used education to strengthen the feeling of national unity in Germany. The history of Japan indicates to what extent a nation may progress by the feeling of national unity. The defeated Japan in the Second World War sprang up in the category of advanced countries within two decades because of the feeling of national unity. In this process education has played a very important role.

Many countries of the South East Asia and Africa have become free after the Second World War. All these countries are trying hard in their respective lands to promote and strengthen a feeling of national unity. But, in each of these countries, there are some political factions which work as impediments in the achievement of this goal. Needless to say that in the educational systems of these countries those elements should be incorporated which may promote the feeling of national unity. Only then the feeling of nationalism will be safeguarded. Evidently, for protection of a nation the promotion of national feeling is very necessary. Education will serve as a main basis for the realisation of this goal.

**Financial Aspects**

In the national system of education of any country, the economic security of the land cannot be ignored. The educational system is always developed according to the economic condition. If the economic condition is not good, educational system remains inadequate and it does not meet the aspirations of the people. The history of poor countries is an eloquent testimony to this. Educational aims and the curriculum have to be organised in a particular manner in order to make the country prosperous. The educational systems of U. S. A. and the former U. S. S. R. testify this. After completing one's education in U. S. S. R. the individual generally knows which job he has to choose in view of his assets and limitations. After receiving education, a citizen of U. S. A. does not find himself so helpless as a person finds himself in India after completing his education. This is so because in their educational organisations U. S. A. and U. S. S. R. have paid especial attention to their needs and economic security. In India the educational system almost remains the same as the British rulers left it in 1947. As a result even after 38 years of independence in 1985, the students after obtaining their graduate or post-graduate are facing acute problem of unemployment. Most of the students in India join Universities and Degree Colleges in order to postpone their problem of employment for two or four years further.

In the development of an educational system we have to keep in mind the economic needs of the country. Education must contribute to economic growth. In India, it has not yet been possible to adjust education according to the economic needs. We are preparing engineers, technicians of various types, teachers and other kinds of skilled workers in thousands every year, but we are not able to provide jobs to them corresponding to their qualifications and preparations for life. Indeed, that educational system is defective which in place of solving the unemployment problem aggravates it. In fact, it is necessary, first of all to ascertain the type and number of workers we need for various areas of national reconstruction. Accordingly, we should organise our educational system. Only then our education will be helpful in making the nation prosperous. It is true that many other things are required for national prosperity. Nevertheless, the importance of education in this process can never be denied.

The national system of education should be such as to enable the various citizens to develop their capabilities to the maximum extent. Only then they may contribute to the national growth. This must not imply to jeopardise the freedom of the individual to mar his development. This implies that the educational system should not be such that a few capitalists and influential people are helped to concentrate wealth into their hands and the common man is exploited. We want such an educational system which may develop the individual and the nation both. For the realisation of this aim, we shall have to pay due attention to the economic potentialities of the nation in our educational reorganization.

**Discriminatory Attitude**

Due to class-distinctions many nations, though very prosperous, are not able to pay due attention to the welfare of the general people. For example, due to class-distinctions in U. S. A. in many areas of the land, the educational requirements of the poor people are not met properly. In U. K. as well, at the secondary stage of education, class-distinction is clearly perceptible.

**The Profile**

It has to be noted that a national system of education cannot be developed on the basis of national potentialities alone. In the absence of a good national character leadership and co-operation of the public will not be forthcoming. Due to this lack the national system of education will not succeed in achieving its goals. On the basis of a strong national character, even when economic facilities are wanting; good leadership and co-operation of the public may help us to achieve good progress in the field of education.

The above discussion clarified that there is a close relationship between national system of education and national prosperity. However, we have to remember that in modern times due to unprecedented development of science and teachnology huge amount, of wealth will be required for educational reconstruction. Poor countries, will, certainly, feel the inadequacy of the required wealth. In this context bigger nations of the world have to play a constructive helpful role. This role appears to be active in some sense in some poor countries through the UNESCO.

The political situation influences its national system of education. Political changes have their inevitable marks on the educational system. The history of education of the former U. S. S. R. is an eloquent testimony to this. In India after the achievement of independence, there have been many attempts to revolutionise the system of education although, we are still-far behind our goal. In fact, it is true of any country that the administrative setup influences the pattern of education.

**Public Pulse**

Feeling of the people is of special significance in the development of a national system of education. The rulers try to provide that kind of education which the public demands. In this attempt, there is a constant demand for the same through some kind of agitation.

**Elements of Change**

Changes in the political situation may be brought about through education, just as education is influenced by thy political setup. We know that Rousseau's educational ideas became instrumental in the French Revolution.

In the second decade of the twentieth century education was made an instrument in the former U. S. S. R. for fulfilling certain political ends. One of the chief aims of education there is to make each citizen loyal to communism. When through education an attempt is made to propogate a particular political faith, then the freedom, of the individual is lost. We have to be very careful about this phenomenon.

The democratic system pays adequate attention to the freedom and development of the individual. Opposite to this position, communism thinks that the state will think for the individual and whatever it does will always be for the welfare of the individual in all respects. So it does not give any freedom to the individual and wants that the individual should be ever ready to obey the State. These two different political setup have close relationship with education. In fact, any political system influences education. Therefore, in order to understand the national system of education, it is necessary to understand the political system of the country.

**Effective Elements**

Current educational views always influence an educational system. Upto some extent this influence is dependent on the social and economic situation also. If the country is ridden with old traditions and is economically backward, the current educational system will not influence much.

In countries where the administration is democratic or communistic an attempt is made to make education available to all individuals. In a dictatorship progressive views are generally not found in the educational organisation. In such a system education is meant for some special classes and the needs of other individuals are generally ignored.

**Language Factor**

Generally a number of languages are spoken in a country. But only one language is chosen as the national language. In some special case some other one may also be accepted as its associate. In a national system of education, the place of the national language cannot be ignored. In every country special importance is attached to the study of the national language. Education in science and technology is generally given through the medium of the national language. The government also tries that each citizen becomes able to express his feelings and ideas in the national language. No country can be powerful without having a national language of its own. Therefore, in the multi-lingual country U. S. A., English was accepted as the national language and Russian was given the status of the national language in U. S. S. R. In order to make the country stronger, Hindi has been declared as the national language in India. However, because of certain differences English has also been accepted as the associate language of Hindi for the , Central Government. Evidently the place of a national language is very important for strengthening the national feeling in a country. Therefore in a national system of education especial attention is paid on the study of the national language.

There is a close relationship between the national language and the culture of a country. In fact, the National language is regarded as the chief means for expressing the various aspects of culture. Therefore, for the development of cultural consciousness and national unity national language is especially used. Every self-respecting nation feels pride about its national language. Therefore in international gatherings the delegates feel proud in speaking in their own languages.

In a system of education the problem of language is given special importance. When the national language is the medium of instruction, the development of individual is facilitated. Opposite to this, when a foreign language is the medium of instruction, the development of the majority of citizens is satisfactory. Therefore, an attempt has to be always made that the medium of instruction is the national language. If in a certain area the majority demands another language as the medium of instruction, then this demand must be conceded. If the national language is, not the mother tongue of a certain group of people, then for those people their own mother tongue may be accepted as the medium of instruction. But the study of national language should always be encouraged at all the stages of education, in order that citizens not speaking the national language as their mother-tongue may also contribute to the growth of the country.

In a country where there are various regional languages, a difficult language problem has to be faced. This situation creates difficulty in the development of the national language, because then the people speaking other languages do not co-operate in its development. For solving this difficultly it has been suggested by some people that the national language and the various regional languages should have the single script. This suggestion, if implemented will encourage all the types of citizens to learn the national language and also the various regional languages. Thus the feeling of national unity will be strengthened and people will also feel encouraged to learn the national language.

We are still facing in India, today, the problem of a single script for various regional languages. Some people are of the view that the same script for the national and regional languages will strengthen the national unity. Some others opine that the scripts of the various regional languages should not be disturbed and they should be accepted as they are, but a judicious attempt should be made to persuade the people to accept only one language as the national language gradually and no haste should be made in this matter. No language should be imposed on any group of people. In fact, they may be intelligently led to accept a certain language as the national one, even when it is not their mother tongue. In this process, we shall have to be very democratic in mobilising the public opinion in favour of a certain language for the status of the national language.

It may be noted that only that language should be made the national language which may succeed in expressing the national feelings and ideas. It should be left on the people themselves to accept a certain language as the national one. Whatever language is made the national, we have to keep in mind that the problem of national language is always related with national unity. In fact, one cannot be thought of in absence of another. One is complementary to another. Therefore we shall have to pay especial attention to the study of national language, no matter whatever language is. The development of national language is indicative of the national growth.

**Global Behaviour**

Because of the ever-developing scientific investigations, the various countries of the world have become closely related with each other. An event at a certain place may affect other parts of the world. Inter dependence of various countries on each other has increased as never before. Howsoever prosperous a country is, it depends upon some other country for the fulfillment of some of its needs. Now we are knit together in some common feelings. Thanks to the modern means of communications, these feelings may spread throughout the whole world within seconds. Normally the more prosperous nation extends a helping hand to a less privileged one and the latter also expects that the stronger nation must help in its development. The existence of U. N. O. is indicative of this feeling. UNESCO and some other committees of U. N. O. are striving for helping the poorer countries in many areas through its various programmes. In the development of national system of education the importance of international co-operation has now increased. Now in the educational, systems of many countries there are mutual exchanges of teachers and students. For strengthening the national systems of education in various countires UNESCO is co-operating substantially. In the field of science and technology each developing country is expecting co-operation from some advanced country. So it has become necessary that the countries of the world co-operate in the development of national systems of education. For strengthening this feeling, now in each national system of education emphasis is laid on promoting international understanding. Towards this end students are taught some such subjects which may help them to understand the unity of the world and the necessity of international co-operation in all types of human endeavours. Evidently, in the national system of education international co-operation is of great importance.

**The Interaction**

There is a close relationship between the national system of education and national character. For example, the national character of U. S. A. is democratic. Therefore its national system of education is also democratic. The national character of U. S. S. R. is communistic, therefore its national system of education is coloured with communistic ideas and goals. If the national character of a country is imbued with class distinctions, then its national system of education too, will strive, to perpetuate the same distinction. In short, the philosophy of life of the country is always manifested in its national system of education. In fact, the relationship between national character and national system of education is so close that one influences the other. Therefore the national character may also be accepted as the basis of national system of education. In various contexts in this book, we shall see how the national character has influenced the national system of education of a certain country. In this connection, the examples of U. S. A., U. K., France, the former U. S. S. R. and Japan are worthy of note.

National elements and national system of education have close relationship.

***Cultural Consciousness.*** Culture developed by forefathers is promoted through education. The permanent and changeable aspects of culture. During the foreign rule period the permanent elements of culture were not given any place in the educational system. As a result, India began to forget its own culture. It is necessary to create love for one's own culture because it strengthens the national feeling. Blind nationalism is harmful. Development of nationalism is possible only through a national system of education. The current system of education in India is not based on its culture.

In the educational systems of U. S. A., U. K., Russia, France and Japan marks of their culture are clearly perceptible, cultural basis necessary. Sub-cultures may be developed through education.

***Consciousness of Unity.*** National system of education strengthens the feeling of national unity. Necessary to forget regional differences. Education is helpful in realising this goal. Reorganisation of the curriculum is necessary accordingly. U. K., U. S. A., Russia and Japan are good examples.

***Economic Capacity.*** Development of education according to economic condition. Education may be used as a chief means of fulfillment of economic needs. Prosperity of the nation is possible only through planned education. Capacities of citizens should be deve-loped. Class-distinctions should not be encouraged. In the absence of appropriate national character the required leadership and general co-operation will not available.

***Political Consciousness.*** Political situation influences education. Educational system is controlled through public opinion also. Through educational ideas changes are possible in the political setup.

***National Language.*** The study of national language is necessary for development of national feeling. So the national language has a especial place in the national system of education. National unity is strengthened when the national language is the medium of instruction. National unity and national language are interrelated.

***International Co-operation.*** Various countries of the world are interdependent. The prosperous nation helps the poor countries through mutual exchange of teachers and students and educational help to poor countries through UNESCO. Hence the place of international co-operation in the national system of education is very important.

***National Character.*** Philosophy of life of the people is manifested in the national system of education. Close relationship between national character and national system of education.

## QUESTIONS

1. Explain any two basic elements of national system of education.
2. What is the place of cultural consciousness in the national system of education?

3. How national unity and national system of education are inter-related?

4. Explain the importance of economic capacity in the development of national system of education.

5. Discuss the relationship between the political situation and system of education of a country. Give some examples.

6. Discuss the place of national language in a national system of education.

7. How is international co-operation necessary in the development of national system of education?

# PART–TWO

# EDUCATION IN GREAT BRITAIN

# 6

# Teacher Training

In the British educational sphere, the status of teachers rose with the gradual development of education there. About a century ago, teaching was considered as a private affair. It was not considered as a professional work like medical and legal practice. At that time the condition of teachers was quite different from the one that exists in the modern educational world. There were no norms for a teachers efficiency and he was not under any control.

With the development of education, the importance and necessity of teachers has been felt. The Royal Society of Teachers of England has made an important contribution in enhancing the status of teachers. This Society is a national voluntary organisation which has been trying to make the teaching profession dignified and to bring all the teachers on an equal level by emphasising the training of teachers and prescribing minimum qualifications for all categories of teachers.

Educational progress, establishing of various schools and educational reforms have been contributing a great deal in increasing the qualifications of teachers. The feeling in the guardians educating their children by qualified teachers has helped in standardising of their qualifications. Various government commissions have laid emphasis on improving educational standards and qualifications of teachers. Today, the demand for qualified and trained teachers in every British school has been made. Now the teachers do not require any professional licence. Only a systematic training is considered necessary.

In Great Britain before the enforcement of the Education Act of 1944, the teachers' training system was voluntary and independent. At that time teachers' training institutions were attached to the church or some religious organisation. The teacher got himself trained only for self-satisfaction or increasing his teaching efficiency. The churches or religious organisations had to bear the expenditure of teachers' training centres. Today, the management of these teachers' training institution is in the hands of L. E. A. which they have accepted voluntarily. The teachers' training system in Great Britain has developed gradually from the recent past. Now economic' stability has been established in the field of teaching training.

In Great Britain, teacher training is not necessary for teaching profession but the standard of teaching must grow up continuously. Generally, it is possible only when the teacher is trained in a planned way it is the duty of the education ministry of Britain to prescribe the minimum qualification for teachers. A National Advisory Council of Education has been formed to consider the problems of teachers' training, in order. It determine suitable course of training and to advice the Education Ministry in the matter. The Education Ministry pays attention on the following aspects:

1. To attend to the needs of the teachers training institutions regarding admissions and to prescribe training programme in order to maintain the desired training standard.

2. To increase training facilities according to the needs of schools and arrange their proper distribution.

In Great Britain, to maintain proper standard of education and to conduct teacher training programme is considered to he a national responsibility. The Institute of Education, London is a pioneer in the training of teachers. All teacher-training institutions are affiliated to it and it, examines all teacher training courses. Two types of training institutions an found here:

(1) Those educational institutions which are run by L. E. A. and all expenditure is borne by it.

(2) Those institution which are run by voluntary organisations and there expenditure is met from public funds.

The institutions of the first category get partial grant-in-aid from the Education Ministry and the rest of the expenditure has to he borne by the L. E. A. The second category institutions get half the expenditure from the Education Ministry and the remaining 50 per cent lis compensated by voluntary organisations. In meeting out the expenditure of the institutions the pupil-teachers are also expected to contribute their own share. Generally the education-Ministry gives grant-in-aid to the extent of 60 percent according to the percentage of pupil-teachers receiving training in the institution run by Local Education Authorities. To solve- the war-time unemployment 30,000 boys and girls were trained in short term courses. But that arrangement was not permanent.

The present aim of Great Britain is to provide for the traning of teachers, keeping in view there retirement of teachers in schools. The universities; too, help in the training of teachers through the Teachers Training Departments. In general, they train 2 to 3 thousand male and female teachers every year. An Area Training Organisation has been established for every university. The Area Training Organisation looks after the training work and provides the necessary advice in this regard. All the provisions offered by this Area Training Organisation are located as that of the Institute of Education. The Area Training Oragnisation includes the representatives of L. E. A., Training colleges and training schools.

There are about 300 training colleges and schools in Great Britain which train nearly 30 to 35 thousand teachers every year. Now a need is being felt for trained lady-teachers to meet the demand of infant and nursery schools. With the increase in training facilities, the importance of educational institutions and Area Training Organisation goes on increasing. The education ministry, too, is active to share its responsibility. It will be still better if the responsibility of providing training facilities is given to professional organisations instead of education ministry. It will be in the fitness of things if teachers' efficiency, training programme, standard of teaching and determination of divisions is done with the co-operation of Area Training Organisation. This organisation can successfully supervise the teacher training programmes in its area, conduct them and control the programmes of the entire area.

**Various Types of Teachers**

In Great Britain the following classes of teachers exist on the basis of the level of teaching and sphere of education: (1) Teachers of Primary Schools. (2) Teachers of Secondary Schools. (3) Specialist teachers and teachers of Art and Vocational institutions. (4) Teachers imparting Further Education.

***Teachers of Primary Schools***-The teachers of this stage are trained in training schools. For admission the age is 18 years and it is necessary to obtain the General Certificate of Education. Two years teacher training is given after general education. And then the teacher is considered fit and qualified to teach. Training is not considered necessary at this stage but mostly the teachers are trained.

***Secondary School Teachers***-Training is not compulsory even at this stage, but most of the teachers are trained. These teachers are called trained-graduates. They are so trained that they can work in any secondary school or university after their training. Now training is considered necessary for the teacher this stage. The duration of training is one year. The training is imparted by Teacher Training Departments of universities.

***Teachers of Special Subjects, Art and Vocational Schools-*** Teachers in subjects, like art, music (vocal and instrumental), home science dance, painting and physical education are trainee in separate training institutions. At this level, there are other training centres having national recognition, such as-Royal College of Music or Royal College of Arts. Their certificates are considered equivalent to that of other institutions. The duration of training in these subjects in not the same. The training course' ill physical education and home science is of 3 years duration while that in an and music is of 4 years duration. The pupil teachers (male and female) are free to take admission in any of them. General qualification for admission is General Certificate of Education.

***Teachers for Further Education-***Mostly the training of these teachers depends on work-experience. The experienced persons of the concerned subjects are appointed from industrial and commercial instilled's. It is not necessary that they should possess high level qualifications. Then experience is more important. The Education Ministry has laid down some minimum qualifications for them according to the suggestions of National Advisory Council. This minimum qualification is mainly their efficiency in the subject concerned.

**Criteria of Selection**

There is no regular system of selection of persons for training. Female trainees are selected from those girls who have completed their education and have an experience of 1 or 2 years in some industrial or commercial institution. The number of female trainees is almost one third of the total trainees ale trainees are selected directly from Schools. The demand or lady teachers is increasing day by day. For training in techinical subjects the student s are selected from industrial institutions on the basis of the knowledge of the subject and experience. After training, they have to work on one year's probation. After completion of the probation period, the appointment becomes permanent.

In the Held of teacher-training, the Teachers' Association, too, gives valuable co-operation. The Associations of the teachers colleges and Teachers Training Departments have planned to extend co-operation to students willing to get training. This association gives valuable advice to Education Ministry and students regarding teacher training. It also helps the young boys and girls wandering about for admission. According to the scheme, the willing candidate applies to the Teachers' Association for admission and the association after considering his application, tries to get him admitted ill some training institution at some place.

**Conditions of Service**

In Great Britain, the teachers are neither appointed by the Education Ministry nor by the administration. L. E. A., no doubt, disburse salaries to the teachers of aided schools but they do not interfere in their appointment. Ordinarily, the teachers are appointed on the basis of service agreement between the teacher and management. The managing committee is free to appoint teachers. In the aided schools, the manager alone appoints the teachers but in the schools run by voluntary organisations, the entire managing committee appoints the teachers. The teachers' associations and L. E. A. help in determining the service conditions. According to the suggestion of the Burnham Committee, the Teachers' Association and L. E.

A jointly determine the service conditions of teachers. The suggestions of the Burnham Committee have been incorporated in the Education Act of 1914 also. It has made the position of teachers stable. In practice the L. E. As. determine the service conditions and obtain the approval of teachers.

According to the service conditions, a headmaster may be removed at three months' notice and a teacher at two months' notice. But for the termination of services of a teacher, the approval of the L. E. A. concerned is necessary. If a teacher is to be removed immediately, he has to be paid 2 months' salary in lieu of the notice and the headmaster will be paid three months' salary in lieu or the notice. Ordinarily, the teachers may be removed from the post at the end of the session and the matter of termination is kept completely confidential. So long as the approval is not received from the Education Authority, even the teachers may not know about it. The termination of the services of a teacher is not publicised, because the management does not want that the teacher may find it difficult to get an appointment in some other school.

A teacher may be removed only when his conduct is against the interest of students and the school. In the beginning, he is warned not to indulge in anti-student activities and the education-ministry, too, is informed of such activities. If even after warnings the teacher does not improve his behaviour, he is charge-sheeted and given an opportunity to clarify his position either himself or through his representative. If any teacher fails to give a satisfactory explanation of the charges levelled against him, he is removed from the service. Even the Teachers' Association does not intend to support a teacher whose activities are against the interest of the students. The education ministry, too, takes disciplinary action against such teachers and cancels the teaching certificate of the teacher.

If some injustice is done to a teacher, the Teachers' Association struggles for him. Generally the post of the teacher is more socure than other profcssional services. If injustice is done to the teacher, the L. E. A. opposes it. The objection is raised on the basis of service contract between the teacher and the management. The Teachers' Association tries to patch up the differences created between the teacher and the management. Because of such efforts cordiality is maintained between the teachers' management.

The teachers along with their usual salary get leaves and other facilities also. A teacher gets three months leave in one year and in serious illness such as T. B. or some other serious disease, he gets one year's sick leave with pay. This one year's sick leave includes six months leave on full pay and 6 months' leave on half pay. If necessary, the sick leave may be extended at the recommendation of the L. E. A. When needed the teacher also gets financial help which is paid back by him in instalments Such facilities are available to the teachers throughout the country. Thus teachers in Great Britain are happy and enjoy prestige.

According to the Act of 1944, the Education Ministry determines the salaries of teachers. For determining the salary-scales of teachers, advisory committees are appointed which give necessary advice to the Education Minister. The trust committee to recommend regarding salaries was the Burnham Committee which was appointed in the name of Burnham Technical Committee. This committee included 26 representatives of L. E. A. and 26 of the teachers.

Similarly, another committee which included representatives of Teachers' Association; training schools, education departments, L. E. As was appointed regarding the salaries of teachers of teachers' training institutions and universites. The chairman of this committee was Sir Henry Pelham, Secretary to Education Ministry. This committee also included the representatives of voluntary organisations. The recommendations of this committee were quite significant and they were accepted immediately.

In Great Britain, the salaries of headmaster, teachers, lady-teachers and male teacher are slightly different. The salaries are determined on annual basis. The amount payable during the year is divided into twelve months and the amount due monthly is paid at the end of the month. Taking into consideration the sick leave, the salary is paid in such a way that it does not exceed the annual salary. If any teacher possesses some higher educational qualification or some special training, he is paid additional salary. Additional salary depends on the number of students. The salary of the headmaster of rural and urban areas Knot the same. The headmaster are paid more because they have to look after the work of the school and manage other affairs.

The salary of secondary and higher secondary teachers is determined on the basis of their qualifications. There is difference in the salary of university teachers and teachers *or* teachers' training colleges, no matter they may be of equal standard. This difference was removed by the Benham Committee. The lady-teachers get less basic pay, annual increment, maximum pay and additional pay than the male teachers. Annual salaries are as follows:

***Salary of Primary and Secondary School Teachers***-Under-graduate teachers' pay scale per year ranges between 700 to 1000 pounds under-graduate lady teachers pay scale falls within 500 to

800 pounds; Graduate male teachers 900 to 1200 pounds per year, graduate lady teachers pay scale 700-1000 pounds per year.

Teachers having special qualification are given additional increments. The post of the headmaster is considered to he a better remunerative post because he gets additional remuneration. This additional remuneration ranges within 300 pounds to 800 pounds annually which depends on the number of students and the expansion of the school. The L. E. A. tries to expand thouse schools which are very limited in size in order that the headmaster may get some additional pay.

***Teachers in Great Britain***-In U. K. the status of the teacher is honourable. Services are secured. In the early period the teachers had personal importance. Now they have governmental, social and national importance. They enjoy freedom.

***Teachers Training in Great Britain***-In the beginning, teachers were trained by Church and Voluntary Oragnisations. Now the trainingis imparted by University Departments of Education, Training Colleges and Training Schools which get government aid. L. E. A. manage them. The education ministry also fulfils its obligations.

***Classification of Teachers***-(1) Teachers of Primary Schools: General certificate of education and 18 years of age is necessary. Two years teacher-training in training schools is available. (2) Teachers of Secondary Schools : One year training course in University Teacher Training Department. (3) Teachers of Special Subjects : Separate training for art. music physical education etc. Certificates of Royal Arts College are adequate for this. (4) Further Education: For them experience in their training.

***Selection for Training***-Selection through Teachers' Associations, directly selected from schools also. Lady-teachers one third in number.

***Appointment of Teachers***-In schools of voluntary organisations appointments are made by managements and in aided schools L. E. As appoint the teachers.

Headmasters and teachers may be terminated at three months' and two months' notice respectively. The teacher is removed only when he does not improve his conduct even after repeated warning's. The Education Ministry is kept informed. It cancels the teaching certificate of the teacher. Teacher cannot be removed without the approval of L. E. A. Charge-sheet is given before dismissal. Services are terminated, if the explanation is not satisfactory. The information is confidential.

***Salary of Teachers***-The headmasters are paid more than the teachers. Male teachers get more salary than the lady teacher. Three months' leave every year. Sick leave is on full pay for six months and on half-pay for the other six months. Financial help is also given, which is deducted from the salary in instalments. Burnham Committee prescribed the pay scales.

## QUESTIONS

1. How are the teachers classified in Great Britain? How is their training conducted ?
2. Write an essay on teacher's status and conditions in U. K.

# 7

# University Education

In the United Kingdom the development of higher education has been much higher than other developed countries. Upto the middle of the twentieth century, there were 12 universities in England, 4 in Scotland, one university with four affiliated colleges in Wales, and one university in Ireland (thus 18 universities in all). In the beginning of the nineteenth century Oxford and Cambridge were the only two great universities worth mentioning. So, these universities are considered to be the oldest in England. Later on, Durham University (1832) and ;London University (1836) were established. Other universities were established in the later half of 19th century. In the beginning some college were in the form of affiliated university colleges. Subsequently, in the beginning of 20th century, they were converted into universities.

The universities of Britain such as Leeds University, Briston University, Manchester University, Shefield University, Nottingham University, Birmingham University, Liverpool University and Reeding University were constitutionally established in the 20th century. Thus the universities in Britain are a gift of the 20th century. The Belfast, *i.e.,* Queen's University of Ireland was established in 1909. The Glasgow, Aberdeen, and St. Adrews Universities of Scotland were established in the 15th century and the fourth university in Edinborough was opened in the year 1583. The Reports of the Census of 1832, 1867 and 1885 reveal that the population in the 19th century has risen three times over that of the above three years. The population of Great Britain at the time of establishing Oxford and Cambridge Universities was one crore. The number of universities went up with the rise in population.

**The Conceptions**

The main nature of the universities of Great Britain is that they are autonomous. The State does not interfere with their work and administrative systems in any way. The universities are completely free in the appointement of teachers, financial matters and administration. Ofcourse, the State continues to provide them financial and other necessary co-operation for their smooth conduct of affairs. These universities were voluntary organisations.

All the British universities may be divided into four categories on the basis of their functions:

(1) Oxford and Cambridge Universities provided the highest level of education traditionally.

(2) The four universities of Wales, Ireland (Belfast) anti Scotland work as Central Universities.

(3) London University.

(4) Universities of England, Menchester, Birmingham and other Stall Universities.

For some reasons, the above four categories of universities fail to admit all the students (boys and girls) willing to take admission. Firstly, some seats are reserved for foreign students in these universities. Secondly, then is an acute problem of providing accommodation. Only 25 per cent of the students are able to get accommodation facilities. These universities provide various scholarships and financial help to the students. Because of this, these universities attract a large number of foreign student. On the basis of the previous data available, it seems that almost 80 per cent of the students get financial help in one form or the other. The practice of affiliationg colleges with the universities is also there. Several affiliated colleges providing education of university level are established even in some foreign countries. Thus the universities in Britain are a model for many universities in some other countries.

## Institutional Control

It has been pointed out above that the British Universities are autonomous and are free in administrative and financial matters. We may divide the administrative aspect in two categories: (i) general establishment and management and (ii) financing.

***General Establishment and Management***-In the universities of Great Britain, the Senate House has an important hand in the administration. For general administration, the governing court is mainly responsible.

The Heads of different departments work as members of the senate house. Sometimes teachers are also enrolled as members of the house. The function of the senate house is to prepare project, devise programmes and advise the governing council or governing court on some problems.

The members of the governing council or court are separate from that of the senate house. The council is free and independence in the matter of university administration and management. The State may interfere only when requested for. In specific matters, such as reform or change the state government may appoint some commission for submitting a report after enquiry on the concerned subject. The members of the commission, generally, are people concerned with the university or local authorities of the Education Ministry. When this commission gives it suggestions or recommendations, Ex-Officio-Commission tries to implement them. The members of this Ex-Officio-Commission are the officials of these university and teachers.

***Financing***-Universities are autonomous and voluntary organisations. Even then they get sufficient financial help from the state government and local education authorities. Sometimes it is as much as 50 percent of the total expenditure of the universities. The amount of financial help needed by the universities is determined by a Universitiy Grant Commission. The members of the University Grant Commission or those public men who have no concern with education ministry and are free from the influence of the education ministry. For State representation in the commission, one or more officials from the education ministry are also included in the commission.

The Grants Commission after considering the financial demands of the universities presents its recommendation to the government. The commission is empowered to accept or reject the proposals of financial help of the universities.

The financial problems of the universities are solved by 50 per cent help from the state and local authorities. Rest of the requirements are met through tuition-fees, endowments and direct donations. On the third portion of expenditure of universities is covered by tuition-fees and rest 2/3 protion by endowments and grants etc. During the war period 50 per cent of the expenditure of the universities was met out from State grants-in-aid. These grants were given through university Grants Commission. Now the aid from the State is continuously increasing because other sources of income of the universities are decreasing.

The governing council is responsible for the income and expenditure of the university. Universities are completely autonomous in this regard.

## The Syllabi

The universities and affiliated colleges of Great Britain have complete autonomy in their teaching work and curriculum formulation. It will be proper to describe them here.

***Teaching Method***-There are no uniform teaching methods in the various univerisities of Great Britain. In order to maintain contacts with affiliated colleges, the Oxford and Cambridge universities have devised tutorial system. Mostly lecture method is followed. Tutorial classes are held once a week. This provides an opportunity for revision of lessons taught, consolidation of knowledge and research work. The teacher holds a key place in the tutorials. He solves the problems of students in a particular subject and removes their difficulties. This provision exists only for arts students. For the students of science classes, the demonstrator gives them practice in experiments and demonstrates some important experiments.

In Post-graduate classes, the system of tutorial classes is different. Here the students are given individual instructions or practice, In place of teachers, supervisors, who look after the work of students individually are appointed. In this way the tutorial system has become very important. Through this system, efforts are made to inculcate democratic feelings and make up the inadequacies or the lecture method. The student who are not benefited by lecture method, are above to gain by the tutorial system.

***Curriculum***-The graduate course of studies in all the university's is of three years duration. The graduation course has been classified as B. A. (Honours) and B. A. (Pass). Honours course provides specialisation in any one subject. Students of both arts and science faculties can offer Honours course, but B. A. (Honours) is mostly offered by arts students. In Scotland only 25 per cent students offer Honours course, rest 75 per cent offer pass course. But in England 60 per cent students are found in Honours course, the rest 40 per cent offer pass courses. The honours course in science includes subjects like engineering, physics, chemistry, mixed courses of physics and mathematics and natural science. Arts students offer law, history, classics and English language in honours course. But now these courses are being changed substantially.

In the B. A. honours course now instead of specialisation in any one subject, knowledge in humanities is being emphasised. With this point of view, by giving prominence to modern science and humanities in arts subjects, efforts are made to clarify the impact of science on human life. Subjects under social sciences are taught to science students. By such a provision, the impact of science on the activities of human society is studied. Both arts and science students of Honours course have to study philosophy of nature and philosophy of man.

B. A. pass course includes literary subjects, English language and literature, modern languages, history, economics, mathematics etc. There are many varieties in these courses. All the universities donot have uniform courses. The same thing applied to honors course also.

After the completion of the course, the examination council of the university examines the students. This examination council consists of the teachers and head of departments of the university. In order to make the examination just and proper, external examiners life also appointed. By doing so, the fear that the internal teachers would be biased in evaluation is removed.

For post-graduate students, provision of research and three years course of Doctor of Philosophy has been formulated. This provision was made in the first decade of 20th century, when the first world war had come to an end.

A university is the highest centre of knowledge from the point of view of education. A centre of education should be well-organised so far as research and dissemination of knowledge is concerned. Research work is an indicator of teacher's level of knowledge. The highest centre of knowledge should have persons possessing the highest knowledge. So provision of research work is considered very necessary.

In all the British universities, there is a provision of research in both arts and science subjects. In this regard the Oxford University leads all other universities. In this university an affiliated college has been established simply for research work in games and sports. No student receives education in this college. Here the teachers, whether they belong to universities or any other institution engage themselves on projects of national importance and progress. Research work is not limited to university people only, but any post-graduate citizen can take up this work. All facilities for research work exist for teachers and professors in Oxford and Cambridge Universities. Such facilities are being provided by other universities also.

The universities teachers keep themselves engaged in inventions and research work for discovery and dissemination of knowledge. Finding the class lectures uninteresting, the graduate-students often absent themselves from the classes. In order to inspire them for acquiring knowledge and learning, discussions are held on the lectures delivered. In the post-graduate classes, the students in groups of 10-15 get opportunities for discussion in the presence of the teachers. Libraries and study-apartments are provided for teachers and students. After the research work, the teacher delivers a lecture before the graduates and post-graduates in a big lecture-theatre. The lecture is related with the research problem. This stimulates the students for acquiring knowledge.

**Life at Campus**

Students admitted in universities are both residential and non-residential. In England, except Oxford and Cambridge Universities, residential accommodation is not available for most of the students. For residential students, facilities of study are available in the university but non-residential students have to miss such facilities. Thus only 20 percent students get residential study facilities. Even then, by establishing community centres near their homes, the non-residential students have been provided such facilities. At such centers, the non-residential students participate in discussions, games and sports, cultural programmes and gymanstics. The residential students get opportunities of national and international contacts because there the students, both native and foreign belonging to different societies, cultures and languages, live together. Thus residential students are better than non-residential students.

On Oxford and Cambridge universities, the students-day is divided into four time-schedules: First part-lecture and study period, Second-games and sports and participation in gymnastic. Third period of study in library and reading-rooms. Fourth-community and group activity. The working hours in these universities are forenoon and evening hours. The forenoon period is spent in discussion, cultural seminars, games, sports etc.

In all the universities except Cambridge where 10 percent girl students receive education, the girl students population is nearly 25 percent. In London University, there is a separate girls section otherwise in all other universities, the courses are common. Separate living accommodation is provided to girls. They are also provided opportunity to study courses suitable to their interests.

***Development of University***-Total 18 universities-12 in England, 4 in scotland, one each in Ireland and Wales. All the autonomous. They were organised in the 19th century. One third of the total population of-students study here. The universities are affiliating and residential both. They are free from State interference.

***General Nature***-Four types, Oxford and Cambridge belong to one class, Wales, Belfast and Scotland universities belong to another class, the London University is of the third type and the universities of England, Manchester, Birmingham etc. may be included in the fourth type.

***General Administration***-(1) General Establishment and Management-Senate house and governors council perform educational and administrative duties. The State Government interferes only at the request of the governors council. (2) Financing from donations, fees and government aid.

***Teaching and Courses***-(1) Teaching Methods-Lecture method prevails; Seminar or discussion once in a week, complementary classes for research work and experiments are organised. Supervisors of post-graduate classes. (2) Courses-B. A. Pass and B. A. Honours courses of 3 years duration. 60% students in Honours courses, specialisation in anyone subject. General course in B. A. Pass course. Examination by the examination council after the completion of the course. External examiner are also appointed.

***Research and Dissemination of Knowledge***-3 years course for Doctor of Philosophy. Most of the teachers and professors do research work and deliver lectures. For dissemination of knowledge discussion and seminars are held on lectures delivered. The teacher works as a guide.

***Life of Students***-Residential and non-residential, two types. Residential life is better then non-residential one. Working-day divided into parts-Teaching and study in the fore-noon and evening. Cultural programmes, games-sports etc. are held in the afternoon. For Girl students 25 per cent of the residential provision is separate.

## QUESTIONS

1. What is the nature of education administration and management of universities in Great Britain?

2. "The universities of Great Britain provide higher standard of education because of their autonomous character." How?

3. Explain the system of teaching-methods and courses in the universities of Great Britain.

4. Describe the life of students in the universities of Great Britain.

# 8

# School Education

Secondary education as today in Great Britain is an outcome of the Act of 1944. According to this Act, the age limit was raised from 14 to 15 years; which finally was extended to 16 years, to understand the present form of secondary education it will be necessary to have a knowledge of the Act of 1944.

## The Background

The credit for the beginning of universal secondary education in Great Britain goes to the Act of 1944. According to this Act, the responsibility of establishing primary and secondary educational institutions vested in Local Education Authorities (L. E. A.). According to this Act, the L. E. As. were required to provide sufficient education in their respective spheres. Here sufficient education means that education which is available in primary and secondary schools according to the ability and aptitude of students along with the provision of necessary apparatus and equipment in sufficient quantity. Thus a great responsibility has been entrusted to L. E. As. in the field of primary and secondary education. It became the duty of L. E. A. to perform experiments in their respective spheres for a system of education which could cater to the needs of specific children and thus decide what sort of education would be suitable to them. Firstly secondary schools, secondly junior technical schools, junior art and commerce schools and thirdly promoted elementary schools were established. The people considered them us upper, middle and lower level schools respectively. In the schools of third level only these boys and girls who were not in a position to spend much on education, received education.

**Various Schools**

According to the Education Act of 1944, secondary education was .sought to be re-organised and all secondary schools were divided into 3 categories- (1) Grammar Schools, (2) Modern Secondary Schools and (3) Industrial and Technical Secondary Schools. After that, these schools were classified in a planned way. The present form of prevailing schools in England and Wales may be described as follows :

After 1950, in the already existing grammar schools, modern secondary schools and technical schools, courses of academic importance had begun to be introduced in the field of secondary education and bilateral schools had come in vogue. Bilateral schools were those schools in which out of the above grammar, modern and technical schools, comprehensive schools being established by integrating any two of the above schools.

These bilateral schools consisted of two types secondary schools-one recognized and the other unrecognized. These bilateral schools were not very much different from grammar, modern and technical secondary schools. Many a modern secondary schools have adopted the curriculum of grammar schools. Such bilateral schools were maximum in number. In these schools students desirous of obtaining General Certificate of Education, were mainly educated. These schools were unrecognized. In the year 1982, 40,000 students for General Certificate of Education (Mixed courses of grammar and modern schools) were admitted by about 1200 modern schools out of a total of 4200 modern schools. These students were imparted education of grammar school curriculum along with modern school curriculum. The number of schools recognised by the Education Ministry have always been increasing out it has ever remained less than the unrecognized schools.

These bilateral schools were considered comprehensive schools. But in fact, they were not comprehensive schools. In reality, only those schools were considered comprehensive which impart general education to all the boys and girls in its area and were based on the individual needs, interest and abilities of the students. But these schools did not possess this characteristic. Some of these schools gave education to students of one sex only either boys or girls. Even today some parents like to send their wards to the private grammar schools in their vicinity but do not like to send them in bilateral schools. The reason is that these schools do not cater to their needs.

Apart from the above bilateral schools, multi-lateral or multi dimensional schools are found in U. K. They are called multi-dimensional because they include the combined elements of grammar, modern and technical schools. These schools cannot be said to be progressive because it is not easy to provide every kind of course for them.

Besides these bilateral and multilateral schools there are other types of schools, too, and they are situated at different places, *e.g.*, intermediate schools, central schools, area or higher grade schools etc. They have been categoriesed separately on the basis of Ministry Report of 1958.

The students in these schools are selected on merit basis. The curriculum prevailing in these schools is less academic than that in grammar schools. At some places there are schools norms and the boys and girls are admitted on selective and non-selective basis. Mostly there are such independent schools which adopt mixed curriculum of grammar, modern and technical school education.

Now, one more experiment is being conducted in the secondary education system in U. K. This experiment was first conducted in Leicestershire and it was accepted by several L. E. As. in 1959. According to this experiment the secondary schools have been classified into two groups:

***Junior Comprehensive Schools***-In these schools students who have received primary education are taught till they reach the age of 14-15 years. These are called high schools.

***Higher Grade Comprehensive Schools***-In these schools, the boys and girls above the age of 14-15 years having received in junior comprehensive schools are admitted.

The above experiment is considered good by most people because in this system services of trained teachers become available and at the, same time passing the eleven plus examination is no more necessary. Even then, grammar secondary, modern secondary and technical secondary schools are, more popular.

**Religious Institutions**

These schools were started during the seventeenth century. They are the oldest schools of secondary education. In these schools such as-English literature and language, modern foreign languages, *viz.*, French, German, Italian, Spanish and Russian languages, applied and basic mathematics, chemistry, physics, zoology, history, geography, art, music, wood-craft etc. are taught. These schools prepare students for University education. Girl students are taught domestic-science. Religious education is compulsory for all. In all these schools physical education and outdoor games are provided. For girls lawn tennis, basket-ball, hockey and for male students cricket and foot-ball are specially provided.

**Private Efforts**

In grammar schools, various voluntary clubs, literary and scientific debates, music and dramatics and such other activities are organised. Similarly, mountaineering, chess, German or French circle clubs etc. are also prevalent. The speciality of these social activities and clubs is that they do not interfere with the school activities in any way. These activities are organised after school hours and the students take part in them enthusiastically on their personal responsibility.

The studies of General Certificate of Education are given to only those boys and girls who are desirous for the same. This certificate system has been divided into ordinary, advanced and scholarship levels respectively. The three levels are examinations of separate subjects.. The students may appear at the examination in the subjects of anyone level out of the above three. The age of the students should be 15 or 16 years. According to the School-Regulations of 1959, if the headmaster permits, the students below the age of 15 may also offer this course otherwise no student below the age of 15 years is allowed to offer this course.

***Importance of General Certificate of Education***-The students (boys or girls) are very much benefitted by passing this examination. The students who is awarded this certificate, is not required to appear at the University Entrance Examination and preliminary examinations of vocational institutions. The only thing required is that he should have received the certificate only in the subject in which, he intends to take admission. Along with the subject the certificate, too, should be of desired level. In universities examination is to be passed in four or five subjects in addition to English language. Out of these four or five subjects, advanced level certificate at least in two subjects has to be obtained. Only then the students is entitled to admission in a university. The same thing applies for procuring scholarship. The education minister selects the students eligible for scholarship on the basis of the result of general certificate of education. Only selected candidates are awarded scholarships.

## Vocational Schools

The number of technical is much less than the grammar schools. There has been notable increase in the number of these schools from 1970 to 1982. But the number of students in these schools almost doubled. However, there seems to be hardly any reason for a decrease in the number of these schools, it is possible that due to establishing of bilateral and multilateral schools, the number of technical schools may not have increased. The British people believe that grammar schools are more important than technical schools. Therefore, their number could not increase. Although, it was announced by the education ministry that the children having the same I. Q. may be admitted in any of the schools of grammar or technical. But in practice it is seen that the guardians prefer to send their children in grammar schools. They send their wards to technical schools only when they are not admitted in grammar schools even after great efforts. One more reason that reduces the popularity of technical schools is that the age of admission here is 12 years whereas in other secondary schools, a child of 11 years of age may be admitted.

One more reason that can be assigned for non-expansion of secondary technical schools is that these schools had begun to run their classes in technical colleges. These classes used the technical apparatus of adult education and allowed their teachers to remain engaged in the expansion of adult-education. The result was that these technical secondary schools could not have their own buildings and there was always a dearth of teachers. These conditions have been depressing for the people and they have grown averse to these institutions.

***Evaluation of Secondary Technical Schools***-Only a few of these schools could earn some reputation. Most of these schools could not make any appreciable contribution towards the development of secondary education. Even so, they are important for the development of technology. Scientific and technical education has been provided by these schools to a great extent. These technical schools, prepare the students for universities, Royal Society of Arts, Technical and Commercial Examinations, after preparing them for General Certificate of Education. The students who receive education in technical colleges, mostly come from these secondary technical schools.

***Modern Schools***-In 1945, senior secondary modern schools prevailing in U. K. were converted as modern secondary schools in order to make education modern. Gradually, these schools made sufficient progress since they organised education to cater to the needs of the people. Therefore, people also helped them. In these schools specific whole time and part-time vocational courses were run, e.g., art and craft, home-craft, needle work and design, practical art, craft-manship, house maintenance and furnishing, mechanical trades, automobile engineering, rural science, gardening, nursing, musk seamanship, commercial subjects and other subjects for general certificate education were taught in these schools.

***Modern Secondary Schools and General Certificate of Education***-These schools have been preparing students for general certificates of education after qualifying them in Royal Society of Arts Examinations such as-School Certificate, Commercial Certificate and Technical Certificate. In 1977 about 10,000 students from modern school and in 1983 about 40,000 students from 2,000 modern secondary schools appeared at the General Certificate Examination. Out of these about 800 students belonged to advanced level. Thus these schools have played important role for General Certificate of Education.

Certain institutions such as Regional Institutions, Union of Education on Institutions, Eastern Middle and Educational Institutions (Union) Lanchasirean Chesire Institutes, and Northern County Technical Examinations conducted various school certificates examinations. Those modern schools which were tinder L. E. As. were conducting Local School Leaving Certificates Examination. After four years of education, the students appearing at the above examinations, appeared in the examinations of secondary modern schools. Out of these schools, many or them prepared the students for armed forces and Apprenticeship Examination of H. M. Dockyards.

***The Form of Secondary Modern Schools in 1959***-These schools have no definite form. They were found in many forms.

The following four forms of these modern schools are found:

***Secondary Modern Schools of General Courses***-In these schools, emphasis is laid on art, craft, social and moral activities and general courses. There are no special courses in these schools.

***General Education and Specific Education Modern Schools***-In these schools general education is given for first two or three years and finally some specific education is provided to boys and girls.

***Modern Schools like Senior Elementary Schools***-In such schools courses were conducted with slight modification in the courses of senior elementary schools.

***Modern School imparting Advanced Education in Basic Subjects***-In these schools major basic subjects are taught. Advanced knowledge is also given in one or two subjects.

The above four types of modern schools have continued till today. However, these four types of schools have affected by the expansion of specific education courses which have become quite popular. Now many modern schools have converted into bilateral (comprehensive) schools. In 1959 there was hardly any difference in the courses of bilateral secondary schools and modern schools. Like bilateral schools, the secondary modern schools also taught specific subjects and prepared students for General Certificate Examination.

**Development and Growth**

We shall understand those landmarks which have led to the development of secondary education in Great Britain.

**Charity Schools**

In the beginning these schools were established by bishops. The City livery company or Guild had also actively co-operated in the establishment of these schools. Endowed schools are also caned Grammar schools. They existed during the Roman period also. Classical languages were taught in these schools.

During the Tudor period of the fourteenth and fifteenth centuries, the business community also took interest in the starting of these schools. In due course the public was attracted towards these schools. In fact; private enterprises played the main role in the development of these schools. For example, the Lady Manners School in Bake well was established by a lady. The Winchester Public School was started by William of Wykeham in 1382 and the Eton Public School was established due to the efforts of Henry VI. These two institutions were working as residential schools in Winchester and Eton from the very start. It is because of this characteristic that these two schools we different from other public schools. Some local communities had also opened some public, schools which were known as Town-Grammar schools. Out of these town grammar schools some developed into residential schools. The public schools at Rugby, Harrow and Shrewsbury are such residential schools.

**Role of Teachers**

Only teaching licence holders could be teachers of a grammar school. Upto the eighteenth century this teaching licence was considered as compulsory. But due to the indifference of Churches, the teaching ,licence was was accepted as a necessary qualification. The bishop of he school area was alone considered as competent to issue a teaching licence. He would first examine the ability, morality and the religious attitude of the teacher before granting a teaching licence. The system of granting teaching licence prevailed since the medieval period and this system was followed in other European countryside.

**The Syllabi**

In the begining the term 'grammar' stood for those places where classical languages were laught. There of classical languages were given special places in these schools. These classical languages are considered as keys to further knowledge. The teaching and study of Latin was the special feature of the curriculum in Great Britain. Upto the eighteenth century there was no difference between the curriculum of the endowed schools and that of the public schools. In both the types of schools Latin and Greek were taught. But in the Merchant Taylors School Hebrew was also taught along with Greek and Latin.

In due course, an attempt was made to effect a change in the curriculum. In 1805, in the public school at Leeds, it was thought to teach modern languages, writing and mathematics. But inspite of the Grammar School Act of 1840; no changes were introduced in the curriculum of public schools. This Act empowered the headmaster to include other subjects in the curriculum, but the teacher were not to be compelled to teach these subjects. As a result, these schools were victims of bitter criticisms. Locke and Sidney Smith drew the attention of the public to these shortcomings of public schools.

**System at Work**

Discipline in the Grammar schools was not good. The school management was also not satisfactory. No suitable arrangement for meals was made in the students' hostels. Discipline was maintained through fear. Severe corporal punishment was very common in these school Some headmasters were famous, for giving severe corporal punishments to students. There was no suitable arrangement for sports and games. No attempt was made to advise the students about utilizing their leisure pours in a worthwhile manner. Some students in some hostels sometimes were victims to drinking and gambling. However, there were many grammar schools which were free from this defect. But it will have to be admitted that most of the Grammar Schools were not in good condition.

**Private Schools**

In addition to the Grammar schools the necessity of opening private schools was also felt because of the following reasons:

(1) Poor people were not able to send their children to Grammar Schools, as this education there was quite expensive.

(2) Some people were against the Grammar schools because of the evils existing in them. So they did not like to send their children for education there.

(3) Certain parents wanted to keep their children away from the contact with children of businessmen in the Grammar schools.

(4) Private schools were better managed. More subjects such as history, geography, modern languages, arts and mathematics were taught there. English and French occupied special place in the curriculum. Students were encouraged to do voluntary labours in order to develop their special interests and abilities. Within the subjects of voluntary labours, music, painting, modelling, printing and surveying were included. Thus the students were given opportunities for natural development in private schools.

(5) Modern methods of teaching were employed in private schools. In a way, they were also centres of experimental work in education.

(6) In the private schools discipline was maintained on democratic lines. The students themselves were made responsible for the maintenance of discipline in their classes. On breach of some discipline, the erring student was submitted, before a jury. This jury under the chairmanship of a judge used to award some financial punishment which had to be met from whatever the punished student had earned through his labour. Sometimes he was also deprived of certain facilities as a punishment or sometimes he was locked into some dark room. The jury consisted of students only and judge was also some student.

There were a number of students' committees which used to look after many affairs relating to the school and its activities but some critics have criticised this system on the plea that it made the students prematurely adults.

Private schools were run for girls also. These girls were mostly from the middle and upper class families. The purpose of education for girls was to make them good housewives. Accordingly, the curriculum for them included various types of domestic arts along with other common subjects. French and Italian languages, instrumental and vocal music, painting and embroidery were also taught to them. Opportunities were also provided to, them for acquiring general knowledge.

Upto 1840 it could not be possible to introduce any remarkable reform in the condition of endowed and public schools. In the beginning of the nineteenth century Bentham Jeremy and Mills advocated the philosophy of utilitarianism. Under the influence of this philosophy, the curriculum of the classical languages was bitterly criticised. The missionaries also criticised the curriculum. This criticism influenced those people who used to send their children to public schools. Simultaneously, due to the industrial revolution, a new class of producers and mill owners was coming up which favoured education through private enterprises. Thus the public, schools came under bitter criticism.

**Corrective Measures**

Due to the discontent of the people about the public or private schools, efforts were directed towards their reforms. Samuel Butler, till headmaster of the Shrewsbury School and Thomas Arnold, the head master of the Rugby School tried hard to introduce reforms in public schools.

At first attention was given on the defective currieulum. Thomas, Arnold tried to introduce progressiveness in the curriculum and methods of teaching. Butler and Arnold wanted that teaching method should create a spirit of self-dependence in students, fulfil their individual needs and encourage self-expression in them. They further suggested that through individual activities in the teaching process natural development of students should be promoted. They considered the study of classical languages very important as they regarded then very necessary for study of such subjects as political science, history and philosophy. In the popular mass education they gave a special place to Christianity. They wanted that Christianity should be the main basis of education throughout whole Great Britain. They did not like any other system of education than this.

***Royal Commission of 1861***-In 1861 a great exhibition was organised in Great Britain. This exhibition indicated how much advanced France and Germany were in the fields of primary, secondary and technical education. A great discontent spread in the public-at this realization. The efforts of Thomas Arnold could not improve the situation in any way. Hence during the premier ship of Lord Palmerston a Royal Commission was appointed in 1861 under the chairmanship of Lord Clarendon. This Commission was requested to look into the curriculum, management and financial position of such nine public schools as Eton, West minister, Winchester, Harrow, Charter house, Shrewsbury, Rugby, Merchant Taylors and St. Paul and suggested measures for reforms. The Commission submitted its report in 1864. The Commission did not condemn the whole system of education prevalent in public schools. It suggested reforms only in the curriculum and the teaching methods. The Commission observed that during the last twenty five years these nine public schools had introduced reforms in them upto a considerable extent and good discipline and moral atmosphere existed in them.

***Recommendations of the Royal Commission of 1861***-The Commission recommended that the existing curriculum and the governing bodies of the public schools should be reorganised on the pattern of German Classical Secondary Schools. The Commission considered the study of classical languages and religious education as very important, but it suggested that mathematics, science, natural sciences, pure sciences, music, arts and German and French languages should also be given due place in the curriculum.

The Public School Act passed in 1868 incorporated most of the suggestions given by the Royal Commission of 1861. Excepting Merchant Taylors and St. Paul schools, this Act was introduced in all other public schools which were required to reorganise their governing bodies on suitable representations of all concerned. The new governing bodies were empowered to appoint and dismiss headmasters, to formulate the curriculum and determine the nature of tuition fees. The headmasters were made responsible to the governing bodies but they were empowered to appoint their assistant teachers. The decision of the headmaster regarding his assistant teachers were to be accepted.

***School Enquiry Commission of 1864***-This Commission was appointed in 1864 under the chairmanship of Lord Taunton for submitting a report on the working of elementary, public and other schools: These other schools were those which were not examined by the New Castle and Clarandon commissions. The commission of 1864 examined the working of 942 schools and submitted a big report. The commission examined 800 endowed schools also. The commission submitted its comprehensive report in 21 parts in 1868:

In the first part of the report, findings and recommendations have been given. The following three types of schools have been recommended in the report:

(1) The first type of schools were meant for children of rich people.

(2) The second type of schools were mean nor children of those parents who had limited means but wanted to give some vocational education to their children.

(3) The third type of schools were those in which children of labourers farmers and ordinary businessmen were to study Generally, these schools were meant for poor

people. The commission had especially emphasised the establishment of such schools.

The teaching of classical languages was emphasised in the first type of schools. Along with these languages, the study of modern languages, sciences and mathematics was also included in the curriculum. Eighteen or nineteen years of age was fixed as the age limit for leaving schools of the first type.

In the curriculum of the second type of schools English, mathematics, modern languages and natural sciences were alsc included. However, the study of Latin was especially emphasised, Sixteen years of age was fixed as the leaving age for this type oi schools.

In the curriculum of the third type of schools along with English, some other language, mathematics and natural sciences were included. Religious education was recommended for all the type of schools. But any guardian was made free to withdraw his ward from any religious instruction. It was also recommended that control over the Holy orders should be removed. Thus there type of schools were recommended for three classes of people.

**The Setup**

The Royal Commission gave recommendations with regard to recognition of secondary schools. An administrative board in the form of a central authority was recommended. The commission advised that the administrative board should be organised in two forms. Fristly, the Charity Commission should be given more power and should be entrusted with the responsibility for organising education. Secondly, some new administrative board should be established. The administrative board was to be related with educational endowments. It was further recommended that at the provincial level also this provision should made. An administrative board was empowered to appoint inspectors for inspecting endowed secondary schools. Its work area was restricted to registrar general division. There would be an officer of the registrar general division who would inspect the endowed secondary schools at least once, every three years and would report on their conditions and functioning. This officer would be known as the district officer. A town with a population of one lakh or over would be outside the control of the provincial board and much a town itself form a province for the purpose.

Special recommendations were made for private schools. A private school was empowered-to have its own governor who would appoint the headmaster, arrange for, the financial resources and finally determine the nature of the curriculum. The secondary schools were required to be under the L. E. A. but their Teachers would enjoy full autonomy in their internal affairs. The trustees were advised not to interfere unduly in their internal affairs. Each provincial authority should decide the standard of the schools within its jurisdiction. The private schools should be inspected according to their own standards. Their examinations should be organised accordingly. The Parliament should enact laws for ensuring proper utlization of endowments. Necessary facilities should be made available for education of girls through the endowments. The governor should fix up minimum fees for schools. Only those boys and girls should be given free education who could benefit themselves from the same most. Education imparted through minimum fees should not mean useless and meaningless education. The importance of education should be continually maintained.

Suitable teachers should be attracted towards the secondary schools. Therefore, good scales of pay should be given to teachers. There should be a criterion for determining the suitability of a teacher. A teaching certificate should be given to a teacher on the basis of examinations passed by him. Teachers' names should be entered in a relevant register. The Commission recommended that there should be medical register for teachers, wherein the names of teachers obtaining medical aid should be entered. The age of retirement for the teacher should be fixed either at 60 or 65.

**Evaluation and Measurement**

The Commission recommended that examinations should be properly organised for finding out the ability and educational achievements of studetns. The examination and inspection should be conducted by separate authorities which should be appointed by the Central Administrative Board. The formation of an examination council was also recommended. But all these recommendations were immediately implemented.

***Endowment Schools Act, 1869***-The Gladstone Government enacted this Act in 1869 for prescribing certain endowment rules. This Act totally ignored the recommendations of the School Enquiry Commission of 1869. Three special endowment schools commissioners were appointed for ensuring proper utilization of school endowments. In this Act it was laid down that maximum benefits should be obtained from, endowments for education of girls. These commissioners were empowered to supervise the use of only those endowments which were not older than 50 years. The Commissioners could exercise their power only on the permission of school administrators. They have absolutely no jurisdiction over elementary and public schools. The Parliament did not co-operate with these commissioners in their functioning. There was no arrangement for the registration of teachers and no local committee was appointed for co-operating with schools regarding improvement of their conditions.

Thus, the Public School Act of 1868 and the Endowment School Act of 1869 could not be successful because no work was done on the basis of the recommendation of the Royal Commission and the Enquiry Commission. However it will have to be admitted that these Act generated an awakening for improvement of secondary education.

**Role of World War**

The world war of 1914-18 affected education in U. K. adversely. However there were some indirect advantages also for education. The war generated an interest in the public for education and it helped in redetermining its form and nature. Elementary education was not much influenced by the war. Secondary education was much more affected by it. The evil effects of the war on education came over on the surface in the following ways:

(1) Due to war many of the school buildings and equipments were badly damaged. This situation created a crisis for education.

(2) The war created a dearth of teachers and it also impaired the ability of many of them; because many teachers had to go on battle fronts leaving behind their teaching work. This created a dearth of male teachers.

The relieving features of the war period was that it did not influence the elementary schools and it led many secondary schools' students to co-operate in national building enterprises by helping in agriculture and factory work. The activities of students were deeply apprecited by the general public and it thought that education should be suitably developed for producing such nation builders.

***Fisher Act of 1918***-This Act was passed by the Parliament although the world war had not ended and its results could not be ascertained in advance. Fisher was the president of Board of Education at the time. This Act occupies a special place in the national educational system of U. K. This Act made elementary education free. It emphasised the necessity of reorganization of grant-in-aid system, local education authorities and tuition fees.

This Act accepted only that education scientific which was prescribed and accepted by the Education Board. This was also decided that the local education authorities would be given as an aid at least half of what they spent on education. This Act increased the powers of local education authorities which were now made free to make any plan of education and send it to the Board of Education for approval. In this plan it was to be decided whether the control over this plan would be exercised by a single local authority or by some authority group. This would be clarified in the plan. On pre-approval of the Board of Education, the local education, authorities either themselves make arrangements for vacation school camp physical training, school swimming bath, play-centres day and evening social education or get these arranged by some other units or committees.

The Fisher Act provided that no child below the age of twelve years would be employed as a labourer either in some factory or any other commercial establishment. Rules for working hours were fixed for children over twelve years of age. The local education authorities were required to fix up a maximum age limit for day continuation schools and compulsory whole time schools. The local education authorities fixed up this age limit respectively at 18 and 16 years. In the day continuation schools education was made free for boys and girls within 16 years of age and for each student it was compulsory to attend the school at least for 320 hours a year. The local education authorities were authorised to reduce the hours of attendance from 320 to 280 hours for the first seven years of education. This plan increased the possibility of developing more frequency contacts between industries and schools; because after working in commercial establishments,or in factories the children could attend a continuation school.

***An Evaluation of the Fisher Act***-This Act developed greater co-ordination 'between industries and schools, but its various recommendations were not fully implemented due to the following reasons :

(1) Dearth of teachers and school buildings, and

(2) The industrialists did not encourage this plan.

However, this Act brought in the forefront the importance of nursery education and continuation schools in the national system of education. Due to this Act, the age limit for school was also increased.

**Labour Party in Action**

After coming into power in 1924, the Labour Government tried to implement its educational policy. This party wanted to make secondary education universal and it believed that education was a great instrument for effecting reforms in society. It regarded elementary and secondary education as two levels of a single educational process. Therefore the Government advised the advisory committee of the Board of Education to make the necessary survey and experiments about elementary education at the elementary level itself. It required the advisory committee to submit a report on nature, form and aims of elementary education. It was further emphasised that this report should be altogether different from the influence of secondary schools. This report had to be related with education of children of fifteen years of age. On the basis of this report, the government wanted to fulfil two major objectives, namely:

(1) To provide education according to the requirements of the nation, and

(2) To provide a curriculum according to the interests of children.

***Hadow Committee Report, 1926***-W. H. Hadow was the chairman of the Consultative Committee in 1926. This committee is known as the Hadow Committee which was entrusted with the responsibility for suggesting reforms in the, educational system.

This committee submitted its report in 1926 on education of juveniles. By, this only ten per cent of children were receiving secondary education. The committee recommended that all the children within the range of 11 to 15 years should receive education. upto the first 11 years of age children should receive elementary education. Afterwards they should receive post elementary education according to their individual needs and interests. Therefore, the opening of a number of new secondary schools was considered necessary. These schools were called grammar schools, modern schools, senior classes, junior technical schools and trade school. Those schools, were called grammar schools, which were founded due to the Act of 1902. All the endowed and county schools came under the group of grammar schools. In these schools, the teaching of science and literature was particularly emphasised. Modern schools were like the then prevailing selective or non-selective central schools which were opened in London and Manchester respectively in 1911 and 1912. These schools were meant for children between 11 and 15 years of age coming from preparatory schools. The Hadow Committee particularly emphasised the establishment of such schools, because their curriculum had an industrial bias but not narrow. The committee recommended that their curriculum should be of four years duration. The committee rightly remarked that opening, of a modern school was not possible everywhere. Therefore it suggested that at places where a modern school could not be established, senior classes should be opened. The objective of these senior classes was to provide post-primary education to those boys and girls who could get education in schools stated above.

The Hadow Committee recommended for opening junior technical and trade schools also. In these schools children of 13 or over 13 years of age could get admission.

The Hadow Committee also recommended that in place of elementary education the term primary education should be used. Primary education was fixed for the first eleven years of age. For this purpose selective and non-selective schools and senior classes were considered necessary. For admission technical schools of lower category, the committee suggested the introduction of an examination test for children of thirteen years of age. If possible, viva voce test was also to be taken. The committee suggested that all schools imparting post-primary education should be called secondary schools. A new leaving examination was also recommended for meeting the requirements of selective and non-selective schools and senior Classes.

***Implementation of the Recommendations of the Hadow Report***-The recommendations of the Hadow Committee were regarded as very useful and from 1926 attempts were made to make secondary education more popular. The Board of Education published a new pamphlet in 1928, which indicated the difficulties in the implementation of the Hadow Committee Report. This new pamphlet was entitled 'The New Prospect in Education'. It was not easy to provide for secondary education separately. For this two paths were possible and both of these were beset with difficulties. The first path was that of establishing new school buildings and the, second was to utilize the very existing school buildings. Both of these ways were difficult. The financial condition of the country was quite bad. The grant that was received from the Exchequer since September 1, 1929 was completely stopped from 1931, because the nation was facing financial crisis. However, some progress was made. By the beginning of the fourth decade of the twentieth century 63.5 per cent of the children above eleven years of age rad begun to receive secondary education, whereas before 1926 the percentage was only ten. Construction of new school buildings was left on voluntary bodies which could not bear this burden.

Both the traditional and new school systems were prevailing. This situation was not good. It was extremely difficult to start new schools in rural areas. All standard church schools and senior church schools were existing in the country. The All Standard Church Schools were converted into junior schools. The children of eleven years oblige passing out of this school were not being admitted in a senior church school. In such a situation the student as compelled to seek admission in a post primary council school. This created great difficulties.

***Education Act of 1936***-It was necessary to find out solution of difficulties created by the implementation of the Hadow Report. So the Government passed the Education Act of 1936. This Act fixed the school leaving age at 15 from September 1939. But if any child was gainfully employed in some establishment after attaining the age of 14, he was exempted from this rule.

But the situation created in the following years due to the Second World War affected adversely the implementation of this Act.

***Spens Report of 1938***-In 1938 Sir Will Spens became the chairman of the Consulatative Committee. This committee published a report on secondary education in 1938. This report is known as the Spens Report. This report pertains to the organisation and inter-relationships of those schools which used to impart education to children over eleven years of age.

The Spens report briefly traced the development of secondary education and remarked that secondary education in the country was repatterned on the basis of the Act of 1902. In this repatterning the old grammar schools were accepted as models. The Spens Report observed that secondary education should be given according to the interests and abilities of children. The Report further emphasised that in the process of education reaction and experiences of the students were more important than the contents of education. The Report observed that the existing grammar schools were more interested in meeting the requirements of the certificates to be given to the students who passed. However, the Report recommended for the continuance of the grammar schools and urges for establishing secondary technical schools. The junior technical schools could be allowed to exist, but after them the Report considered the establishment of technical high schools very necessary: These schools should teach 5 year course and children over eleven years of age were to be admitted to them. This suggestion was bitterly criticised on the ground that eleven years of age was not ripe for receiving technical education. The committee suggested that after admission at the eleven years of age, the child would be given a new suitable curriculum according to his interests on attaining thirteen years of age.

For the children of thirteen years of age the liberal education was to be given. Accordingly, the curriculum had to be repatterned. In the technical high school some such leaving certificate should he instituted which could facilitate the transfer of students from technical schools to grammar schools, if students so desired. Like the Hadow Committee, this Committee also opined that the post-primary education should be like secondary education no matter through whatever type of school it was imported. This would help the public to choose any school for its children, without being especially attracted towards a particular type. This would also ensure education to children according to their needs, abilities and interests. Furthermore, all schools would fall in the same line in a way.

***Multilateral Ideas of the Spens Report and Administration-*** On principle it was quite appropriate to provide education to children according to their interests and abilities and to bring all the post-primary schools into close relationship with the public, but practically this work was extremely difficult. A multilateral school could he so widely expanded that it would have been difficult for the headmaster-to control the students and teachers in the school. The Spens Committee had recommended to introduce the following things in a multilateral school:

(1) To emphasise practical education particularly.

(2) To establish higher technical schools and to introduce three years technical course for younger children.

(3) To introduce a number of subjects in order to cater to the verying needs, interest and abilities of children.

(4) Thirteen years of age should be fixed for admission of younger children.

***Norwood Committee, 1941-*** The Board of Education appointed a special committee under the chairmanship of Sir Syril Norwood for studying the recommendations of the Spens Committee and other committees. This committee submitted its report in 1943 outlining the nature of secondary education for all the children of the country. In this report all the students were divided into three categories:

(1) Those children who are interested in practical education and do not believe theoretical things.

(2) Those children who are especially interested in applied art and applied science. They do not like long explanations, but they do understand the work-processes very clearly.

(3) The children who want to obtain knowledge for the sake of knowlede. They like to reach the bottom of an issue and understand its causative factors.

The Norwood Committee recommended that separate schools should be established for these three types of children. For the first category of children modern secondary school, for the second category secondary technical school and for the third category grammar schools would be appropriate. But the question arose as to how to categories such students? The committee opined that the teachers of primary schools would categories studetns according to their particular abilities, interests and aptitudes. Intelligence tests and performance tests were also recommended for this purpose.

Like the Spens Committee, the Norwood Committee also recommended for interrelationships between various secondary schools and for similar curriculum in all the schools for children between 11 and 13 years of age in order to facilitate transfer from one school to another. The Norwood Committee further suggested that a lower school should be organised in these schools under the control of only one teacher who would classify the children according to their abilities and interests. The recommendations of the Norwood Committee were consistent with the political, economic and historical conditions of the country.

***Criticism of the Recommendations of the Norwood Committee***-The critics held that the implementation of the recommendations of the Norwood Committee would widen social disparities in the country leading to social disturbance in the nation. This plea was opposed on physical basis also. It was held that it was quite on psychological to classify children into three groups at the young age of eleven. So classifying children was considered difficult, but to administer schools into three different categories was not regarded so difficult. Unless a general intelligence base was prepared, it was not possible to categories children into the above three groups.

***Flening Committee of 1942***-R. A. Butler, the president of the Board of Education appointed a committee under the chairmanship of Lord Flening in 1942 for suggesting measures for establishing close relationship between public schools of England and Wales. After studying the public schools, this committee suggested the following measures:

1. Boys and girls should be admitted in public schools according to their abilities and interests. Admissions should not be permitted on the basis of financial' conditions of guardians. The financial position of a guardian should not be an impending factor in admitting his ward.

2. The schools should be classified into A and B groups.

Under the 'A' group all those schools would be included who obtained direct grants from the government. These schools should be recognised as associated schools by the Board of Education. In these schools either the tuition fee should be abolished or should be fixed according to the economic condition of guardians. The same policy should be followed about the maintenance charges in boarding schools. The local education authorities should be empowered to reserve certain seats in these schools and pay for their tuition fees. The same power should be given to them in boarding houses also. Those local education authorities whose candidates would be admitted in the 'A' group schools would be entitled for one third representation in the management of the school concerned.

Under the 'B' group, it was dedicated to group all the public schools which were to conduct the general education of the-country. If necessary, certain seats for the students of those primary schools might be reserved who were on the grant-in-aid list. Such students might be only 25 per cent of the total admitted students. But this percentage was prescribed only for those students who bad studied at least for two years in some grant-in-aided school. The Board of Education decided to award certain bursaries to students of the 'B' group. A provincial committee was appointed to select students for bursaries which were adequate enough to meet the varying educational an boarding expenses of the students concerned. But the bursaries were to be awarded only when the guradians gave their partial contributions for their wards education. Any guardian could apply for admission of his ward to any school under the 'A' group. By applying through the local education authorities seats might be reserved in the 'B' group schools for students of the 'A' group.

Through its recommendations the Flening Committee tried to effect a harmony between the traditional schools and the new educational system. Evidently, it did not choose to start any new plan of education. The public still harboured the notion that the facilities of the public schools were meant only for the wealthy and higher class people. The public schools had created a class-group. It is true that the committee had recommended the reservation of 25 per cent of seats in the public schools for those students of the aid primary schools who had obtained education at least for two years, but the general public was not at all satisfied by the recommendations of the Flening Committee. This discontent arose because of the fact that still 75 per cent of the students in the public schools were to be admitted from the higher class people. The bursary plan for the government controlled secondary schools created another discontent in the people, because this plan was likely to affect adversely other schools. Therefore the recommendations of the Flening Committee were bitterly criticised. Evidently, the Flening Committee failed to strike a balance between the state institutions and other general schools. However, the committee did prepare a background for this balance to be effected in future.

***Education Act of 1944 and Local Education Authorities-*** According to this Act, provision has been made for whole-time compulsory secondary education. The maximum age is fixed at 15 years.

L. E. A.'s responsibility increased. New educational experiment enhanced their responsibility for providing education and the expansion of the sphere. Primary and secondary education became their responsibility.

***Kind of Secondary Schools-***Schools prevailing before- (1) grammar secondary schools, (2) modern secondary schools, (3) technical secondary schools. Later on the following schools sprang up :

***Bilateral (Comprehensive) Secondary School-***The school offering courses by integrating the courses of any two of the above schools. They prepare students for general certificate of education.

***Multilateral Secondary Schools-***They included the courses of all three types of schools. They have two categories of schools- (1) Junior Secondary Multilateral Schools (2) Higher Secondary Multilateral Schools.

***Other Types of Secondary Schools-***Grammar Schools, Voluntary Clubs and Social organisations, General Education Certificate and Grammar schools.

***Secondary Technical Schools-***Their number is less than that of grammar schools because the people had little faith in them.

***Secondary Modern Schools-***4 types-Those with (a) General Education, (b) General and Specific Education, (c) Senior Elementary Schools and (d) Advanced Education Schools.

***Endowed or Grammar Schools-***The teachers of these schools were to obtain a teaching certificate. This system continued till

1869. Classical languages were emphasised. Un psychological method of teaching.

***Private Schools-***Their own educational system. Modern languages, art, geography and history etc. in the curriculum. Progressive methods of teaching. Student themselves maintained discipline. Girls were well educated in domestic arts. Sanuel Butler and Thomas Arnold tried to reform private schools. Arnold wanted to make education psychological and to base it on Christianity.

***The Royal Commission of 1861-***This commission was appointed under the chairmanship of Lord Clarendon for suggesting measures for reforms of nine particular public schools. The report submitted in 1864. Many recommendations for public schools.

***The Public schools Act of 1863-***Recommendations of the Royal Commission of 1861 were incorporated in it.

***The Enquiry Committee of 1864-***Under the chairmanship of Lord Taunton to enquire into the affairs of those schools which were not covered by the Royal Commission of 1861. The Report submitted in 1868. Three types of schools were emphasised. Reorganisation of examination system, secondary education and teachers qualifications were emphasised.

***Organisation of Secondary Education-***The Royal Commission and the Enquiry Committee emphasised the necessity of reorganising secondary education.

***The Endowed School Act of 1869-***The recommendations of the Enquiry Committee were ignored in this Act.

***The Impact of the First World War-***Secondary education was reorganised. The services rendered by the student during the war period impressed the public about the great utility of education.

***The Fisher Act of 1918-***This Act made changes in the tuition fees, grant-in-aid system and the powers of local education authorities. The industrialist did not co-operate. The Act could not succeed.

***The Labour Party and Education***-Tried to introduce social reforms through education. Many attempts were made to introduce reforms in education.

***The Hadow Committee Report of 1926***-Emphasised the need of secondary education for all children between 11 and 15 years of age. Stressed the establishment of grammar schools modern schools and senior classes.

***The Education Act of 1936***-For implementing the recommendations of the Hadow Committee this Act was passed.

***The Spens Report of 1938***-Emphasised the classification of students on the basis of examination. Suggested reforms in education of children over eleven years of age.

***Multilateral Ideas of the Spens Report and Administration***-The Spens Report was related with education according to the needs interests and abilities of children. This created administrative difficulties.

***The Norwood Committee of 1941***-gave recommendations for secondary education for children of various classes. Grouped all the children into three categories and recommended education for each. The public rejected this plan on the plea that it was likely to create class differences in the people. The suggestions were regarded as un psychological also.

***The Flening Committee of 1942***-This committee was appointed for suggesting measures for establishing inter-relationship between public schools and general education. This committee prepared a plan for education of all children through puhlk schools. The committee suggested the grouping of 'A' and 'B' type schools. It did not give any new scheme, but tried to bring in a harmony amongst the existing schools. The general public did not like the recommendations. However, it prepared a base for co-ordination between public schools and government schools.

## QUESTIONS

1. "The Education Act of 1944, determined the form of Special Secondary Education." How? Show the impact of this Act on the educational system in U. K.

2. Describe the system of modern secondary education in Great Britain.

3. Grammar schools have become more important than other schools, why?

4. Describe the Bilateral, Multilateral and Modern Schools established in U.K.

5. Describe the chief characteristics of Grammar Schools of U. K. Explain the reforms then were suggested for their improvement from time to time.

6. What were the better points in public schools in comparison to private schools. What measures were suggested for their reforms by various committees appointed by the Government?

7. Write short notes on :

   (1) Enquiry Committee

   (2) Hadow Committee Report

   (3) Norwood Committee Report

   (4) Flening Committee Report

   (5) The Impact of the First World War on Education.

# 9

# Basic Education

In this chapter we shall understand the nature of some important events which have led to the growth of primary education in Great Britain. Upto the middle of the eighteenth century in England and Wales. Private Day Schools and Common Day Schools were prevalent. Ladies were working as managers of these schools. Teachers in these schools were mostly cruel in their behaviours with children. Every week some money was received from each student as tuition fees. Most of these schools were not satisfactory. However, there were a few ones providing good education. Later on, the conditions of many schools improved when the system of regular tuition fees was adopted. For convenience of the reader, the development of primary education in U. K. may be understood into two phases as under:

(1) Development of primary education till the eighteenth century, and (2) Development of primary education during the nineteenth century.

**Historical Background**

Below we are describing those schools for primary education which existed in Great Britain upto the eighteenth century.

According to the difference in age two types of schools existed at the time. For infants there were Dame schools and for older children other type of schools-was known as the Common Day School. Only those children were admitted in these two types of schools who could pay some tuition fees. Although the tuition fees charged were not much; but the poor children were not able to pay them. Therefore for poor children charity schools were opened. Charity schools were dependent on charities for their functioning.

**Various Types of Schools**

In 1698 some charity schools were opened for propogating the elements of Christian religion and also for fulfilling the minimum educational needs of poor children. The teachers of these schools were generally kind and generous bishops. They had their own managing committees. But the condition of these schools was not good, because they depended only on charities.

***Curriculum of the Charity Schools***-It consisted of reading, writing, simple arithmetic and religious instructions. Some practical manual labour was also made a part of the school activities. Ploughing fields, gardening, weaving and spinning were done by the school children. The purpose of these activities was to make these children suitable to undertake domestic services in some homes after completing their education in charity schools.

***Financing of Charity Schools***-Due to lack of school buildings these schools were generally held in church galaries. These schools did not charge any fees. So they were entirely dependent on charities from the public. The teachers used to place their demands before the public from their church galaries mostly on Sundays before or after the church services.

***Importance of Charity Schools***-As we have already said earlier, the purpose of charity schools was to educate the poor and illiterate children. Hence these schools rendered a unique service to poor children. The general public had great faith in these schools. These schools were generally opened it that area which was inhabited by poor and illiterate people. In the beginning of the nineteenth century an attempt was made to run these schools on the monitorial system. These schools served the public well. The Pietism Movement of Germany drew inspiration from these schools and started several institutions like charity schools of Great Britain. These schools were in Great Britain generally over-crowded with students. In 1760 there were more than 30,000 students in these schools. Gradually, this strength was reduced.

Besides the charity schools, there were some other schools also run on charities, but they were not related with the church in any way. These schools were run by non-conformists and Roman Catholics. There was no central organisation to control and run these schools. Consequently upto the eighteenth century, these schools were bitterly criticised by the public as it did not had sympathies with them. Hence they declined gradually.

***Industrial Schools***-In these schools, children of those persons received education who were generally engaged in small industries. These were opened after the industrial revolution. Students received free education here and were trained in spinning, weaving, sewing and gardening etc. They were given religious education also. Expenditure of the schools was met by the income received from sale of articles produced by the students. Sometimes the students were also taught reading, writing and arithmetic. They were given meals in schools. In due course, the attention of the government was drawn towards these schools. The Pit government of 1769 has suggested that students should take admission in industrial schools. By this time the industrialists had started to employ children in their industries on salaries. So the parents were happy at this assistance received through their children employed in mills and factories, therefore the parents preferred to send their children to industries instead of to industrial schools. As a result, the industrial schools suffered a set-back.

A section of the people were interested in improving the condition of industrial schools and giving some facilities to their students. An ideal industrial school was started in 1786. Inspite of reforms in these schools, only 20,336 students came for education here upto 1804. These students were between the age group of five to fourteen. Gradually the growth of these schools stopped.

***Sunday Schools***-As a result of industrial revolution mills and factories began to employ children. By and by a large number of children began to work in industries. So some device had to be found out for education of these children. The children used to work throughout the week. They could get leisure only on Sundays. Therefore, for their education such schools were opened which would be in operation especially on Sundays. Robert Raikes was the first person who opened a Sunday school in 1786 for educating children working in industries in Gloucester. A Sunday school organisation was, constituted for organising the various Sunday schools. In 1803, this organisation was named 'Society for Establishment and Support of Sunday Schools'. Local committees were organised by the Society. Fifty percent of membership of these committees was given to bishops and fifty per cent to persons interested in public welfare.

The main purpose of Sunday schools was religious and social. They were not so much interested in the mental development of students. therefore, in these schools, the children were given religious education, were trained in handicraft and taught reading, writing and arthmetic. People of higher class were sympathetic towards these schools and they used to give financial help to them. In the beginning the teachers of Sunday schools were given some remuneration. But as the number of these schools increased in due course many persons became teachers in these schools without accepting my remuneration.

***Importance of Sunday Schools***-The importance of Sunday schools lay in the fact that they made the beginning of free and universal education. They tried to work in mills and factories of their adverse circumstances. Gradually these Sunday schools became centres of meeting places of workers in various industries, foremen and industrialists. In 1787 there were about 2,50,000 students in the various Sunday schools. In 1801 only in London, there were about 1,56,490 student in Sunday schools. In the development of these schools the liberal attitudes of industrialists was of great importance. The industrialists understood that they were nothing to lose if the children-labourers were educated. Therefore they very often encouraged them for receiving education. As a result, the life of children working in mills and factories became more disciplined and cultured. This situation also helped in making the environment of the mills and factories more cultured. Thus the Sunday schools helped the development of primary education immensely.

Griffith Jones established these schools in 1737 in Carmar then of Wales for teaching Bible to poor children through their mother-tongue. He wanted to give religious education to children through catechism (questions and answers). When he noted that the parochial schools of Wales were not fulfilling this objective, he started his circulating schools. These schools were called circulating because the teachers of these schools were to move from one place to another for teaching children of various places. As considered necessary; teachers used to stay at one particular place for 3 to 6 months and do teaching work in some hired buildings or shelter. These schools were set in operation either during the day time or in the evening. Both children and adults came to receive education in these schools. These schools were maintained through charities and the assistance received from the society for the promotion of Christian Knowledge. Due to the indifference of successors of Griffith Jones, these schools began to disappear and their place was taken up by the Sunday schools. These circulating school existed from the second half of the eighteenth century to the first half of the nineteenth century.

The Monitorial system was adopted from the Indian education by Andrew Bell and Joseph Lancaster who utilized it on a higher plane. This system was started with a view to educate children of poor people. In this system the senior student used to teach the junior ones. This system partly solved the dearth of teachers.

***Andrew Bell and Joseph Lancaster-***Andrew Bell (1753-1832) a bishop and Joseph Lancaster (1778-1835) were members of the Peace Committee. Andrew Bell was a head master of some school at Madras. During his head mastership, he used the monitorial system for meeting the dearth of teachers. He enlisted the co-operation of senior students for teaching younger students. Some classes were fully entrusted to the care of senior students. After his return to Great Britain, he adopted this method in some charity schools. This method gave satisfactory results.

Joseph Lancaster also opened a school in South Wark. When the school because overcrowded with students, he entrusted the responsibility of teaching some junior students to senior ones.

***An Evaluation of the Work of Andrew Bell and Lancaster-*** Both Andrew Bell and Joseph Lancaster contributed immensely to the development ,and universalisation of primary education in Great Britain. New method of primary education by grouping into classes was started. However, it will have to be admitted that inspite of certain merits of the monitorial system, its defects also came out on the surface. It is true that the monitorial system made the primary education cheaper, but its standard fell down. The teachers lost contact with students who could not be benefited by the knowledge of the teachers.

***Robert Owen, Wilder Spin and David Stow-***These three lovers of education contributed to the growth of primary education. We shall understand below their role in the same:

***Robert Owen and Primary Education-***Wilder Spin (1771-1858) was a practical man, he organised the Ignorant Factory Community. He used the monitorial system of primary eduction for working children between 5 to 10 years of age. Under the influence of some progressive educationists he made some changes in his method of teaching.

***Wilder Spin and Primary Education***-Wilder Spin (1792-1865) was a progressive educationist. He did not believe in the monitorial system. He believed that a teacher could be successful in his teaching work only when he brings himself down to the level of children he has to teach. He did not like that children should be advised to behave like adults. He felt that the teacher should deal with his students with sympathy and kindness. He wanted to introduce activities and some recreation, in the method of teaching.

***David Stow and Primary Education***-David Stow (1793-1860) was a businessman of Glasgow. He established some Sunday schools for teaching poor children. He did not succeed much in this enterprise, so he established the Glasgow Infant Society in 1826. Due to his efforts primary education developed in Scotland.

Efforts of Andrew Bell, Joseph Lancaster, Robert Own, Wilder Spin and David Stow were very slow. So greater efforts were needed for accelerating the growth of primary education. There were some social factors also due to which development of primary education was obstructed.

Each section of the society did not feel enthusiastic for contributing to the growth of primary education. Particularly, the higher class of people did not like that the children of poor people should be educated. They thought that their education would ultimately jeopardise their interests; because in due course they would revolt against the superior position of the high class people and would demand equal status. The industrialists and businessmen also thought that if the poor children admitted in schools, they would not come to work in mills and factories. The various church groups had contradictory approaches to religious education. This situation worked as an impediment to the growth of primary education. The monitorial system, too, was not taken kindly and it was thought that this system emphasised memorisation instead of developing natural powers in children. The State was neither showing any interest in primary education nor did it interfere in the efforts of private enterprises. This position, too, was unhelpful to the growth of primary education.

**Role of State**

Upto the eighteenth century the State did not take much interest in the development of primary education. So the role of private enterprises alone had been helpful in this sphere. But there was an awakening in the people due to the industrial revolution. So the common people asserted their legitimate right for primary education. Hence the government compulsorily thought to do something in this field. The cruel and inhuman treatment given to child labourers in mills and factories attracted the notice of some social workers and educationists. So they pressed the government to do something for education of such children. The industrialists were exploiting the children by exacting from them hard labour day and night. The children had to live in dirty and unhealthy surroundings. They were getting neither proper nutrition nor healthy living accommodation. there was no arrangement for their mental, moral and religious education.

***Robert Peel Act of 1802***-Sir Robert Peel submitted a bill in the Parliament for removing the inhuman conditions of the factory child-labourers. Many mill-owners and some members of Parliament opposed the bill vehemently. But the bill as passed under the name Factory Act. This Act, though very much limited in scope, had far-reaching consequences on development of primary education. The Act led to the passing of several other bills for improving the condition of the children working in factories. In the Factory Act of 1802, the following were the main items of reforms:

1. The child-labourers were not to be employed now during night. Only twelve hours work could be given to them during day time.

2. The mill-owners were required to make the necessary provisions for light, fresh air and cross ventilation at working places and from now onwards they were also required to colour or whitewash the walls of the factory building at least once a year.

3. It was laid down that the child-labourers should be taught reading writing and arithmetic for some time every day.

4. The child-labourers were to be given at least one hour's religious education on every Sunday, and they were also to be sent in the church at least once every month.

Thus the Factory Act of 1802 proved very helpful. This Act became the basis for the Education Act or 1870.

***Parochial School Bill of 1807-***This bill was presented in the House of Commons by White bread in 1807. This bill contained the provision that for children between 7 and 14 years of age, there should be at leat 2 years of education in some rural school to be opened for the purpose. But this bill could not be passed due to opposition of capitalists and the Church.

***Robert Peel Bill of 1815-***Robert Peel again submitted a bill in the Parliament for improving the deplorable conditions of children working in mills and factories. The House of Commons appointed a Select Committee in 1818, for enquiring about the conditions of children working in factories. This committee found that the working children had to work for 12 to 14 hours a day. At some places, these children were complelled to work for 100 hours per week. On some mistake they were severely punished. Robert Peel's bill was discussed in the House of Commons in 1818 and many changes were made in this bill and its original form was considerably changed. In 1819 this bill became an Act. But this Act, too, was not implemented earnestly as was done with the Act of 1802. The Act of 1819 was made limited to the working children in cotton mills. According to this Act no child below he age of nine years could be employed in a mill nor any child within the age range of 9 to 13 years of age could be compelled to work for more than twelve hours a day.

***Parliamentary Committee of 1816-***Samuel White bread started an education movement in the Parliament in 1816. After his death Henry Brougham (1778-1816) continued his work in the parliament flue to his efforts a Parliamentary Committee was appointed in 1816. This committee inspected into the education given to the children of lower orders. This committee reported that such children sent to school were not given even the minimum educational facilities. Their attendance in schools was not regular. The endowments of the various schools were being misused. On these informations Henry Brougham demanded an immediate probe into the school endowments. Brougham maintained that education of children would not be properly managed if the school endowments are not properly utilized. Brougham further observed that if this was done, there would be no need of levying any education tax. Many schools opposed bill. But in 1820 this bill was brought before the parliament under the name Parish School Bill.

***Brougham's Parish Schools Bill of 1820***-The purpose of this bill was to make education available to the poor children of England and Wales. But the Roman Catholic people and the Established Church opposed this bill tooth and nail. As a result, this bill was withdrawn. Later on, this bill was supported by John Arthur Roeback.

***John Arthur Roeback and Popular Education***-John Arthur Roeback supported the point of view of Brugham. He asserted that only organizing the equipments for education was not development of education. He emphasised that education meant development of moral and mental qualities which the educated should he able to use in his own life. John Arthur Roeback recommonded the establishment of four types of Schools, namely, (1) Infant Schools. (2) School's of Industry, (3) Evening Schools for adults and adolescents and (4) Normal Schools for training of teachers. He said that from the economic point of view financial position might be improved through charging fees (or school pence), levying taxes and organising endowments. The whole country should be sub-divided into school districts and each school district should elect a school committee for its schools. The whole education affair should be managed and controlled by the education minister of the cabinet. Several people supported the proposal of Roeback, but his bill could not be passed.

## Growth and Development

During this period the Government contributed to the growth or education. So there was good progress of education. The Government gave £ 20,000 in 1833 for construction of school buildings. This state grant was gradually increased. In 1846 it became £ one lakh and in 1833 it was raised to £ 836920.

***Elementary Education Enquiry 1833-***A State grant was made available for the first time in 1833. Efforts were now started for the development of primary education. For finding out the necessary things for this development an enquiry committee was appointed in 1833. This committee reported that there were no good schools for primary education both in rural and urban area. In big cities only one out of ten children was receiving suitable primary education, two out of ten children were going for education in unsuitable infant schools and three out of ten to private day schools and the remaining four were not receiving education in any school. The 'Education Mad' group was very much surprised at this deplorable situation. So they demanded that the state should take up the responsibility of running schools. They asserted that throughout the whole country there should be a central education authority which should be open new schools, distribute grants and levy educational cess. They also emphasised the need of a Central Teachers' Training College and a model school for practice teaching. They, further suggested that religious education to be imparted should be of two types denominational (special) and undenominational (general). In the first type only those would impart religious education who are entitled for the same and are also ministers of religious institutions. For the second type, all qualified teachers were considered suitable. In 1836 the Central Society of Education was constituted. This society was authorised to see that the above suggestions were implemented.

***Committee of Privy Council in 1839-***The Queen established a committee of privy Council in 1839 for considering the problems relating to general education. The Privy Council was empowered to consider all those factors which in any way affected the progress of education. The Council was also requested to look .into the utilization of grants-in-aid given to schools. As a result a Central Administrative Authority was appointed. Dr. Kay was appointed the Poor Law Commissioner. Dr. Kay studied the schools meant for poor children both in Great Britain and some European countries. He thought about the satisfactory way's for promoting education in poor children and felt that it was a state responsibility to provide education to children.

Dr. Kay recommended that schools should be made community centres. He further realised that good education could be imparted only through trained teachers. So he emphasised the need of opening a teachers' training college. He tried his best to give a practical shape to his ideas. His friend E. C. Tufnell gave a hand for implementing his proposals.

The Home Secretary James Graham prepared a Factory Bill for improving the poor condition of labourers in mills. The following were the essentials of this bill :

(1) Children within the age group of 8 to 13 working in work houses or mills should not be required to put in more than six hours labour per day and they should be taught at least for three hours every day.

(2) The School Trustees will be empowered to appoint teachers in their schools. But the appointement will have to be approved by the Bishop. The clergyman of the rural area and the patron of the church would be the members of the board of trustees.

(3) The students will have to attend the religious services of the established Church of England and their attendance will be compulsory in church on every Sunday.

(4) The financial necessities will be met by the State. School building will be constructed by obtaining loans from the state.

The above features of the bill indicate that the church had a prominent place in the organisation of schools. Church wardens opposed this bill. But a conscience clause was included in the bill to the effect that the desiring parents might keep their children away from catechism. But because or bitter opposition the bill was withdrawn. Thus the cause of education suffered.

**Private Efforts**

Voluntarists movement advocated that state interference in education should be checked but they, too, accepted religion as the oasis of education. They wanted to implement the principle of Free Trade in education. They felt that freedom and competition was necessary for reform in education. They collected money from the public and opened schools. They did not take any aid from the government. Upto 1851 there were about 384 such schools. Gradually people began to find fault in their educational programmes and they became sceptical about their success.

***Kay Plan of 1846***-In 1846 Dr. Kay prepared a plan of education which was announced by committee of council education. The following were the main features of this plan:

(1) Pupil-teachers selected for 5 years apprenticeship should be given stipends.

(2) Her Majesty's Inspector of Schools should inspect the work or pupil-teachers.

(3) Grants should be given to teachers training pupil-teachers.

(4) After completing five years' apprenticeship the pupil-teachers should sit in the scholarship examination of Her Majesty.

(5) The teachers trained in a government training college should be given proficiency grants.

(6) After completing 15 years of teaching, if a teacher chooses to retire he should be given a pension.

(7) A teachers training college should be given annual grants.

The above plan was liked by many. One lakh pound were approved as grant for educational development. Within 1848-50 this grant was increased by twenty five thousand pounds. Thus the government began to take interest in education.

***W. J. Fox Bill of 1950***-This bill regarded as a secular one, was presented in the parliament. This bill gave no place to any denominational school. It was stated In the hill that the tax-payers of those places where schools were very necessary should be given unequivocal rights. The taxpayers who arranged for free and secular education of, children between the age group 7 to 13 should be empowered to levy educational taxes. But due to opposition from the Church and denominational people this bill could not be passed. After this bill, some other bills were also submitted to the Parliament but the problem of popular mass education could not be solved.

**Departmental Setup**

The Government realised the need for development of education in the country. So on February 22, 1856 on the basis of the Council order in place of the Committee of Privy Council the Education Department was established. Its establishment was for finding out solutions to educational problems of the day. The Lord President of the Council was made the head of Education Department. A deputy head was also appointed to assist him. The deputy head had to be a member of the House of Commons. Intimately connected with the ruling party, affairs relating to expenditure of the Education Department: The deputy head was responsible to the Parliament. Thus the head was only a nominal head of the Education Department.

***Royal Commission of 1858***-Under the chairmanship of the Duke New castle a Royal Commission was appointed in 1855. This commission had two major aims. The first aim was to study the condition of the prevailing primary education. The second aim was to suggest sources for making good primary education available to all. Below we are giving some of the main recommendations of the Commission:

(1) The government grants sanctioned in 1833 could not yield desirable results. Hence this was not a successful plan. For development of education greater government grant is necessary.

(2) The system of primary education then prevailing, though defective, was useful.

(3) The prevailing system of education is difficult. It should be made simpler.

(4) Schools should be given grant-in-aid on the basis of examination results.

(5) Schools which are regarded as unsatisfactory by her Majesty's Inspector of Schools should also be given finanical assistance. This assistance should be in addition to the grants that the pupil-teachers were already receiving.

(6) Local grants to be given to counties and boroughs should also be determined.

(7) The sanctioned grants should not be more than the tuition fees and income received through donations taken together.

(8) The system of charging tuition fees should be continued. The counties and boroghus should be empowered to see how the grants were utilized, but they must not interfere in the internal affairs of the school process and the kind of religious education imparted.

Many of the above recommendations were good. But due to bitter opposition, they could not be implemented and they remained as suggestions on paper only.

## Free Trade Rule

In 1869 Robert Lowe became the vice chairman of the Education Department. He believed in the principle of free work. So he implemented this principle in education. Thus the work of education came in the hands of those who were opposed to the principles advocated by Kay. The ability of a student from now on was to be determined on the basis of examination result. The local examination of Oxford and Cambridge were started in 1859. Examinations in Science and Arts were also started in 1865. Open competitions were also started for civil services in 1855. On the principle or demand and supply, Robert Lowe wanted that the public education should remain denominational. He did not favour the principle of educational grant according to the recommendations of the Royal Commission.

***Act of 1870***-On the election ill 1865 the Liberal Party again came into power. Hence many changes took place in the area of primary education. Primary education under the school boards developed remarkably. At that time school boards and voluntary organisa-tions were working simultaneously for primary education. The primary schools run by voluntary organisations were more in number than primary schools under school boards. In 1880, out of 17,614 primary schools, there were 14,181 schools under voluntary organisations and 3,433 under school boards. In 1897 great changes were made in the schools run by voluntary organisations. Still there were students in them than in schools under the school boards. But in due course because of good management of students in them went on increasing. By the end of the nineteenth century, there were only 46 per cent primary school students in the schools of the voluntary organisations and 54 per cent were under till school boards. The schools under the school boards were getting girl grants than income through taxes. Hence they were benefited most. As a result, the schools under the voluntary organisations were left behind.

**Public Schools**

In 1882 the Education Code was framed. So many changes Were made in the grant-in-aid system. In 1882 the grant to a school was determined according to the number of students present in the middle of the school hours and not at the beginning. On the report of the Inspector of Schools on this point, the nature of grant was decided. The Inspector used to submit his report keeping in view the following three factors:

1. The organisation and discipline of the school,
2. The methods of teaching, and
3. The general standard of the teaching work.

On the basis of the above three points, the inspector would write 'fair good' or 'excellent' in his report. By 1882 the arrangement for education upto the seventh class was made. On the basis of the inspector's report two types of grant was being given-merit grant or fixed grant.

The schools under the school boards were receiving greater grant than the schools under the voluntary organisations. For the board schools more qualified teachers were available as the emoluments there were more attractive. Good conditions did not exist in the schools under the voluntary organisations. Only a few schools under voluntary organisations could get sufficient grants due to its good standard of work. The other schools of voluntary organisations received insufficient grants.

**Kindergarten System**

In Bloomsbury some schools on the Kindergarten pattern were established by the disciples of Froebel in 1854. Such schools developed very slowly. Children of only rich people were getting education in these schools. Within 1874 a number of such schools were opened in several parts of London. In 1874 Maria Grey founded the Froebel Society. She opened many Girls Public Day Schools. Croydon's high school was one of them. One Kindergarten school was also associated with each of such schools. Schools under this system became very popular and many people opened such schools. The children of high and middle class people preferred to go to these Kindergarten schools to public elementary schools.

In the beginning the Froebel system of education was not being implemented in these schools. Activities relating to reading, writing and arithmetic were more emphasised. Gradually Froebel's principles were understood and incorporaned in the educational procedures.

***Royal Commission of 1886***-Under the chairmanship of Sir Richard Cross the Royal Commission of 1886 was appointed for evaluating the work of primary schools. This commission submitted its report within two years under two categories majority report and minority report. About religious education only one report was submitted. Primary education was defined unanimously and the necessity of giving grants was emphasised by all the members of the commission.

Some school boards were running some secondary schools also. A few members of the commission suggested that these secondary schools should also be given public grants. But most of the members of the Commission were of the view that these secondary schools should not be given grants from the public funds, because children of rich people were receiving education in these secondary schools. So the majority insisted that the necessary funds for these secondary schools should be procured through higher tuition fees.

***Implementations of the Recommendations of the Royal Commission of 1886***-Many reforms were effected in primary education on the basis of recommendations of the Royal Commission of 1886. In 1890 au education code was framed. The system of 'Payment by Result' was stopped, because the grant relating to reading, writing and arithmetic was discontinued. Now grants were introduced for teaching elementary science, physical science, geography to students of advanced age. Teachers' training centres were opened in universities and colleges affiliated to universities. Those recommendations of the Commission which were not unanimous could not be implemented due to opposition from various groups.

***Common Day Schools and Dame Schools***-Those children who could pay tuition fees were educated in these schools.

***Charity Schools***-To teach, reading, writing and arithmetic to poor children. Religious and industrial education were also given. The purpose was to spread education. Financed by charities. Monitorial system was used.

***Industrial Schools***-Free religious education and training in domestic industries.

***Sunday Schools***-For children working in factories and mills. On Sundays teaching of reading, writing and arithmetic. Religious education and training in handicrafts. Public education received encouragement.

***Circulating Schools***-To teach Bible through the mother-tongue. To spread literacy Teachers would move from one place to another after a few weeks or months.

***Monitorial System***-Andrew Bell and Joseph Lancaster. To teach junior children through the help of senior students under the supervision of one teacher.

***Robert Owen, Wilder Spin and David Stone***-Contributed to the growth of primary education through their ideas.

***Development of Primary Education During Nineteenth Century***-Due to the Industrial Revolution children between 10 to 14 years of age began to work in Mills and factories. Their education was stopped. The high class people and big industrialists opposed their education.

***State and Education***-The state did not interfere in education till the 18th century. In 1802 the Apprenticeship Act, Parochial

School Bill of 1807, Robert Peel Bill of 1815, Parliamentary Committee of 18th, Parish Schools, Bill of 1820. Development of education remained arrested till 1833.

***The Privy Council Committee of 1839***-To look after the public education and after utilization of the given grants. A Central Administrative Authority was appointed before the establishment of the ministry of education. Dr. Kay was its secretary. He emphasised community development.

***Voluntarist's Movement***-No state interference in education. Follower of the principle of Free Trade in education.

***The State Supervision of Primary Education***-The slate should take Education under its control.

***Establishment of educational Department***-In 1856 it took the place of the Education Committee of Privy Council.

***The Royal Commission of 1858***- Its report in 1861 for reforms in primary education.

***The Principle of Free Trade in Education***-The chairman of Education Department, Robert Lowe was its advocate. Importance to examination. The Education Code in 1862. New problems sprang up.

***Primary Schools under the School Boards***-Financial position and work better.

***Public Elementary School***-Improvement in the condition according to the Education Code of 1882.

***Froebel and Elementary School***-Many Kindergarten Schools.

***The Royal Commission of 1886***-The Report published in two years.

Difference of opinion regarding religious education. Improvement in primary schools.

## QUESTIONS

1. Describe the development of primary education in Great Britain upto the Ninteenth century.

2. Explain the contribution of Robert Owen, Wilder Spin and David Stone to primary education.

3. Trace the development of primary education in U. K. during the 19th century.

# 10

# Initial Education

In England and Wales, there are three types of schools imparting primary education. This formal elementary education starts from the lowermost schools. So it will be better to classify nursery and infant schools in pre-primary education. Infant education cannot be separated from primary education because they are supplementary systems of primary education. Primary education prevailing in England and Wales consists of the following three stages:

***Nursery Schools and Nursery Classes***-Young children of about two years or so are accepted in these schools and they are taught upto the age of 3 or 4 years. The attendance of children in these schools is not compulsory but optional.

***Infant Schools***-In these children of 5 years of age are admitted and are taught for two years, i.e. upto the age of 7 years. Attendance here is compulsory.

***Junior Schools***-In these schools, the children of the age of 7 years are admitted and are taught upto the age of 11 years. The attendance of students in these schools is compulsory.

The above three stages make the primary education complete. A brief description of each types of school is given below:

**Nursery Level**

Two types of Nursery schools are found in the United Kingdom. The trust type of nursery is that which gets all the financial help from the local education authorities. These are called maintained schools. The other type includes those schools which receive grant-in-aid. They do not get full aid but only partly. There are 60 to 80 students in a nursery school. A class does not consist more than 20 students. The age limit of children is 2 to 4 years. Women teachers are employed in such schools and they modify the behaviour of the children promoting tender feelings in them. They provide them food and educate them to put on clothes and help them to learn many other things through games. These schools are established near factories particularly textile mills because the mothers of the children go to work in these nulls for earning a living leaving them in the shelter of these schools.

No formal education *is* imparted in these schools. For their physical mental and social development the children are required to participate in activities like playing, singing, painting, dance and modelling. This leads to their natural development and they become happy and self-reliant. In these schools, constructive games, health and hygiene and activities for amiable nature and behaviour are the basic components of the curriculum, For these. suitable school buildings, apparatus and equipments, corresponding to that development stages of children are provided. Most of the nursery schools are independent but at some place they are attached to infant schools.

**Schools for Babies**

In these schools, a child of 5 years of age is admitted and upto the age of 7 years, he learns reading, writing and arithmetic. Thus formal education begins here. In these schools Montessory and Kindergarten methods of teaching are adopted and the children are provided opportunities of participating in various games. At some places these infant schools are attached to junior schools or primary education centres. The knowledge of different subjects in these schools is given in an integrated and correlated form. Efforts are made to modify the behaviour of the students by correlating their, knowledge of different subjects to their life. Natural and attractive atmosphere are made available in these schools. Efforts are made to develop the power of observation and other sensory powers of the children. The teachers try to develop their vocabulary and speak words in correct pronunciation.

These infant schools are co-educational. Efforts are made to develop Self-expression in boys and girls through the medium of mother-tongue and music. First of all, the boys and girls are prepared mentally and physically and then their psychological behaviour is studied and further education is imparted. The attendance in these schools is compulsory.

**Initial Level**

Primary education is provided by establishing junior schools. Boys and girls of 7 years of age are admitted in these schools and are taught upto the age of 11 years. There are co-education in these schools. The attendance of students is compulsory.

These junior schools are established independently and some of them are also attached to nursery and infant schools, The curriculum of these schools includes, nature study, mother-tongue, mathematics, science, history, geography, music, gardening and health education. The curriculum may be changed according to the local needs. Thus there is no uniformity in the courses of studies of various regions.

The boys and girls receive education for 4 or 5 years together and move about freely in the open grounds of the schools. Importance is given to dramatization and story-telling from the point of view of self-expression. Efforts are made to develop their power of observation and skill in crafts. The boys and girls are provided opportunities to learn spinning-weaving, basket-making, mud-work and domestic crafts. The instructional work is more systematic in these schools than in nursery and infant schools. The number of students in every class is about 40. The teachers in these schools are both male and female.

Primary education has been divided into three parts :

*Nursery Schools*-For the children from 2 to 4 years of age. Attendance option.

*Infant Schools*-For the children from 5 to 7 years of age. Attendance compulsory.

*Junior Schools*-For the children from 7 to 11 years of age. Attendance compulsory.

***Nursery Schools***-Attendance optional; Age, 2 to 4-5 years. Playing, eating, dressing, and rearing tender emotions main activities. School hours 9 a. m. to 4 p. m. No formal education. Schools near mills where mother leave their children in the care of teachers.

***Infant School***-Compulsory attendance. Age 5 to 7 years. Reading, writing and arithmetic part of curriculum. Singing, dance, painting, clay work and play main activities. Kindergarten and montessory methods of teaching. Development of power of observation and sensory organs. Singing and mother-tongue as medium. Attention of psychological processes.

***Junior School***-Attendance compulsory. Age 7 to 11 years, dramatization, story-telling, nature study, mother-tongue, mathematics, science, art, history, geography, health education and gardening as subject, Girls are taught domestic crafts. Number of students in the class 40. The curriculum is flexible.

## QUESTIONS

1. Describe the pre-primary system of education in Great Britain.
2. Describe the system of primary education in U. K.

# PART–THREE

# EDUCATION IN FRANCE

# 11

# Teacher Training

For various levels of education, such as-primary, secondary and higher, there is a need of teachers according to the french system of education. Generally, in France only two types of teacher are found. Those who teach at the various stages of primary education are called teachers and those at the secondary and higher stages are known as professors.

**Various Institutions**

Under the category of teachers come all those persons who teach pre primary and primary classes. In 1830 the system of formal training of teachers was started and about 30 primary normal schools were established for training of primary school teachers. In 1833 some more norm schools were opened and in 1879 some normal schools for training of lady teachers were started.

**Fiscal Aspects**

The national government beras 50 per cent of the total expenditure on normal schools. Salary of teachers, expenditure on teaching materials and school-building are the responsibility of the central government. The government awards some scholarships to the trainees also. The concerned department of the government looks after its general maintenance.

### The Management

The rector of the department is responsible for genetal administration. The rector appoints a council of administration for looking after the administration of normal schools. The officers of this council inspect the normal schools, look into their budget and do the needful regarding transfer of teachers and trainees from one normal school to another. The rector appoints a director of this council who is generally one of those teachers of normal schools who have experience of teaching in normal schools and have qualifications of an inspector of primary education.

### The Syllabi

There are thirty teaching periods per week in normal schools. Sunday is a full holiday and Thursday is a half-day. Fifty half-days a year are given for practice-teaching. Each normal school has a practising institution. Along with instructions in principles of education, certain general subjects are also taught. In all about twenty subjects are taught. These include educational psychology, sociology, philosophy, science, physiology, natural science, agriculture, painting, music, physical education, geography, history, mathematics, French language and literature and a foreign language. During the first year of the normal school supervision and observation are emphasised. In the second year an attempt is made to develop a sense of responsibility of a teacher. During the third year it is seen that the trainee acquires the ability to teach and control a class independently. Thus the three year curriculum of the normal school is completed.

### Evaluation and Measurement

In the normal school every year an examination is held on completion of the prescribed course. In the first year examination, the trainee is examined in more subjects than during the second. In the first year, he is examined in history, geography, education, sociology, physics, practical knowledge and a foreign language. In the second year the trainee is examined in the remaining subjects. In the third year a viva-voce test and examination in practice-teaching are held. After this a written examination in one of such subjects as art of teaching, art, music, physical education, French language and literature, agriculture, home economics is held.

**Criteria of Admission**

Persons within 15 to 19 years of age having passed Brevet Superior Examination or some equivalent examination may be admitted in normal. Before being admitted each candidate has to submit a health-fitness certificate. He has also to sign an agreement form with the government that after obtaining training in a normal school he will serve at least for ten years in some primary school. Every trainee has to stay in the hostel compulsorily. If there is no hostel he has to obtain permission for staying at a particular place. The trainees residing outside a hostel have also to sign an agreement form for doing ten years service after the training, because the government gives them also the allowances as permissible to trainees in hostels. If some trained person does not abide by the conditions laid in the agreement form, then he has to refund all the sums to the government received as allowances.

Because of the heavy curriculum and strict rules of hostels, the trainees do not have time for other activities. The trainees are permitted to go out only during holidays. The lady-trainees have to observe stricter rules. They have to submit in advance a list of acquaintances whom they may meet on request. Only a person from this list is allowed to visit the lady-trainee. The correspondence of a lady-trainee is censored with great care and vigilance.

After the Second World War, recreational activities have been encouraged for trainees. Before the war little attention was paid to such activities for trainees.

## Model Schools

Superior normal schools train teachers for normal schools and for higher primary schools. For males there are superior normal schools named as Saint Cloud and for women there are Fountehay-Aux-Roses. A person of at least nineteen years of age who has passed either higher primary education or secondary education may sit at the admission test of a superior normal school. This admission test is generally very stiff. Generally about ten per cent of the candidates who take this test are able to pass. For this test one year's curriculum is taught in the normal schools. The trainees of the superior normal schools, too, have to submit a health-fitness certificate. They have to reside in hostels wherein there is usually adequate arrangement for boarding and lodging.

***The Curriculum and Examination in Superior National School***-There is a two year curriculum of literary and science group in the superior normal school. A trainee may choose either the literary or science group. Practice-teaching, educational psychology and principles of education are compulsory for all. Each group of studies (literary and science) has been divided into two parts. In the first part of the literary group are placed history and geography and in the second group French language and literature. In the first part of the science group natural science, physics and physiology and in the second group are kept pure science and mathematics.

As regards examinations, separate arrangements exist for various groups and parts. A certificate is awarded after the completion of the two year course.

## Teacher Education

The secondary school teachers in France, as we have already remarked in the preceding pages, are known as professors. Their training is of the following two types:

(1) One is considered competent to teach in secondary schools if he possesses the B. A. (baccalaureate) and obtains the prescribed university education.

(2) To obtain training either in the Grand Ecoles or Ecoles Normal Superieure after obtaining the B.A. degree (baccalaureate).

For admission in the Ecoles Normal Superior, one has to prepare himself while teaching in a Lycees; after having obtained the B. A. degree. After passing the admission test, one has to study a, four year curriculum during which one may earn a number of certificates. Under, this curriculum after studying for two years, one gets a license and on completing the third year one is awarded a diploma d' eludes superieures. During the fourth year, one prepares himself for the government aggregation examination. For women there is a separate system which is known as severs. Those women trainees who obtain good marks in competition are given scholarships and other facilities in hostels and others are sent to the Sarr'doune University or to some other schools for education. The university also prepares students for the aggregation examination and grants licenses to successful trainees. Some special education courses are also taught.

***Ecoles Normal Superior School***-This school was established in Paris in 1795. This school alone used to give training to teachers of secondary schools. This school admits about 48 trainees-28 in the literary group and 20 in the science group. This school awards license, diploma, stage pedagogic and aggregation degrees which some universities also award. After the aggregation degree one is qualified to teach in a lycees or he may become an educational administrative officer. There is adequate arrangement for co-curricular activities in the Ecoles normal superior school. The educational atmosphere is kept at a very high standard. Special importance is attached to teaching in a lycees. Therefore the lycees in Paris generally appoint teachers with aggregation degrees. The college teachers are considered as inferior. According to the modern developments in France, arrangements have been made for training of teachers of industrial and vocational schools. Training in physical education also has been organised.

**Working Conditions**

There is a great difference between the qualifications of teachers meant for different stages and types of education. On the basis of service and their mode of appointment the teachers in France may he grouped under four categories, such as-(1) probationers-those who are under training, (2) long-term substitute teachers hut without permanent appointment, (3) regular substitutes and (4) short-term substitutes for one day or longer service to help out in case of sickness or other cause of temporary absense of the regular teacher.

The teachers of public schools are government servants. They are appointed by the government or its representative. The prefect of the department appoints teachers of primary schools. The teachers for industrial and vocational schools are appointed by the central education minister. The education minister appoints teachers of higher primary schools and secondary schools also. The president appoints the teachers of universities.

The special types of teachers (professors) are appointed by the officers of the concerned department.

The teachers of universities have to reach for fewer hours. Their promotion is dependent on seniority and teaching experience. A teacher generally retires at the age of sixty years. On retirement some pension and allowance are given. If one is requested to teach beyond sixty years of age, he is given additional remuneration.

On breach of discipline, a teacher may be demoted or his license may be cancelled or he may be suspended. There is a committee of judge of the institution for recommending a suitable punishment. Its recommendation is considered by the councilor board concerned.

Teachers have their unions for pressing their legitimate demands before the government. There is a federation-general d' el Enseignement for protecting the rights of teachers and this federation works for unity amongst teachers.

Financially, the teachers in France do not feel frustrated. They enjoy suitable pension after retirement. They are respected by the government and public in general.

Those who teach upto the primary stage are called teachers and the rest are known as professors. Normal school started in 1840. Separate normal schools for training women teachers.

The government gives 50 per cent aid. The rest is the responsibility of the department or the local municipality.

***The Administrative System of Teachers' Training***-The departments are responsible for administration. The rector appoints an administrative committee. The inspector of schools acts on behalf of the rector.

***The Curriculum***-Three year curriculum. Twenty subjects are taught. Practice-teaching, educational psychology and principles of education are compulsory for all. The other subjects are taught in different groups.

***Examinations***-Examination every year. Written, oral and practical.

***Admission in Normal Schools***-An admission test has to be passed. For admission one should have passed secondary course. The age should be at least 19 years.

Residence in hostels compulsory. Strict discipline in hostels.

***Superior Normal Schools***-To train teachers of normal school and higher primary schools. Stiff curriculum. Only 10 per cent of candidates get admission. For admission success in admission test is necessary.

***Grand Ecoles***-B. A. degree; holders are admitted on admission test. The Government responsible for expenditure.

***Condition of Teachers***-Retirement on attaining sixty years of age. Satisfactory economic condition. Teachers of public schools are government employees. The university professor is appointed by the president of the nation Promotion based on seniority and teaching experience. Pension is granted.

Union and federation for pressing demands before the government.

## QUESTIONS

1. Describe the teachers' training system in France.
2. Compare the teachers' training system in France with that existing either in U. S. S. R. or India.

# 12

# University Education

To acquire knowledge after completing the prescribed course of studies may be regarded as the chief aim of higher education in France. Ofcourse, to acquire a degree or certificate is another aim of higher education there. So along with knowledge for the sake of knowledge aim, the objective is also to obtain degree for some professional purposes. Three types of students are found in France at the higher stage of education. One group is of those students who want to earn a degree for some professional purpose after studying the prescribed courses. The second group of student are especially interested in acquision of knowledge and they do not desire any degree of certificate. The third group of students are those who do care about admission requirements in universities and they just attend lectures of earning some knowledge.

## Basic Principles

Higher or university education is a responsibility of the provincial government concerned but it is directly controlled by the education ministry of the central government. Hence they are adequately financed and maintained by the centre.

Arrangement for higher professional training is made for the interested students. This training is separate from the university education. The provincial government is responsible for this training. But this is controlled by the professional or industrial department concerned. Separate educational institutions are established for industrial and professional education. These institutions are run under instructions of national departments concerned.

In France there is always an attempt to maintain a high standard at the higher level of education. So their degrees and certificates have won recognition. The first two years of the four year courses of American colleges may be regarded as equivalent to the French secondary education. There is a consistent effort in France to maintain a high standard of education and to keep the spirit of acquisition of knowledge alway at the top. This spirit has relegated degrees and certificates to a secondary position and has led to a high standard of education.

**The Setup**

The universities in France in their external forms are almost like universities in other countries. In all the French universities, there are separate faculties of Arts, Law and Science. Only in one university, there is no law faculty. In the old university of Paris, the students do not get easy facilities for studies, whereas in other universities students enjoy all the necessary facilities. In this respect other universities are much better than the Paris University. In the Straitsburg University, separate arrangements exist for Protestant and Catholic theology even when the number of students is quite small. Some universities have separate faculties for medicine and surgery.

In France, there are seventeen such universities which affiliate about 150 educational centres which provide facilities for higher professional education, training and research. Thus, at the higher level in France there are provisions for various types of vocational and professional education.

**The Administration**

A university in Franc imparts higher education through its various faculties which are independent in themselves. There are some other independent institutions also which impart higher education and they are not inter-related. Each one has its own laboratories, workshops and libraries. Since there is no interrelationship between them, one institution does not get the co-operation of another. Therefore, their laboratories and libraries are in a way inadequate. So students usually feel the lack of necessary facilities at various stages of their education.

There is a committee formed by the heads of various faculties. This committee looks after the internal affairs in relation to the university . The rector of the academy under Which the university happens to exist is the chairman of this committee which determines all the policies pertaining to the various types of managements. This committee also looks after the affairs of those institutions which are affiliated with the university.

However, these affiliated institutions are independent like the various faculties of the university.

**Award of Degrees**

There is no prescribed national policy in France to degrees on completion of various courses of studies at the higher education stage. Normally these degrees are indicative of some professional skill or some kind of special ability. It may be noted that these degrees are simply licenses or license-degrees for a specific period. These licenses may be earned on studies of less than one year duration. The duration may be even four or five months. If some foreigner completes his studies for some duration, he too is awarded a license. In the absence of a national policy, each university has it own separate degrees or licenses. These degrees are so varying in nature that even the separate faculties of the same university may award degrees with spectacular differences.

The French baccalaureate (B. A.) degree may be regarded as equivalent to the matriculation certificate of U. K. The highest degree of a French university is a doctorate. The doctorate degree in France is awarded after obtaining a number of licenses and also on producing of two theses on the basis of an intensive research work done for a number of years. Between the first degree of baccalaureate and a doctorate, the doctoral candidate has to earn a number of licenses certificates. The examinations for these certificate are conducted by the central government. The duration of conducting a research for a doctorate degree has been now reduced. This duration may be even as short as two years. However, some students take more time. But because of the reduction of the period of research the doctorate course has become more attractive to foreign student.

***Aims***-Knowledge for the sake of knowledge and dissemination of knowledge is the chief aim of univeristy education in France. For some, obtaining of certificates or degrees may also be the aim.

***Higher Education Standard and University Faculties***-The French public stands for a high standard and wants to enhance the value of univeristy certificates. Separate faculties for arts, science, law, medicine and surgery. These faculties are independent in their internal management.

***Higher Education System***-No prescribed national policy. Variations in the degrees and certificates granted by the various faculties and institutions. Baccalaureate (B. A.) the lowest and doctorate highest degree. Degrees are just licenses for obtaining some jobs.

## QUESTIONS

1. Describe the system of higher education as existing in France.
2. How is the university education system in France different from that in U. K. or India? Explain their salient points.

# 13

# School Education

### Different Schools

Napolean Bonaparte had realised the necessity of able citizens for running administration efficiently. So he organised secondary education on a sounder footing for preparing an elite class of people who could help in-running the administration smoothly. The system introduced by him continued till a new one was evolved. The new education system does not aim at only intellectual development but at full physical and mental growth for enabling one to perform his duties as a useful citizen in the desired manner. Secondary education in France is complementary to higher education. Provision for vocational education is also made at this stage.

***Lycees and Colleges***-Lycees were establishes in 1809 for imparting secondary education. The central education ministry is responsible for these institutions which prepare students for higher education. In them there is a seven year curriculum. Teaching of classics and mathematics is especially emphasised in them. Since the tuition fees in them are charged at very high rate, so they have not been available to all. In 1812 municipalities established a number of colleges for removing the inadequacies of Lycees. The municipalities were wholly responsible for their maintenance. However, the government used to give them some grant. When the new scheme of education was introduced, the grant for these colleges was also increased. These colleges did not give any place to teaching of ancient languages and literatures.

The teachers of colleges were generally of lower qualifications and abilities than those in Lycees. The teachers of Lycees were holders of aggregation degrees. But the college teachers were holders of licenses of a lower order. Therefore, guardians used to prefer Lycees for education of their wards. But, for most of the people, Lycees were very expensive.

**New Trends**

After the Second World War under the influence of the existing Lycees and colleges some College Moderne were started. The main purpose of these modern colleges was to raise the existing standard of primary education. These modern colleges are under the control of Lycees and colleges but in them modern language and science are also taught. These colleges also prepare students for passing the baccalaureant degree in addition to training them into modern citizenship.

At places where Lycees and college are not established, the primary school students who pass the entrance examination at eleven years of age are given secondary education. The classes run for giving secondary education in this manner are called complementary classes. This arrangement is generally found in rural areas. After completing the courses of the complementary classes the students are awarded either elementary certificate or lower secondary certificate. On the basis of this certificate the student may either get admission in some normal school or in some secondary school at another place. The courses of these complementary classes vary according to local needs. The facility for introducing the necessary modification and change is available for all complementary classes.

**Vocational Schools**

The college technique has been established for imparting technical education at par with secondary education. If students for technical education are few in number, then arrangements for them are made in modern colleges. However, their courses are kept different according to the requirements of technical education and their classes are also run separately. Orientation Classes in the beginning, the courses for secondary schools were not chosen on a psychological basis. In them no attention was paid on individual interest, aptitudes and abilities. This kind of curriculum was like a load on students. So in order to remove this defect, in 1937 crientation classes were run. In 1945, a scheme was made to develop this plan with co-operation of about 200 teachers. A journal was also started in relation to this. Now these classes are considered equivalent to the beginning classes of Lycees and Colleges. In this new plan particular attention is paid on the interest, ability and aptitude of a student. For this purpose psychological tests are administered. These tests are conducted at the secondary level now. But some conservative people are opposing this procedure.

**Education for Females**

Education of girls belonging to traditional families was principally under private religions or sectarian institutions. Their education was conducted by the convent people also. According to the education law of 1880 separate Lycees and college were organised for education of girls. Where the number of girls was small, co-education was permitted. Neighbouring areas young girls whose elder sisters were getting education could also be admitted in these institutions. An examination board was constituted with teachers as its members. This board used to award certificates to these girls.

In the courses of studies for girls, language, literature, dancing, painting, music, feminine arts, home science, home economics, sewing and cooking etc., were emphasised. After passing the prescribed examination, the girls could become inspectresses or teachers. During the twentieth century, according to the changed situations of life, arrangements have been made to bring education of girls at par with that of boys and provision of awarding the B. A. (baccalaureate) degree to girls has also been instituted. For this degree, the girls, too, have to pass the same examination which the boys have to do. Now the girls were also prepared for higher education. Subjects which suited the feminine nature were introduced in the system. Some vocational courses were instituted for boys.

**School Management**

The Lycees and Colleges are very well governed. The head of Lycees is called provisor and that of the college is known as the principal. The head of the Lycees and college meant for girls is called doctrice. The teachers of these schools are known as professors. For the help of the Lycee provisor there is a committee constituted by the rector of academy, prefect, academy inspector and the principal. Some representatives of guardians also serve on this committee. This committee is responsible for financial affairs, construction of buildings and appointment of school inspectors. For the help of the principal also, a committee of a similar nature is constituted.

For distribution of scholarships there is an alumani association. Similarly a class committee is organised. All the teachers of the concerned class are its members. An education committee to effect a correlation between various subjects is also organised. This committee also tries to see that a balance is maintained between the school work and home task. All the teachers of a particular subject are members of the education committee which decides about a suitable curriculum of the subject for various classes.

This committee also tries to create a balance between the various subjects of the curriculum. This committee has also to see that there is a uniformity of standard in various subjects in comparison to the same in other schools.

**The Syllabi**

The curriculum of secondary education may be divided into two pre-primary and secondary. In Lycees and colleges the primary courses are of four years and the secondary of three years. After completing the primary course, the student is given a certificate which entitles him for admission in the secondary course. In the primarystage, Latin is compulsory and Greek is optional. At the secondary stage in place of these languages greater emphasis is laid on teaching of painting and science. At this stage, there are not too many optional subjects. French, algebra, chemistry, physics, history, geography, painting and physical education are taught at both the primary and secondary stages. Provision has been made for technical education which is generally equivalent to other subjects in standard. The technical classes are known as class de mathematics. They are arranged for all desirous students.

In the first year of the secondary stage of education the curriculum is generally of 23 hours per week. In this programme six hours are deveted to teaching of Latin, 2 for algebra, 2 for physical education, 2 for painting, 1 for natural science, 1 for geography and 4 for chemistry and physics. Similarly, for children of 15 or 16 years of age in the first part of the baccalaureate (B. A.) degree course 3"2 hours for French, 2 for history, 2 for geography, 3 for mathematics, 2 for physical education, 4 for Latin, 4 for physics and chemistry and 3 for Greek per week are given.

At the secondary level in France the classes are numbered in the reverse order. For example, Class I is not known as class I but as class VI. Similarly the second class is V, the third class is IV, the fourth is III, the fifth is II and sixth is I. The curriculum of these classes is the same as in other schools. The courses prescribed for obtaining the baccalaureate (B. A.) degree are taught in the last two classes *i.e.,* class II and I. The baccalaureate (B. A.) degree is the highest degree of the secondary stage of education. For this degree, four subjects are taught, out of which one is optional. After this one may prepare himself for admission to a university. Suitable arrangements are available for this admission test at the secondary level of education. Mathematics and literature are taught for this test. For this test, girls are taught some foreign literature translated into French. The secondary part of the baccalaureate teaching is co-educational. But now arrangements are made for this test in girls' school also. Feminine arts are particularly taught to girls.

**Teaching Methods**

Particular emphasis is laid on development of logical ability in students through the methods of observation, thinking analysis and generalization. The student makes notes ,in his exercise books about the subjects taught to him. His notes are made generally in such a systematic manner that in due course they assume the form of a book. Writing of essays is started from the third class. Spacial emphasis is laid on speaking and writing French accurately. Some portions of the lesson have also to be memorized by each student.

Teaching of Greek and mathematics is done with a view to develop intellectual capacity. The teaching methods of Greek and Latin are the same and they are arranged according to the capacity of students at various levels. Greek is considered to be a difficult language. So it is taught at a mature stage of child development. Correctness of pronunciation is especially emphasised. The life of the literary figure concerned is taught with due emphasis and care.

History is taught with a view to acquaint the student with French history and historical developments in foreign lands. In teaching of history an attempt is made to develop an international understanding in students. Art is taught for cultural development. There is no vocational bias in its teaching. Geography of France and of other parts of the world is taught with a view to develop basic geographical concepts. Economic geography is generally taught in higher classes. In the beginning descriptive geography is emphasised more.

Science is taught in order to ,develop a capacity of making scientific insvéstigation and research. Philosophy is aught at a higher stage according to the Socratic method in order to develop the power of finding out solutions of problems oneself. The various class committees and education councils contribute immensely in imparting knowledge of various subjects.

***Types of Secondary Schools***-Lycees and Colleges oldest institutions. High tuition fees in them. So they are not within the each of all. They are considered better than other types of secondary schools. Teachers in Lycees are more qualified and are considered more competent. There are other secondary schools such as complementary classes modern college, orientation classes, technical secondary schools. The modern colleges were established to meet inadequacies of Lycees. They are governed by Lycees.

***Secondary Education for Girls***-After 1880, Lycees and colleges were organised for girls also. If girls are small in number, co-education is permitted. Girls too, have to sit for examinations. They also get B. A. degree.

***Administration of Secondary Schools***-The head of Lycees is known as provisor and the head of the college is called participial. The lady head is called doctrice. There are many committees for their assistance. Prefect, inspector of schools and representatives of teachers and guradians serve on these committees. There are class committees and education committees also to help the administration.

***The Curriculum***-Few optional subjects, Latin, Greek and French languages and literatures, mathematics, science, history, geography, painting and philosophy are taught to boys. For girls feminine arts, home science, home economics, dancing, music, sewing and cooking are emphasised. The curriculum is of 7 year duration.

***Method of Teaching***-For development of logical power and intellectual capacity, the teaching is done on a psychological pattern. The students are guided to make systematic notes in their exercise books on the basis of their text-books. Correctness of pronunciation is particularly emphasised'. Greek and philosophy are taught to students who appear to be quite mature. Socratic method is followed for these two subjects.

## QUESTIONS

1. Describe the various types of schools that impart secondary education in France. Why are Lycees and colleges considered of a higher order ?

2. What are the specific features of secondary education for girls in France ?

3. Explain to what extent secondary education is modernized in France. What are the points worthy of incorporation in them for any other system of secondary education. Illustrate by giving examples of either U. K. or U. S. A. or India.

# 14

# Basic Education

Primary education in France was declared free before 1881. In 1882 it was made compulsory and in 1937 its age limit was fixed between 6 to 14 years of age.

There is a primary education department under the ministry of education for looking after the primary education affairs. The stage of primary education is the middle point of early education of the child as pre-primary, primary and higher primary stages complete the primary stage of education. After completing 14 years of age, the child's secondary education may be started. Though the age limit for primary education is 6 to 14 years of age, but it is not necessary that primary education will end at 14 years of age. It may be continued even much further. However, this arrangement of continuing primary education a little further is meant for those boys and girls who are able to go further for receiving secondary education.

**School Organisation**

Under each municipality there is at least one government primary school. Separate arrangements for boys and girls exist. But where the number of boys or of girls is small co-education is accepted. Now there are only government and private primary schools. If at least twenty children are available at a distance of about 3 kms from a big village, a primary school is opened for them. The government is fully responsible for constructing a building for a government school, but it also gives grant to private bodies for construction of buildings for private primary schools. This grant may be anything between 11 per cent to 90 per cent of total expenditure on the building. The body which obtains government grant for construction of building has to follow government specifications for the same and they are as under:

1. The class-room should be so big as to permit at least 1.25 sq. meter space for each child.

2. The lawn of the school, too, should be so big as to allow at least 1.25 sq. meter space for each child.

3. The school should be much away from graveyards and places of noise.

4. The ceiling of a class-room should be at the height of at least 4 metres. I should be ventilated at least from two sides. If it is not possible to have cross ventilation from two sides, then the light should come from the left side.

5. The playground should be so big as to permit at least 5 sq. meter space for each child.

The grant for the building is sanctioned only when the site and the plan of building is approved and the site is duly inspected.

Compulsory school attendance law for children between 6 to 14 years of age has been passed in France. Before starting the session, the local children are counted. It is the responsibility of guardians to supply a list of those children to education officers who are within the compulsory school attendance age. On violation of this law financial punishment or imprisonment may be awarded. If a guardian wants, he may arrange for education of his child at his own place. Guradians are informed about the absence of their wards from the school and this information is also given on the notice board.

A student may be granted leave if he cannot come to school because of illness or due to some adverse circumstances at home. For encouraging attendance a student giving maximum attendance is rewarded with many articles of daily use. If a student of a farmer comes from a long distance, he is granted two days per week leave and a scholarship. On recommendation of the school inspector a student of a farmer may be granted 3 months leave during the year by the departmental council. In rural ureas the attendance is still poor due to the following reasons:

(1) Lack of faith in the school system due to narrow conservative and religious outlook.

(2) Due to bad climate and other natural difficulties.

(3) To exact agricultural labour from children by big land-holders or to compel them to graze cattle.

The school hours are determined keeping in view the tender age of children. The time-table is framed for six hours per day according to the courses of study. The first part is from 8 A. M. to 11 A. M. and the second from 1 P. M. to 4 P. M. after two hours interval in between. Both in the first and the second parts separate leisure time is permitted, Thursday is full holiday every week. At east 2 hours per week are devoted to physical education.

### The Syllabi and Books

The French public gives national importance to primary education. It regards it not only as general education but the basis of democracy established in the country. The public feels that primary education should be such as to produce able citizens and leaders for democracy in the country. French language is the medium of instruction at the primary stage. Primary education of France may be divided into the following three parts after which course superior is started:

(1) Course Preparative of Elementaire

(2) Course Elēmentaire

(3) Course Moyen

It is true that education in France is not so developed from psychological point of view as in U. K. or in U. S. A. But there practical psychology is given more importance. The balance between the courses of studies is effected beautifully. For example, for the mental development of the child provision has been made for education in mathematics, handicraft and domestic craft. For physical development, provision of physical education is worthy of note.

The necessary variation is allowed in courses meant for boys and girls according to their different needs in life. Under general subjects, language, mathematics, reading, writing, elementary science, history, education in citizenship, moral education, painting and geography are taught. But in the higher primary classes the curriculum has been made more extensive by introducing handicraft, physical science and agriculture etc. According to some local requirements education in some commercial and industrial areas may also be arranged. In place of agriculture girls are taught domestic science. Thus a unitary curriculum is current in the whole country.

The French government is very careful in the selection of text-books at the primary stage of education. The central ministry of education has appointed a separate committee for determining the suitability of text-books at the primary stage of education. The inspector of schools for primary education is the chairman of this committee and the teachers are its members. This committee holds its meetings in July when the session starts and determines the suitability of various books for various classes for the whole year. In this determination the available and universally approved books are selected. This selection is never changed during the session.

In the course elementaire the student is given a piece of slate and, elementary text-books. At the course moyen level the student is provided with exercise books and books relating to mathematics, geographical atlas and elementary grammar etc. In the course Superior the students are given books, exercise books, a book on history of France, book on moral education and training in citizenship, books on mathematics and French grammar. Students of all classes are given pens, pencils, note-books and some pieces of paper. A provision of giving other material aids exists in the school for all the students.

**Measurement and Evaluation**

An examination system has been considered necessary for the evaluation of educational achievement of students of all government and private schools. There are generally two types of examinations-(1) general examination and (2) competitive examination.

***General Examination***-This is taken when the courses are completed. On success in this examination a certificate is awarded to each student. In addition to the examination taken for awarding a certificate another examination is also taken for testing specialization done by the student. The student who passes the test of specialization is given preference in giving a teaching position. There is a departmental examination committee for examining those children who were receiving education at home and now want to get admission in some school. The representative of the canton, teacher and the primary education inspector are the members of this committee. This examination may be regarded as an admission test also. The primary education examination is taken at the age of twelve years and the student is given a certificate of passing it. At the primary stage the examinations are both written and oral. These examinations take different forms which are changed according to place and sex differences. The examinations arranged in schools in rural areas are different from those meant for municipal areas. At the higher primary stage the examination is oral, written and experimental. In this examination children within the age of 15 to 18 years alone are permitted because the experimental examination is difficult for younger children.

***Competitive Examination***-The students who want to get admission in normal schools for training to become teachers have to pass a competitive test. Such a test is also arranged for award of scholarship and teaching certificate. This test is both written and oral.

**Higher Level**

After completing the course of primary education one has to receive higher primary education. For this type of education there are superior primary schools proper and complementary classes. Under the compulosry attendance law the Superior Primary School Proper Course is for three years. After completing this course a certificate of capacity is awarded. This certificate is essential for government administrative services and for teaching positions. The course for complementary classes are for two years. The student passing this course may get admission in a normal school.

At the higher primary education stage, there is a provision for recreation, sports and games, library, exhibition, gymnasium and agriculture. A workshop is also organised for handicraft at this stage. The course for the first year at this stage is general, but that of the second year is different and more difficult. Courses for boys and girls are varying. They may be related to technical education, social sciences and vocational education. The head-master is empowered to select courses and subjects for the same. In this selection due attention is paid on local needs. The head-master is a person who has passed at least the higher primary education. He is regarded as the director of the courses. A teacher for this stage must be of at least 25 years of age and he should also have at least five years' teaching experience. He must also possess the superior license of teaching the brevet superior.

A committee of patronage looks after the school management. The headmaster is appointed by a cabinet minister. The local municipality or the administrative unit is responsible for construction of the school building. On the recommendation of the committee of patronage the government gives 50 per cent grant.

In maintenance of the school discipline, punishment may be given to erring students. Through prizes and certificates the students are induced to maintain good discipline. Generally corporal punishment is prohibited. On some charge of indiscipline the student may be detained for some time after the school hours. Moral education has been made compulsory at this stage. Each student is given training in good citizenship for strengthening democracy in the country. There appears to be a judicious harmony between the spirit of individualism and corporate life on acceptable social principles.

***Primary Education System***-It is after pre-primary education, but before higher primary education. It is under a department of primary education which works as an independent unit under the central ministry of education. Previously, it was given by preparatory classes.

***Opening a school and its Building Construction***-Separate schools for boys and girls. Co-education is accepted if the number of students is small. Local municipalities and boards responsible for construction of buildings, but the government gives 10 to 90 per cent financial help. For this help prescribed rules must be followed.

***Attendance of Students and School Hours***-Compulsory attendance rule in force. The guardian is made responsible. If his ward does not go to school, he is given financial punishment or he is sent to jail. Thursdays and Sundays are holidays. The school are from 8 A. M. to 11 A. M. and 1 P. M. to 4 P. M. Teaching hours are 322 per week.

***The Courses of Study***-French is the medium of instruction throughout the whole country. Emphasis on physical, mental and moral education. Differences in rural and urban curriculum. Sex difference in curriculum *is* also maintained. Handicraft, art, language, mathematics, history and geography are given main importance.

***Text-books***-A committee selects text-books. Teachers and the school inspector are its members. Text-books are chosen once a year. They are not changed during the session.

***Examination System***-General examination both written and oral. Admission test *is* also arranged. Competitive test for scholarship, financial help and admission in normal school.

***Higher Primary Education***-This is conducted by the committee of Patronage. The headmaster determines the curriculum and chooses text-books. The teacher should be at least 25 years of age and should have at least five years teaching experience. The government gives 50 per cent grant.

## QUESTIONS

1. Describe the nature of primary education in France.

2. What features of French Primary education are worth incorporation in any system of primary education and why?

# 15

# Initial Education

The current nature of French education is an outcome of a consistent development. In the beginning, there was a lack of articulation in the various stages of education in France. This feature presented great difficulties before students who wanted to get admission in some higher school after completing his education in a lower one. In getting admission in a new higher school he had to repeat certain courses which he had already studied. Thus his time was wasted. In the new educational set-up in France, this difficulty has been removed and each stage has been made complementary to another. Thus, pre-primary primary, secondary and higher education are inter-related with each other, These day pre-primary education in France is given in five types of schools as under:

(1) Kindergartens

(2) Children's classes

(3) Special pre-primary education

(4) Primary classes in secondary schools.

(5) Special schools for physically and mentally handicapped children.

According to the instructions received from the central ministry of education primary education was made free and compulsory between the ages 6 and 14 years. Formerly, the age limit was 13 Pre-primary education is complementary to primary education. In the above five types of schools pre-primary education is imparted. At places where there is no arrangement of pre-primary education for children within 6 years of age, admission in a primary school starts at the age of 5 years. Formerly Lycees and colleges used to impart primary education also in some form. But, later on, this responsibility fell on institutions known as Salles Asile. In 1881 the names of these institutions were changed to Ecoles Matetneles. In addition to these institutions, there are some other pre-primary institutions known as Class Enfantine. These schools impart primary education also. We are describing below the various types of pre-primary schools.

**Various Institutions**

Lycees and calleges also provide pre-primary education to children below six years of age. The lycees and colleges run pre-primary classes on the old pattern. But with the evolution of a new pattern of pre-primary education lycees and colleges are losing their importance as additional centres for pre-primary education.

These are old institutions. In 1881 their name was changed to Ecoles Matetneles. These schools teach children of 2 to 5 years of age. Education imparted here is quite psychological. These schools were made free in their organisation and they had their own inspectresses to supervise the teaching work. Here children enjoy sweet parental affection.

**Institutions for Babies**

This is only a part of primary school and it is held in extra hours after the primary school being over. Children between 3 to 6 years of age receive education here. The headmaster of the primary school looks after its entire arrangement.

## Kindergarten System

Children of about 3 years of age are generally admitted in these schools. According to age two groups are organised in a kindergarten. In the first group for physical and mental growth the children are given lessons in handicraft, painting and general manners of behaviour. They are also given some language exercises. In the second group the children are taught reading, writing and arithmetic. It is particularly seen that the children do not feel education as a load on them. So the whole thing is so conducted that the children are happy to be in such schools.

## Teaching Methods

The pre-primary schools in France provide education to all such normal children who fall within the age range of 3 to 6 years. Within this age range the rate of physical and mental development of children is quite fast. So an attempt is made to effect a balance between the physical and mental development of children. This is done through plays. In this way playway method of teaching is generally followed in these schools.

In France there are still some persons who want to run pre-primary education on traditional lines. They regard play methods as waste of time. So they stand for giving instructions in 3 Rs through memorization. But in quite disregard to traditional method now Montessori and Decroly methods are followed at this stage. Besides, the latest psychological methods are also used in giving pre-primary education.

## The Organisation

According to the statistics available in 1983 about 8,00,000 young boys and girls were receiving education in pre-primary schools. Out of this number, about 6,00,000 children were in government pre-primary schools and the rest were in private pre-primary schools. The Second War had paralysed the total educational structure in France. But a new type of maternal schools were opened based on the spirit of the Red Cross which had also established some Creches and Missions d' enfanee for teaching young children of 3 to 6 years of age. This pre-primary education began to develop with great speed.

Primary education is organised by communes and the government does not interfere with this arrangement. A commune may have a number of pre-primary classes attached to primary schools and get additional grants for the same from the government. All types of pre-primary schools get government grants and their work is inspected by government inspectors. Thus pre-primary education is organised by a commune but it is controlled by the government.

In the beginning in France the various stages of education were not complementary to each other. The lycees and colleges used to run pre- primary classes for preparing students for primary classes. Afterwards this work was done by Salles d' Asiles which were known as Ecole Matetneles in 1881. Now children classes, Kindergarten, special pre-primary school, pre-primary classes affiliated with secondary schools and schools for physically and mentally handicapped children. General Enfantine class. These schools prepare children for primary stage.

***Method of Education***-Many schools on traditional methods. But now new methods used on Montessori and Decroly styles.

***Arrangement***-Before 1837 private enterprises encouraged pre-primary education. The interference of the government has now improved the situation. Communes open pre-primary schools. The government gives grant. Government controls them.

## QUESTIONS

1. Describe the nature and kinds of pre-primary education in France.

2. Give your assessment of the pre-primary education system in France.

# 16

# Growth of Education

Education in France has shown a continual development from 1684 onwards. Religious and some other organizations have helped the growth of education in France immensely. Jean Baptist de LaSalle, a religious leader founded a school Christian Brothers in 1684. This school developed so much that in due course it succeeded in running a number of primary, secondary, vocational, and teachers' training schools. This attempt served as an ideal for other organizations. The Jesint society, which ended in 1764, did some work in this direction. In the beginning-many cathedral schools were started. The Government did very little for education till the end of the eighteenth century. In 1825 for the first time a university named Mantpelier was established.

In due course the public rose against the schools run by religious and sectarian bodies. The public thought that these schools were imparting narrow religious instructions. They regarded this situation harmful to the development of democratic traditions. Therefore the public began to establish public schools. This step was regarded as an unprecedented revolution in the field of education. The schools run by religious bodies used to produce elite individuals. These individuals were not able to fulfil the needs of the country.

Thus in France two opposite groups came forward in the field of education. One supported the public schools and the other was in favour of schools by religious and sect' an bodies. The patrons, teachers, managers and organisers of public schools became busy in the religious bodies stood for conservatism and fanaticism. Because of these two opposite groups, the cause of education suffered. But this groupism came to a standstill soon and the development of education was speeded up.

Consciousness developed in the public for education led to the demand of universal and useful education for all. In 1789 a movement for centralisation of education was started. So it was not possible for the Government to ignore the public demand and it began to interfere and take interest in educational affairs. Thus the Government fhtbelped the growth of education. But due to lack of adequate financial resources the governmental efforts, too, did not succeed much.

**Role of the State**

The tendency of centralisation in education developed with the tendency of centralisation in administration. LaChaloltais was the first man who in 1763 emphasised the necessity of centralisation in education. Other educationists also stressed the importance of centralisation of education, but the efforts of Napolean Bonapart has been really praise-worthy in this context. Napolean divided the educational organization of the country into twenty seven academies. Each academy was put under the control of a rector. In 1808 University de France was established. The educational affairs of these twenty seven academies were governed by the Grand Maitre de La University. But the rector was still held responsible for the educational activities of his academy. Untill now centralisation of education was limited to secondary education alone. The primary schools were not under the centralisation scheme.

The elementary schools of France were under the local authorities. The government did not give them any help. In 1833 Guizot succeeded in making government grants available to these schools. In the beginning this grant was only nominal. But by 1907 seventy five per cent of the expenditure incurred by these schools was shouldered by the government. After 1907 inspectors of schools were appointed for inspecting the affairs of the schools. The inspectors used to emphasize centralisation of education. Gradually the government began to control the communes and the local public schools. In 1882 an education act was passed which gave freedom to guardians to make arrangement for elementary education of their wards. But these wards were required to sit at the annual examinations conducted by the inspector of schools. It was after passing these examinations that the government used to grant certificates to the successful students. Thus all the independent enterprises in the field of education were compelled to follow the government rules. The religious schools also came under the government control.

In 1904 a new education act was passed according to which no religious or sectarian organization could interfere in educational affairs. As a result the number of students in public schools rose to five times more than the number in private schools run by religious and sectarian organizations. By 1935-36 this number increased further Rousseau's ideas of liberty, equality and, fraternity influenced education all over the world. Condercet's principles of uniformity and Victor Cousin's ideas influenced education immensely. But in secondary schools the principle of university and equality had not been promoted fully by this time. The facility of secondary education could be available to children of some special classes only. In France two types of schools were existing after the primary level. One type was those of higher elementary schools and the other were preparatory schools affiliated with secondary schools. Children of lower classes were admitted in the higher elementary schools and those of higher classes in the preparatory schools. Such preparatory schools were known as Lycees and Colleges.

Thus theoretically the state provision for Universal education existed but the same was not available from practical point of view. It was extremely difficult, if not impossible, for student to get themselves transferred from one school to another. After the First World War efforts were made to ease this difficult situation. But because of uneven comparative examinations enrolment at the secondary level did not increase much.

**Language Problem**

Since centuries there has been a demand in France to make regional languages as the medium of instruction. This demand became more intend as the country made advances in various spheres. The French government thought that making of regional languages as the medium of instruction was not compatible with the policy of centralisation. Therefore, the government did not accept this demand. While the agitation for regional languages was in process, some young teachers founded an institution called LES Champignon de L. Universite Nouvelle. This institution stood for a new educational system which demanded education for each child according to his intellectual, social and economic status: This institution urged that each academy should have such a universal system of education which may be easily available to all. All the academies should have well determined and useful curriculum. These demands could not he met immediately, hut in due course educational reorganisations were made on the same basis. Efforts were made to effect a uniformity on the academies of all the provinces. Admission in secondary schools became easier for children of all classes. Secondary education was made free for poor children. For elementary school the age group was fixed between 6 and 12, for higher elementary school between 12 and 16 and preparatory school about 18 years of age. For all these stages useful an universal education was provided.

**The Syllabi**

With change in time educational philosophy and values of life also changed. After the end of the Second World War great changes appeared in philosophy of life and educational philosophy. This change was naturally mainfested in new social, economic and political concepts. This change resulted into new outlook regarding the physical mental economic and social development of children. Consequently, great changes were introduced in educational methods and organisations. The Ministry of Education began to give more importance to industrial and vocational courses. The standard of examination was prescribed and selection of suitable text books was emphasised. The training of teachers was organised according to the needs of schools. So normal schools were established for training of teachers. As far as possible these normal schools were opened in big cities also and not only in rural areas. The following two proposals were considered with regard to training of teachers:

1. After university education the teachers' training course should be of one year.
2. For teachers of elementary school one year's professional training should be organised after completing secondary education.

On the basis of the above two proposals teachers' training was reoganised and a number of normal schools were opened.

***Algiers Commission***-This commission was appointed in 1940 under the chairmanship of M. Captain after the French Government was established in Algiers. The main purpose of this commission was to suggest measures for reforms in education. This commission suggested to implement the recommendations of Ecole Unique. It further observed that it was very important to introduce suitable changes in the methods of teaching of higher schools and universities. Paris was under foreign domination when this commission was appointed. So when it became free in 1944, the recommendations of this commission were considered for implementation in Paris also. The commission recommended to include technical and science subjects in the course of study. But the Government did not choose to implement all these recommendations on the ground that they were too ambitious. However, some of the recommendations were regarded as useful.

***Langevin Plan***-The French government did not pay much importance to the recommendations of Algiers Commission. So it appointed another commission under the chairmanship of Paul Langevin. This commission studied the educational problems of the country very minutely and gave certain recommendations as mentioned below. Paul Langevin died soon and the chairmanship of the commission was given to Henri Wallon. But the recommendations of the commission were grouped under Langevin's name. So the same are known as the Langevin Plan which had the following main proposals:

1. Universal and identical educational facilities should be made available to everyone.

2. A general system of education should be introduced by reorganising schools and introducing necessary changes in the curriculum.

3. Full time compulsory education should be made available to students of twenty eight years of age.

4. Adequate development of technical and science education should be made.

5. Along with technical and science education provision should be made for cultural education also.

6. The higher schools should not give training in public services. This task should be entrusted to other type of schools.

7. Scholarships should be instituted for techinical, vocational and teachers' training institutions.

8. The pattern of the British Education Act of 1944, elementary, higher and technical education should be reorganised in France also in a graded manner.

Langevin Plan could not be implemented because of its being too ambitious. However, it has been of great historical significance.

**Educational Administration**

***Central Administration***-Central government controls education in the country. The French Parliament consisting of a Senate and a Chamber of Deputies is fully responsible for education in the land. The laws for education are framed by the Parliament. But the same are implemented by the Cabinet. Education Minister is one of the members of the cabinet. The Central administration has the following responsibilities pertaining to education:

1. To arrange for the salaries of teachers and other administrative officers engaged in educational services.
2. To establish all types of educational institutions and to enact laws for governing them.
3. To prescribe, some common aims of education and to frame courses of studies accordingly.
4. To prescribe the methods of examination.
5. To decide about the scale of salaries, service conditions and promotion procedures of all teachers and others engaged in educational services.
6. To prescribe the methods of examination.
7. To co-operate with local bodies in construction of school-buildings.

The education minister is responsible for entire education in the country. The following are his functions:

1. To appoint teacher for higher classes.
2. To arrange for proper distribution of scholarships and grants.
3. To see that laws and rules are followed with regard to the budget for education.

4. To prescribe regulations for examinations and grant of degree and certificates and see that the same are followed.

5. To supervise the working of private schools himself or through his assistants.

6. To consider and to give final judgements on the rules and regulations passed by university councils, school boards and councils of primary education of the department.

7. To formulate rules for discipline and for methods and courses of studies of all schools.

A number of bodies have been appointed to assist the education minister in performance of his multifarious duties. These bodies are Superior Council of Public Instruction and Consulting Committee of Public Instruction.

**Apex Body**

The President of France, ex-teachers, members of the Institute de France, Principal of the college de France, Museum representative, elected members of elementary schools and higher schools and ministers constitute the Board for Higher Education. This board advises the Minister of education on the following subject.

1. Disciplinary and administrative matters.

2. Rules regarding examination procedures, grant of degrees and inspection of private schools.

3. Curriculum, teaching methods and text books.

4. Establishing educational institutions with foreign aids and rules for accepting teaching positions.

This committee is constituted with representatives of teachers, representative secretaries of concerned bureaus, inspectors general, university president and some ex-officio members. This committee has various separate sections for elementary, pre-secondary and higher secondary stages. There are separate committees for technical education and fine arts. There are some other councils, such as council of national museum, Commission of Historical Monuments and Superior Council of the National Conservatory of Music and Oratory. These councils are responsible for constituting new posts, abolition of existing posts and promotion affairs pertaining to their particular jurisdiction. Inspection is considered important for all educational organisations except for higher education. The inspectorate department looks after teaching material aids, method of teaching and appointing new necessary teachers. Fourteen inspectors are appointed for the elementary leveled four pre-elementary stage.

For administrative convenience France is divided into ninety provinces. For looking after the affairs of each academic region a rector is elected from amongst deans of faculties holding university doctorate degrees. The rector supervises the affairs regarding pre-primary education. For advising about the progress of secondary education, there is an auxiliary body which cooperates with the rector in performance of his duties. This auxiliary body is formed with inspector of schools, heads of departments of universities, teachers of private schools, and some ex-officio members. The legislature also nominates some members to this auxiliary body. This body also publishes an annual report on progress of education.

Each academic region is divided into departments. The seventeen academic regions of France are divided into about 92 departments for administrative convenience. The officer of each department is known as the prefect who looks after the general administration of the region. The inspector of school supervises the elementary education affairs. However, the prefect presides over the elementary education council. Sub-sanctions of a department is known as Arrondissements. A subprefect is made incharge of an arrondissement. An arrondissement may be divided into cantons and cantons into commune.

The rector is responsible for secondary education. Inspectors of schools have to assist the rector in performance of his duties.

These inspectors do all the work of the prefect. A doctorate degree holder is generally appointed as an Inspector of School. Besides, some inspectors are selected from the group of administrations of a Lycee, Director of normal schools and inspector of elementary schools.

The inspector of schools has to look after arrangement of teachers, construction of school buildings, opening of private schools, discipline, training of office-workers for schools and adult education. The education minister appoints inspectresses and inspector for elementary schools. These inspectresses and inspectors help the departmental inspector of schools immensely. For technical education there is a separate inspector who is generally a government officer or an artist, engineer or some kind of famous industrial worker. He holds office for four years. Agriculture inspectors are also appointed at some places. These inspectors are also given the responsibility of teaching agriculture, if they pass a competitive examination. Agriculture teachers help the inspector of the region immensely.

General Council of Department, the Council for Primary Education, Committee for Technical Education and Commission for Agriculture have been appointed for administrative convenience. In the General Council of Department, there is a member from each canton. This council also represents the Department Council of Primary Education and the Board of Directors of Normal Schools. This council makes the necessary arrangement of normal schools.

The Council of Primary Education looks after the teaching work in primary schools. Determination of the curriculum, methods of teaching, disciplinary matters and matters concerning association of teachers fall within the jurisdiction of this council. The inspector of schools, director, two school-inspectors nominated by the legislature, prefect teachers of primary schools and director of normal schools are members of the council.

The Committee for Technical Education studies the problem of technical education, sources of income grants and establishing new technical schools. The prefect appoints some of its members who have to be technical teachers or director of technical education or school inspectors or labour inspector or members of some vocational department.

The departmental commission of agriculture organises the post-graduate curriculum of agriculture. The officers of the department of forest and irrigation, some respectable persons from the field of agriculture, school inspector and director of agricultural services are the members of this commission. The prefect is the chairman of this commission.

**Local Level Setup**

The officers of the municipalities perform the following functions with regard to education:

1. To establish public schools and to organise resources for them for their proper functioning.
2. To advise on establishment of schools and about creation and abolition of posts.
3. To run canteen shops and to organise funds for giving away prizes.
4. To open post-graduate class and to make the necessary funds available for them.

The representatives of canton inspect the reading materials in schools, attendance of students, health of students and the position of the schools. The council of primary education appoints these representatives. The mayor and these representatives have nothing to do with teaching work and results of examinations.

Multipurpose schools and Saint Cyr Schools are organised by war department. The navy schools are related with naval forces. The public works department runs the Ecole National Des Mines which is responsible for geological education.

Thus in the French education system along with centralisation the local units also co-operate. But the centre fully controls the administration, method and development of education. In this way the concept of centralisation in education is very strong in France.

## Various Types of Schools

When primary, secondary and higher educational organisations are complementary to each other, then there is no difficulty in obtaining admission in one after completing education at the lower stage. In France the three stages of education were not complementary to each other and each was imparting education in quite disregard to the requirements at the next higher stage. Sometimes the students was requirements repeat the courses that he had already completed at the previous stage. In France, primary education was divided into the following groups:

***Infants Classes-*** These classes were meant for children between 3 to 6 years of age. The children were taught through plays in these schools.

***Kindergarten Schools-***They admit children between 3 to 6 years of age. The children were taught in free and playful environment. These schools prepared children for compulsory primary education which started from the sixth year of age.

***Elementary Education Proper-***These schools are like children's classes. Children get education here between 3 to 6 years of age and become suitable for compulsory primary education.

***Primary Education Classes Associated with Secondary Schools-*** These classes are run along with secondary school classes.

***Schools for the Physically and Mentally Handicapped-***In France arrangements have been made for children who are physically and mentally handicapped. Special schools have been opened for such children. When the child finishes his pre-primary education at the age to six years, his compulsory, education begins. This compulsory education continues upto thirteen years of age.

There are four types of organisation for this compulsory primary education. (1) Ecole Communale which provide education for most of the children, (2) Lycees or college to educate children who are especially privileged, (3) Private schools in which genitally children of rich people receive education, (4) Enseignmentale Maison which provide education for children of rich people at home. After the pre-primary education from 6 to 13 years of age the child gets higher primary education between 13 and 16 years of age; Because of the various types of curriculum taught at this stage, this education is known by the name of the particular kind of education imparted such as commercial education, general industrial education, agriculture education and home economics education.

***Part-time Schools***-Some part-time schools also exist for adolescent children in addition to the above type of schools. According to the Education Act of 1919 it was made compulsory that adolescents from industrial area would receive education in the part-time continuation schools. Therefore in these schools' maximum number of adolescents are found. According to the data found in 1983 about 5,00,000 students were receiving education in these schools.

**The Interaction**

Considerable isolation is perceptible between the primary any secondary schools of France. As we have already said earlier these two stages do not make one ladder and the primary does not lead to the secondary. At some places higher primary classes were run as pre-secondary classes and at scme they were associated with secondary schools. Thus the child who completed primary education hesitated entering a secondary school, becuase there he was required to repeat many such courses which he had already completed. The secondary schools had some peculiar approach. It was very easy for a student to get admission in naval academies, engineering schools and normal schools after completing his secondary education. Thus most of the students after completing secondary education used to obtain salaried jobs on receiving some training in some of these vocational schools.

Gradually in the existing primary and secondary schools isolation came to an end and the admission difficulties were over. Now students after completing primary education began to take admission in Lycees and Colleges. Poor students were given scholarships in these institutions. After completing primary education at the age of 10 or 11, the student used to get admission in a Lycee or College and study there for 7 to 8 years.

There was some difference in the education level of Lycees and Colleges. The education in Lycees was considered to be superior to that in colleges. In these institutions residential accommodation was provided to students. So their importance had increased. Boys and girls had their separate boarding houses. But due to small number of students in classes, co-education was permitted. Lycees were fully dependent on government help. But the colleges used to receive grants and financial assistance from the state, commune and municipal boards. There were variations in the tuition fees charged from students. Students who would not stay in boarding houses were called day pupils and such a student had to pay annual fees which, amounted between 90 to 300 francs. The boarder had to pay an annual fee between 900 to 1,650 francs. Normal schools were especially considered important for teachers' training.

**Changing Trends**

From 1927 onwards we find many changes in the French system of education. In this year primary, higher primary and secondary education were made parts of one series of education and more suitable courses of study and duration of education were determined. The Education Minister Harriot made in 1928 the education in Lycees and colleges free. The system of co-education was also started. In 1930 free education was declared as constitutional.

**New Setup**

The year 1936-37 is of special importance from the point of view of development of education. In 1937 the private preparatory schools were abolished and completing of a six-year curriculum was made compulsory for obtaining admission in a secondary school. This six-year curriculum was only the first year course of the 7 year course of primary education. Primary education was regarded as the first level and secondary education as the second level. Three units were recognised of primary education-(1) elementary school education, (2) revised elementary school education, (3) continuation school education. Primary education was made of six years. But from the examination point of view one more year was considered necessary after completing six year primary education. Thus primary education was made of seven year duration. After completing the seven year duration a student could get admission in a secondary school or in a higher primary school. In the higher primary education three year vocational education was included and in it an attempt was made to effect a harmony with general education. The student who would not be admitted in a higher primary school could be admitted in continuation school. On completing seven year primary education the student was granted a certificate known as "Certificate d' etadel Primaires climentaires". On the basis of this certificate he could get some job in some government offices.

***Secondary Education***-The secondary education in France is of seven year duration. This duration is divided into two types of courses. One unit is of four year course on completion of which a middle examination is taken. The second unit is of three year duration on completion of which the final Baccalaureate examination is held. The seven year secondary education is of three types (1) literacy, (2) modern and (3) technical. In 1937 he admission age was raised to 14 from 13 years of age. This increased the enrolment of students and by December of 1937 about 1,486 new government and municipal schools were established.

In 1937 the then Education Minister reorganised education. So this year is known as the Ameed Orientation year. This year for 50 cities some investigational plan was determined. For this plan one director, five teachers and some subject experts constituted an examination committee for testing the abilities and aptitudes of students. This committee after investigations used to declare certain student as suitable for higher primary education and some for secondary education. Under this plan the first year of secondary education was generally spent in testing ability and aptitude and during the remaining six years the student could study the literacy, modern or mechanical courses according to his ability and aptitude. In fact, the testing revealed only the memory power and not the ability and aptitude.

Under the above plan two types of orientation classes were started. For a class of 25 students; 27 lessons were prescribed for a week and five teachers were appointed for the primary, secondary and technical levels. These teachers used to hold meetings every week for discussing about interests, aptitudes and the future plans of student. If the meeting of these teachers was not able to decide about the interest and aptitude of a student, then the matter was referred to experts for psychological investigations.

Because of the amendment in the labour code children below the age of fourteen years could not be employed in any factory or commercial establishment. At least for half an hour every day per week physical education was given to children in an open field. In 1937-38 the physical education scheme was started for all the departments. But only 29 departments could participate in this scheme. Within the co-curricular activities were included regional plays, historical, geography, industrial and literary tours and music activities. Plays were especially considered more important in the co-curricular activities.

***Developmental History of Education***-Religious and sectarian groups played a leading role In development of education in France. In due course the progressive socialists declared this one-sided conservative education harmful for development, of democracy. As a result centralisation of education was started in 1789; Napolean reorganised secondary and university education in 1808. In 1833 the primary schools were given government grant. In 1882 it became possible for the government to interfere in religious and private schools. By 1904 the control of the government over educational institutions was further tightened. By 1907 the government used to shoulder about 70 per cent of the total expenditure on education.

***Development of Regional Languages***-Some educationists started a movement for making regional languages as medium of instruction. This movement adversely affected the policy of centralisation of education. So the government did not accept the regional languages as the medium of instruction.

***Reorganisation of Courses of Studies and Training Schools***-After the First World War, the agricultural curriculum was changed into industrial curriculum. Industrial education was considered as the basis of social system. Examination system, curriculum and text-books were improved. Arrangements were made for training of teachers for primary schools.

***Algiers Commission***-This commission criticised the educational system which stood for preparing a special class of citizens.

***Langevin Plan***-This plan was influenced by the Education Act of 1944 of Great Britain. Eight-point programme of universal, vocational and technical education was presented by the plan. This plan was rejected on the ground that it was too ambitious.

***Educational Administration Central Control***-Centre controls the entire educational pattern. Appointment of education officer by the education minister or his deputies. A council of education to advise the education minister. The centre makes education laws, organises training of teachers, gives grants, establishes new schools and appoints teachers and other workers in the field of education.

***Provincial Administration***-Prefect controls the department and sub-prefect look& after the units placed under him. The inspector of schools works on the direction of the centre. Role of municipalities, cantons and communes.

***Classification of Schools***-At the primary level-infant classes, Kindergarten, special pre-primary school, primary classes affiliated with secondary schools and schools for physically and mentally handicapped. Part-time schools for adolescent children.

***Inter-relationship between Primary and Secondary Schools-*** The two were not inter-related. One did not lead to another. The two were isolated from each other. One was not complementary to another. Lycees and colleges were meant for rich people at first. But later on they were made universal. Lycees is of a higher standard than the college. Lycees are residential. Co-education started in them now.

***Reorganisation of the Educational System-***Primary education from 6 to 13 years of age. Higher primary changed into continuation education. Seven year curriculum. One year examination after six years of education. After passing this examination during the first year the student was admitted either in secondary, higher primary or continuation school. Seven year secondary education curriculum, four middle school curriculum and three year baccalaureate curriculum. Literary, modern and technical curriculum. Admission at 14 years of age. Physical education along with inellectual education.

## QUESTIONS

1. Discuss the role of religious and sectarian bodies in the development of education in France. How did it come to an end ?

2. How is educational administration in France centralized?

3. Describe briefly how primary and secondary education became complementary to each other ?

# PART–FOUR

# EDUCATION IN U.S.A.

# 17

# Teacher Training

The system of Teacher Education in U. S. A. is not very old. In the middle of the 19th century, the suggestion of teacher-training was put forth and the State made arrangement for teacher-training. Prior to this the profession of teacher was not held high in the eyes of public nor was it attractive to encourage learned persons to join it.

With growth of interest in education, the people began to feel the shortage of teachers. Realising the seriousness of the art of teaching, demand for a system which could prepare skilful and capable teachers began to grow. As a result, in 1839, the Government Teachers Training Institution was established in Massachussets State for the first time. With the establishing of this institution, the need of such one year teacher training schools began to be felt in other States also. In 1857, the State Normal School at Lexington was established in Illinois State. This normal school was meant to provide training to primary and secondary school teachers by upgrading its curriculum. In 1860, the one year curriculum of Lexington School was converted into a two year curriculum. Till then, mostly teachers for primary schools were trained for whom no qualification for admission was prescribed. So the educated and eager persons were selected according to the felt need from time to time.

Till then, the normal schools provide teacher training. The higher education colleges and universities could not make any provision for teacher training. But with the awakening for education professional training began to be emphasised. Consequently, education departments were started in some universities as mentioned on wards to meet the shortage of teachers. In 1873, a training department was started in the University of Iowa by providing short-term and part-time courses. In 1879, the University of Michigan did a praiseworthy work by providing full-time teacher training. In 1887, the University of Columbia in New York not only organised training for teachers, but it also made arrangement for the training of school managers. This provision proved very useful and this teacher training college did remarkable work for the development of teacher training.

In the second decade of the 20th century, due to the efforts of educationists, teacher training was given a techincal shape and education as a subject was recognised as teacher education and it was considered necessary to include this subject in the curriculum of the normal schools.

**Criteria of Admission**

Upto the beginning of the 20th century, no compulsory qualification for admission was prescribed. The status of training schools was equal to that of secondary schools. So candidates who passed primary education, could be admitted in normal schools. Till 1920, 2 year training course continued to be conducted and in order to raise the standard of teaching, students completing two year programme of secondary level continued to be admitted in normal schools. After the duration of 2 years training was raised to 4 years and the teaching methods were revised and modernised. In 1922, the Columbia University brought novelty in the teacher training methods. At that time emphasis was laid on the training of pupil-teachers. Consequently, teacher training institutions and teachers education centres were started. American Association of Teachers colleges passed some important resolutions to impress the need of teacher training. Such resolutions helped significantly in the increase of the number of teachers during the depression period and in maintaining proper teaching standard.

In U. S. A. the teacher training is given a vocational importance like other professional training and by prescribing minimum academic qualification for the teacher-training course, selection of candidates is managed like selection for any other vocational training. For admission to teacher-training course, only academic qualification is not taken into account but attention is paid to other general requirements also. The recommendations of the principal of the school last attended, academic and character records, certificates of co-curricular activities intelligence, personal interview and physical capacity are mainly considered.-In many States, there is no prescribed qualification for admission. At the time of appointment; it is seen that the teachers teaching secondary classes should have completed 4 year teachers training after post-graduation (M. A.). For primary level education those candidates are admitted for training who have obtained 2 year junior college education. In some cities even Ph. D. is compulsory for secondary school teachers.

In 1938, the National Education Association of America emphasised the need of appointing most qualified teachers from the point of view of national interest. In 1938, this Association established an institution named the Future Teachers of America. This institution with this view, too, that the most qualified teachers may be available for secondary schools, laid stress on establishing clubs and chapters at college level which the training schools gladly tried to implement.

The American citizens are very much alive to their educational system. They know that the teachers are the builders of future citizens. So they demand proper training facilities for the teachers. For the purpose of admission, the personality, nature, religion, socio-cultural and political beliefs and their personal life is taken into consideration.

**Various Institutions**

In U. S. A., in the Held of education, private and community efforts have been quite significant. In 1823, fifteen years before the Government effort, private Normal School had been established in Vermont.' Similarly, in 1827, a training school (Normal School). has been opened in Lancasters of Masachusset; State. Till the middle of the 19th century, Normal schools had been established as a result of public efforts. The County Boards had established Normal Schools in their respective areas. Thus before the beginning of the 20th century about 170 Normal Schools had been established. All these efforts'speak of the activities of American people for education. The impact of European progress and environment is quite evident on the estahlishment of these Normal Schools, but it has been changing according to the social needs of American environment

The following types of teacher-training institutions are found in U.S.A:

(1) Normal Schools

(2) Teachers' College

(3) School Education

(4) Department of Education

The nature of these institutions is being explained below:

***Normal Schools.*** In U. S. A., the extension of teacher training has been based on European traditions. The word 'Normal' has been derived from. French language, which means 'Rule'. In Hindi in place of *'Niyam'* we call it *'Diksha'*. So Normal Schools are those schools which give training in 'Rules of Teaching'. Here teacher-training had been organised on the basis of the Report on Public Education in Russia presented by Victor Cousin. In the beginning the Normal School course was of one year in which teaching pertained to general education. But, later on, when the course became of two years, in the first year education was taught as a subject and in the second year teaching methods were taught. In this situation, students who had passed primary level came for admission and after two years became eligible for teaching primary classes. In fact these schools imparted education like lower secondary classes. At that time, there was hardly any provision of any specific teacher-training. Rather education of the first two years of secondary education after the primary education was given. In some places even this education was not compulsory and the tradition of becoming a teacher after completing primary education prevailed.

In U. S. A. during the first 25 years of the 20th century, it was found that during the 2 years of normal Schools, the subjects of primary level were repeated and the teacher-training included methods of teaching, principles of teaching and practical teaching training. But realising that qualified teachers should be prepared for creating future citizens, instead of concentrating on the teaching or education as a subject, attention had begun to be paid on methods of teaching and higher professional training. In 1920, considering the 2 year course as inadequate, it was converted into 4 year course. Thus, by the end of the first quarter of the 20th century,.the training , course became of 4 years duration and all Normal Schools changed into Teachers Training Colleges.

***Teachers' Training Colleges.*** As has been said above, the training of Normal Schools had changed into a 4 year course and their form was changed into that of Teachers Training Colleges. In the years to come instead of Normal Schools, Teachers Training Colleges began to be established but Teachers Training Colleges had already been established in addition to Normal Schools. About 125 years ago, a Teachers Training College had been establtshed in 1857 in Illinois. This college provided higher professional education to college teachers. Upto the American Civil War, this college continued to give higher professional Training to college teachers. During this period in many Liberal Arts colleges, arrangement was made for lectures on the art of teaching. In 1888, a Teachers Training College was opened in New York. The founder of this college was Nicholas Murray Butler. This Teachers Training College after 210 years of functioning was affiliated to Columbia Univeristy. By 1920 the number of these colleges rose to 45. Later on, in the next 20 years the number of these colleges increased considerably. It is said that the Training Colleges were established so rapidly during those 20 years that their number became three times of the then existing training colleges.

The period between 1920 to 1950 may be said to be a period of awakening and expansion from the point of view of development of teacher training. During this period, the importance of education as a subject came down and the importance of art of teaching increased. Thus in the sphere of teaching, pre-service and in-service training was started and training of secondary level changed into training of college level. At that time training courses were revised and such courses were included which could make a teacher skilful, efficient, learned and a man of integrated personality. So general education, specialisation, teaching profession education, teaching practice and other such programmes were included in the training course.

By including humanities in the field of general education, departmental education, physical education, social studies, natural sciences, art, educational sociology, educational psychology, educational philosophy and principles of education, efforts were made to lay teaching foundation for tlie teacher through specific knowledge. With the view of specialisation different types of programmes and courses were instituted. Such a training enabled the teacher to get excellent vocational efficiency. Today in U.S. A. in order to make the teacher-training more developed, modified and utilitarian, the guidance of experienced supervisors and directors is made available. The practice-teaching system is becoming psychological and developed day by day and is changing according to ever-changing national need.

In U. S. A. the training colleges are managed and run by the State Governments. After providing the teachers training for primary and secondary level, they are awarded the Degree of Bachelor. Some colleges are conducting 5 years course instead of 4 years for the sake of specialisation. These colleges also award Master's and Doctorate Degrees. Some of these colleges have earned international reputation because of their specific teacher-training programmes.

***School of Education.*** Schools of Education are like teachers training colleges but these schools are affiliated to one or the other University. In 1879, the Michigan University had organised full-time School of Education. However, even before this the Michigan, Borwn and New York Universities had started part-time teacher training. The Michigan University awarded Degree of Graduation after the completion of raining. In 1888, the New York University, also began to award the Graduation Degree and made the teaching profession more modern by giving teacher-training a vocational form. This changed policy affected all the teacher-training schools and centres of all places and all tried to raise the standard of the art of teaching.

The American Schools of Education are like different departments of education of universities. These departments are quite independent in organisation and management. After completing two years of college education, admission is given in a school of education. In the teaching course along with education subjects, general education, philosophy of education, psychology, language, literature and culture are also taught. During the training period emphasis is laid on skill and efficiency of teaching profession. After the completion of the course, Degree of Graduation is awarded. In these schools of education the curriculum is similar to that of teachers training colleges.

***Department of Education.*** In 1873, the Iowa University started part-time teacher training by recognising pedagogy of science education as an independent subject. Later on, the Michigan University conducted full-time course with a view to make teaching vocational. Thus many Art colleges and universities establish separate Departments of Education considering pedagogy of science of Education an independent subject and conduct teacher training course.

In U. S. A. talk about the development of pedagogy had been started from time to time and changes had been brought about. The educationists laid stress on making teacher training more technical. Consequently, the teachers colleges and universities began to give vocational training in the art and science of education by establishing separate departments of education. The Chicago

University established its independent departments. In the subject of pedagogy, advance courses have been started for the training of school administrators and educational administrators. These departments have research facilities in pedagogy.

## The Syllabi

As has been said earlier, pedagogy includes teaching of general education along with professional aspects of teaching. The courses of teacher education may be divided into two parts—(1) general education course, (2) teacher training course.

***Organisation of Curriculum.*** In about 43 States of U. S. A. 4 year teacher-training courses are run. In some States, the teacher training curriculum is of 5 years. In such a system, after completion of 4 year course, specialisation of one year is provided. General education and teacher training system are not uniform in all the States. There is some difference or the other. In some States general education continues for all the four years and teacher-training is provided simultaneously. In some other States general education or teacher training is provided in the first or last two years.

In U. S. A. there are more than 600 such institutions which by providing advance degree course, try to maintain interest in the teaching profession throughout the life of the teachers and create better skills through teachertraining. These institutions encourage the school teachers to take admission in Higher Degree Course and also maintain contact with them. On obtaining the higher Degree, the salary of the teacher is increased. By such incentives, the teachers are motivated to obtain the highest training and increase their efficiency and knowledge. In order to maintain the spirit of obtaining, training, the managers, college president, administrative officers, teacher specialists and educationists are given opportunities of participating in the higher Degree course.

In U.S. A., it is customary to divide the 4 year curriculum of teacher training in the following form. In the first two years liberal art study and in the last two years opportunity of extensive study is provided. Teacher training is also given with general education. In general education, national and international languages, literature, mathematics, music, science, social studies and economics etc. are taught. The teacher-training subjects include, health education, education for mental hygiene, child psychology, education for internationalism and cultural subjects. They are taught through discussion and lecture method. For practice-teaching, the students are acquainted with old and new class-teaching methods and effort is made to give full practice in them.

For inculcating the spirit of democracy an effort is made to mould the teachers according to democratic environment. Through co-curricular activities, their personality is made sociable and useful. By forming associations and committees on federal basis, democratic qualities are inculcated in the pupil-teachers. For collective information and direction magazines and journals are published. Games, sports and facilities for physical exercises are provided, They are taught to work in the environment in which they have to teach after training. For recreation, music, singing and dancing are arranged. Thus the teachers are moulded there according to national and social ideals of the country.

**Basic Requirement**

The qualifications of teachers are not the same at different levels. In about 36 States, the certified qualification of teachers (much and female) are different. In some States minimum of 2 years college level education is essential and in some completion of 2 years course of the training period is essential. In the remaining States, along with 4 year training certificate, graduation is also essential. In about 48 States, for teachers of secondary classes, 4 year training with graduation is compulsory. In the remaining States, specialisation after the 4 year teacher training is preferred. At the time of appoinment, various training qualifications of teachers are taken into consideration. In some places, teachers trained in new methods as Nursery System, Kindergarten System or Dalton Plan are demanded and in some others specialisation in guidance and counselling is preferred. At the secondary level; the specific capability of the teacher, extra training and Higher Degree Course are given special consideration. Generally preference is given to teachers offering 5 year training course.

After completion of training, the responsibility of awarding certificate or Diploma rests with the State Education Department, State Education Superintendents or State Boards of Education. Only in about 30 per cent of State throughout America, the holding of a certificate is essential. In State where certificates are essential, the certificates are awarded after giving a test before appointment. The certificates are given on the basis of their educational ability and graded ability. In some places, the certificates are awarded for a specified period. After the end of the period, the certificate stands cancelled. These certificates may be given for the whole-life also. In some places, the certificates are conditional. Thus in the system of awarding certificates, probation and conditions are given importance.

For teachers of colleges and universities, certificate is not necessary. But traditionally, two years education after the college education is recognised as the minimum qualification. In some places they are required to possess a post-graduate Degree and three years additional study which while in some States only teachers with a Doctorate Degree are considered eligible for university level.

For encouraging the development of science of education, research work is provided. The universities provide research facilities for trained teachers. Those who are engaged in teaching work, refresher courses and fellowship courses are organised. The Harvard University is doing excellent work in this direction. This university provides opportunity to the university teachers for obtaining specialisation under the guidance of able and experienced guides. It provides special courses for those primary and secondary teachers who have been able to complete 4 year training course due to certain circumstances and have not been able to achieve specialisation in their 5th course. This training is considered equivalent to the 5 year course. The Harward Graduate School by conducting Fellowship Course extends maximum co-operation in inculcating the above ability, following national ideals and earning international reputation.

The Antioch College of Ohio State gives training to those teachers and supervisors who work in other industrial and vocational spheres instead of educational sphere. These persons after receiving training of teachers and supervisors provide vocational guidance and counselling to persons seeking employment This system imbibes the spirit of social service which prompt a person of any sphere to give counselling and vocational guidance to any other person. This programme is a project of National Youth Welfare in which a person benefits other persons by his abilities and skills. Thus the coming generation gets the ability and direction for entering into a vocational field.

In running the above activity, camp system is also adopted in which professors of the Antioch College actively participate. The teachers fulfil their responsibility from one central camp or by visiting other camps. By doing such social work, their outlook and devotion to duty is refined and they are able to solve various problems of student. In the camp system, the teachers are divided into two groups. If one group works at camp centre, the other group performs educational programmes in the college campus. When the groups complete their assignments, their work is exchanged and every group completes its assigned work by replacing each other.

**Teachers' Role**

In U. S. A. as in other countries, the status of a person is determined by his financial position. This applies to teachers also. In the beginning the teacher had no high status in society because he was paid a poor salary and his services were not properly recognised. But by the end of the 19th century, sufficient development took place in the field of education and with this development attention was paid on the needs conditions and facilities of teachers. Consequently, the condition of the teachers began to improve.

Along with educational development in the beginning of the 20th century, attention began to be paid on the academic freedom, service security, medical leave, weekly rest and pension facilities etc. The teachers began to be appointed on long term contract and gradually on permanent basis as well. The teachers at present are working in a more satisfactory and pleasant atmosphere. Like the workers of other professions, they too, have their association and enjoy all facilities and service-security.

In U. S. A., the services of the teachers are based on an agreement according to Government rules between the management and the teacher. In about 45 States of U. S. A., the services are fully secure and may be terminated only in special circumstances. In all other States, the services of teachers are permanent and for their security of service and facilities, there is one or the other statutory provision. In about 30 States, there is a provision of sick-leave and retirement also.

For the appointment of teachers, there are no comprehensive rules from the Federal or State Governments just as in France or Australia. After the completion of training, candidates send their applications to Teacher Employment Agencies. On the basis of such applications, these agencies maintain the record of the educational qualifications, training, experience etc. and by establishing contact with local administrative units recommend the names of the teachers according to their needs. In some places, the candidates send their applications directly to the local administrative units. The units send these applications to the employment agencies for selection according to their requirements. The employment agencies keeping in view the requirement of the concerned unit forward the application of the candidate and the local administrative units appoint the teachers on the recommendation of the Superintendent of Education. The teacher employment agencies are private, community, governmental and public. Some agencies are governed by- teachers associations and training institutions as well.

As has been said earlier, the status of the teacher s assessed on the basis of his salary scale. The salary scale depends on the financial condition of local boards. These local boards decide the salary scales of the teachers according to their condition and needs. The scale of the teachers in rural areas is less than that of teachers in the urban areas, so teacher of lower salary scales migrate to the areas of higher salary scales. The determination of the salary scales of teachers depends on average state income per head and the number of students of school going age. No importance is given to time scale and efficiency bar in the salary scale. The increment in teachers salary depends on the increase of State income. As the State income increases, the scale of teachers is also increased. Most of the expenditure on salary is met from the funds of the local units.

In U. S. A., the lower limit of the salary scale is fixed. According to it, for the teacher of prescribed qualification even if he is a teacher of a primary level or secondary level, salary less than the prescribed limit cannot be given. According to rules, the salary scales are roughly as follows:

| | | |
|---|---|---|
| (1) | President of University and Local Education Superintendent | From 15,000 to 30.000 dollars per annum. |
| (2) | Teachers of Post Graduate Degree | From 9,000 to 15,000 dollars per annum. |
| (3) | Graduate teachers dollars per annum. | From 6,000 to 10,000 |
| (4) | Graduate Teachers but with 10 years experience | From 5,000 to 7,000 dollars per annum. |
| (5) | University Heads of the Departments and Supervisors | From 8.000 to 15,000 dollars per annum. |

Variations are also found in all these scales. Besides these salary scale, a teacher retiring after a fixed period is also given annual pension. At places where the minimum salary is not fixed, there the average annual salary is also different. For example, when the national average annual salary (in 1983) was 6.000 dollars, the average salary in California was 7,000 dollars annually and in Missisipi it was 3,000 dollars per year. In 1983, there was equality and uniformity in national average salary but the salary scales in States differed.

**Conditions of Service**

Saturday and Sunday are holidays in every week in U. S. A. The session is generally of 9 months in a year. Working days are Between 160 to 200 in a session. A teacher does not teach more than 35 periods a week. There are about 25 students in a class. The rest of the day time is utilised in preparing the class room for next working day, in the effort for bringing backward children equal to other students and in conducting and organising co-curricular activities.

The teachers try their best to devise various programmes for solving the problems of students through parent-teacher contacts and co-operation. The post of the teacher is considered dignified and honourable. The teachers enjoy working with youth and spend their leisure in social work and making contact with people. They discuss educational problems with the honourable members of the society and community and organise conferences.

Most of the American teaching staff at the primary and secondary level consist of women and young girls. Even when they are more in number than the male teachers, they are getting higher places in educational services. On the basis of the custom of working as teacher for two years before marriage, every unmarried girl considers teaching work as a privilege. There is no sex discrimination in salary scales and equality of opportunity. Democratic principles are followed as far as status, prestige and salary of both the sexes are concerned. According to the available data in 1983, out of one million primary and high school teachers in U. S. A. about 9,00,000 were women. Thus women teachers are found more in number than the male teachers at the primary and secondary levels. Association of Education has been organised for teachers of all levels. About fifty per cent teachers are members of this Association. The function of this association is to conduct development at work, keeping in view the professional and philosophical outlook of the teachers. For collective progress and security, unions have been formed at different places and there is a national institution known as American Federation of Teachers which fulfils its obligations in co-operation with trade unions.

***Development of Teacher Education.*** Development of Teacher Education is not very old in U. S. A. There the status of the teacher depends on his salary scale. In the beginning, due to meagre salary very few persons were attracted towards this profession. First of all a Normal School was established in 1839 in Messachussets. In

1857, a Normal School was established in Illinois also. In 1873, part-time teacher training programmes were started in Iowa University. In 1879, the Michigan University established Departments of Education and in 1887, Columbia University vocationalised Teacher Education by establishing an education department.

***Admission Qualifications and Selection.*** In U. S. A., there has been no prescribed qualification for admission. 2 year study in secondary classes after the primary education was sufficient qualification. As soon as the training period was raised from 2 years to 4 years, the prescribed qualification for admission was also raised. At the time of admission in normal schools, training centres and training institutions, knowledge about the trainees health, educational qualification, character record, teaching aptitude and conduct etc. were ascertained through interview. The recommendation of the principal is given importance at the time of admission. At the time of selection of teachers attention is paid to various needs at different levels. The selection procedure is not the same in all States. Generally, for primary level, 2 years college education with teacher-training is essential. At the secondary level, 4 year teacher training certificate along with Graduation is demanded. For selection to the post of teacher, the nature, health, religion, political ideals and philosophy of life are considered.

***Teacher Training Institutions.*** *Normal Schools*-Generally, they were equivalent to secondary schools because in the beginning, they imparted two years secondary education after the completion of primary education. In 1925, need for efficient and trained teachers was felt to maintain educational standard. Consequently, the courses were extended. Thus all the normal schools were converted into Training Colleges. *Teacher-Training Colleges*-New York Teachers' Training College was established in 1888. Upto 1920, ordinary training colleges were established to teach education as a subject. These colleges were 45 in number upto 1920. Later on teaching was given a professional form. Training for teaching began to be given with general education. *Schools of Education*-Institutions conducting an integrated curriculum of training along with general education were named schools of Education. These schools are affiliated to some university. In these schools educational philosophy, various languages, literature, culture etc. are taught along with teacher education. The curriculum is quite similar to that of training colleges. *Department of Education*-These departments are a part of universities and arts colleges like other departments. In these departments teacher training is mainly emphasised. Here higher vocational courses are conducted and provision for research is also made.

***Courses of Teacher Education.*** The 4 year training period is divided into general education and vocational training courses. These courses are not similar throughout the land. In some States, training is given in the first two years and in some during last two years and in some States general education and training courses are run simultaneously during all the four years.

***Award of Degrees and Certificates after Training.*** Certificates are awarded by Local Education Boards or Department of Education. Degrees of professional training are awarded by universities and training colleges but ordinary lower standard certificates are awarded for a fixed period on certain conditions. After the expiry of the period, these certificates lose recognition. All examination is held for giving such certificates. The teachers of various levels are examined for distribution of certificates.

***Provision of Research in Teacher Education.*** After four years of training in teaching, one year specialisation course is also conducted. Harvard University provides special training course for trained and in-service teachers. Antioch College is a pioneer in this regard. Many centres and camps affiliated to it have been established, where teachers increase their knowledge through research and social service when in-service. After the completion of this course, it is considered equivalent to 5 year training.

***Condition of Teachers in U. S. A.*** At the present time, an American teacher gets facilities of pension, sickleave and medical aid etc. like persons of other professions. His services are now secure and permanent. The teachers are appointed through Teacher Employment Agencies by Local Education Boards according to their needs. The teacher sends his application to the Employment Agencies of Boards directly. The salary of the teacher depends on the funds of the Boards and the number of students. The teacher's salary increases with the increase in the national income.

## QUESTIONS

1. "The condition of teachers in U. S. A. is satisfactory." Explain.

2. How did teacher education develop in U. S. A. ? What are the institutions providing teacher-training there?

3. What efforts are made to maintain the status of teachers high? What factors are taken into consideration at the time of admission and appointment?

# 18

# University Education

In the beginning the nature of American higher education was like European higher education. In both the systems specialisation and research methods were prominent. But according to needs of the time and change in American philosophy of life, the aims of higher education have also changed consequently, the nature of European and American education is not considerably different from each other.

The higher education because of specialisation and being research oriented was not universal and accessible to all in U. S. A. and proved useless for persons with vocational interests. So it began to be emphasised that higher education should be made universal, accessible and useful far all. So in 1949, Acts were made in Massachussets, New York and New Jersey that no person would be debarred farm receiving higher education an the basis of caste, creed, religion and nationality. According to the Acts, thase columns were removed from the admission farms which required information regarding these. Although this legal provision was made only far higher education, but it began to be followed at all levels of education.

The university education combined with specialisation and research outlook was useful only far brilliant students. Ordinary students were neglected and even the teachers neglected ordinary students. But, later on, the higher education was made accessible, useful and universal so that even average students could receive higher education and the teachers had to change their teaching-methods by changing their indifferent attitude.

Far providing equality of opportunity, the number of universities rose in about 200 in 1983 and the number of higher education calleges became about 1,500. The number of students in Liberal Arts Colleges increased to 50,00,000. In professional schools and separately organized schools which are about 1,800 in number, 18,00,000 students are receiving education. The increase in populating and need far education have affected educational institutions of all levels. In U. S. A., the number of Government colleges is about 35% of the total colleges for higher education. The rest are managed by private, collective, community, religious and municipal agencies. In spite of large number of colleges, there is a huge crowd for admission and sometimes problem of admission arises.

The changed organisation of American higher education has affected the aim of life of the graduates. Earlier the graduate who wanted to be a research scholar, being impressed by specialisation, now tried to become a qualified teacher. Although the educational standard deteriorated a bit but education became practical and useful. To solve the problem of admission in higher education, terminal education, supplementary courses and other specific provisions have been made. An attempt has been made to ease the admission problem by making admission tests simple and easy. The reorganisation of curriculum has been considered necessary for saving the educational standard from deterioration and it has become the responsibility of teachers that they provide education according to the needs and interests of students. Keeping in view the capability of students, useful and practical education have been arranged and their curriculum have been divided into groups so that educational standard might be successfully evaluated.

**Different Varsities**

There are two types of universities for higher education in U. S. A. :

(1) Private Universities, and

(2) State Universities.

***Private Universities.*** These universities are based on old and conservative traditions. They are mainly influenced by European traditions. These universities have specialisation and research provisions. Consequently, only brilliant students can take admission in these universities. These universities have to face the problem of financial stringency due to limited number of students and lack of State interference. The finances are met from tuition fees paid by the students As a result, the fees charged are quite high due to which the common people cannot admit their wards in these universities. Stamford, North Western, Johns Hopkins, Columbia, Prinston, Yale and Harvard universities are some such universities.

***State Universities.*** Some universities are known as State universities. Indiana, Ohio, Minnesota, Wisconsin, California and Mischigan universities are such universities. These universities are controlled and aided by the States Governments. Consequently, the number of students is quite large and fees charged are not very high. Those students who come to these universities from other States have to pay more fee. This fee is almost five times more than the ordinarily charged. At the time of admission preference is given to students of the related State. These universities provide education according to the new and revised curriculum. These universities try to fulfil desired objective based on national ideals. Complete co-operation and contact with affiliated colleges is found. These universities and affiliated colleges fulfil a great need of the nation by trying to make higher education useful for life practical and public. Specialisation and research spirit are getting weaker and weaker day by day in these universities.

**Generation of Finance**

In higher education sufficient income is required for salaries of teachers and staff building-construction and maintenance of laboratories apparatus material aids researches, scholarships, loan scholarships and provision of games and sports etc. Consequently to bear the expenditure the following sources of income are recognised :

(1) Private Sources of income and

(2) Governmental Sources.

***Private Sources of Income.*** In America for development of higher education the following private sources of income are available:

***Endowment.*** This source has been recognised by the State on the basis of its movable and immovable properties pledged at the time of establishing private universities and colleges. These institutions have their own endowments and also receive help and donations etc. from time to time. This endowment may be increased when needed but other sources of income such as fees etc. cannot be increased. As a result the institutions often reduce their expenditure.

***Tuition Fees.*** In private universities and colleges higher fees are charged. This tuition-fee is annual. Private educational institutions determine these tuition fees after careful consideration. In the determination of fees, the number of students educational standard economic condition of local people reputation of the institution etc. are taken into consideration. If in an institution the tuition fees are increased much the students begin to take admission in other institutions. So the institutions have to reduce their expenditure due to decrease in the number of students and the standard of education goes down. High tuition-fees are also a measure of high standard of education. In private educational institutions the annual tuition-fee is from 2,000 to 3,000 dollars while in State Universities, it is about 1,000 dollars. In private universities there are other fees as reading-room fee class-room management fee light, refreshment, transport etc. besides the tuition-fees.

***Donation for Immediate Expenditure.*** Private institutions receive donations from the public from time to time. This donation is known as a gift. It is in two forms-(1) Investment Gift or Endowment which is paid by the public to increase endowment, (2) Indirect Gift which accumulates sufficiently even when given by the public in small quantity. This gift or donation is given for immediate expenditure. This amount may be from one dollar to one lakh dollars or more. The American public pays this gift when becoming prosperous or at some happy occasion and to meet the expenditure on education of some member of its family. This voluntary gift is given for managing reading-room, library, lecture theatre or laboratory or without mention of any specific purpose. This gift is spent by the President and Treasurer of the University who are free to make any expenditure. Now-a-days donations in memory are bocoming popular.

The public donates money to commemorate the birthday or death of some of its dear ones and this donation continues for indefinite period. Various scholarships are given from this donation which are called Memorial Scholarships. This donation is given by commercial and industrial undertakings to private universities. These commercial and industrial concerns help the universities during finacial stringency; These universities co-operate in providing training and education to the employees of these commercial and industrial undertakings.

Although private universities and colleges are entitled to get financial help and grant from the State or Federal Governments, still these universities are hesitant to receive the same, lest their autonomy is hampered with by the State interference. Even then, these universities get many State grants indirectly. No tax is paid on endowment, donation or accumulated amount. Income upto 600 dollars which i received in the form of endowment or memorial scholarships is free from income-tax. Guardians who spend 600 dollars annually on the education of their wards are exempted from the payment of income-tax. After receiving education when the student begins to earn, he give some donation for sake of fulfilling his duty towards the institutions.

## Governmental Universities

Those universities and colleges which are run by State Governments, get their income from municipalities and public exchequer. State universities and colleges are run by State or Federal Governments. Most of the universities are run by State Governments. These universities and colleges charge only nominal fees. Although the State Governments have arranged various sources of income for these universities and colleges, still there is shortage of funds which are met from donations, gifts and fees. These educational institutions demand more gifts and fees from those students who come from other States for study.

## The Establishment

In the field of American education, universities were established to satisfy the thirst for knowledge. Whatever knowledge is obtained by public efforts, is developed through researches in universities and it is made available to others for their benefit and happiness. In those universities, cultural, sociological, scientific and atomic research activities are encouraged.

## Apex Body

The central administration of a university is in the hands of chief administrator called President. The President of the university is elected by a Board of Trustees consisting of elected politicians, teachers and honourable citizens. The term of the President is indefinite and may continue unopposed for several years. Sometimes even less educated person is elected as a President. The President looks after the financial position of the university and solves the related problems. He tries to maintain contact with old graduates of the university. He maintains contact with local administration. State administration, traders, industrialists and donators in order that needed donation may be received from them at the time of financial stringency.

**Various Departments**

The administrations of the university is divided into various faculties. Every faculty has a Dean who tries to solve economic and individual problems of his faculty statutorily and he is also the chief of related departments in affiliated colleges. In some universities, the Dean is not the Head of Department for affiliated colleges rather the colleges have separate Head of Department of the concerned subject. Sometimes a department has to manage two colleges having the same course. For example, the Medical Department of the Harward University manages School of Dental Medicine and Medical School both. Liberal Arts colleges and Graduate School of Arts and Sciences are run under the supervision of only one Department of Arts and Science. In such a system, the problem that arises is that the teacher takes interest mostly in the education of graduate colleges and the other of students are neglected. Such a situation is harmful. To solve this problem the Columbia ,University has organised separate departments for colleges of both levels. Thus separate teachers for both levels have been arranged. This system seems more expensive and there is likelihood of overlooking each other's regulations.

The various departments of a university are fully responsible for the education of the students of their subjects. The admission of students, their examination, determination of educational policy, vocational guidance and ideals of citizenship etc. fall within the responsibility of these departments. For the success of student-life of the newly admitted students the guidance of departments is praiseworthy. Thus the function of the departments is extensive, serious and responsible. In universities where the departmental work is extensive, sub-departments are formed for the sake of administrative convenience by dividing the departments into administrative divisions. These sub-departments hear the responsibility of managing related funds and preparing the annual budget. In the Chicago University, sub-departmental administration is run by dividing departments.

## The Interaction

Whenever any programme requiring the participation of several subdepartments is devised, the Dean calls a meeting of different heads and manages to execute the programme. But when this programme is related to different faculties, the President of the University gets the activity conducted through the joint efforts of different Deans.

## At the Helm

The members of Board of Trustees are generally from businessmen, politicians, professors etc. This Board controls the university. The President of the university is a representative of the Board of Trustees. The Board extends full co-operation to its representatives. The Board of Trustees maintains cordial relations with Deans. The Deans are directly concerned with educational policy determination, but the Board of Trustees is not directly related to it. So there is no question of any disharmony.

## The Syllabi

In the university curriculum, it requires four years for Graduation, one year for Master's Degree and at least four years for a Doctorate Degree. Three years are needed at under-graduate level. Thus the university curriculum is of 12 years.

**Attached Institutions**

The colleges affiliated to universities are of three kinds:

***Liberal Art Colleges-***These colleges award Graduation Degree and mainly controlled and managed by religious institutions.

***Under-Graduate Colleges-***Some colleges are independent and separate from the university system but such colleges as-Engineering colleges, Agriculture colleges, Music colleges, Home-science colleges, Physiology colleges and Physical Education colleges are also within the jurisdiction of universities.

***Graduate Colleges-***A candidate with a Graduation Degree may get admission in a Graduate college. In this also, there are various kinds as-Law College, Medical College and Arts and Science College. The administration and control of all types of colleges is both joint and separate. The administration in joint form is managed by a university college. The Registrar is the administrator of this office.

**Students' Role**

The students do not interfere in university administration. They can simply advise. Every university provides various interesting subjects for selection. The student is free to select any subject of his choice. The Deans do consider the annual report presented by the Students' Union. The old students of the institution can demand details of expenditure at the time of collecting funds for the institution.

**The Time Table**

The period from last week of September to middle of June is the academic year of universities. In the remaining summer days, the universities organise adult education; day classes and night classes are held to conduct Study-Counselling Centres, Health

Centres, Vocational guidance and teaching of English to foreigners. The teachers and students get opportunities of revising their acquired knowledge.

**Life in Campus**

The educational philosophy affects the educational aims and influence the educational system. So American philosophy of education may be sensed from the student life there. The students have to live in hostels for their physical, mental, social and spiritual development. Some municipal colleges have no hostel provision, otherwise all the universities and colleges are residential. The hostels have provision of retiring-rooms, dining halls, libraries and play-grounds. The students unfamiliar to each other try to lead a corporate life. The entire hostel system is based on family mode of living. Daily life activities are fulfilled in a co-operative atmosphere. This system being more expensive, is not available to all. Those students cannot bear the expenses live in nearby houses and rooms on rent. For them some centre established where hostel like facilities are available.

**Professional Courses**

The students have the facility of choosing various subjects of their interest. Three periods per week are assigned to teach a subject. A period is of 50 minutes duration. Besides the class teaching periods, every student gives two periods per week for his studies. At the Graduate level 120 hours regular class-teaching credit is required. Since more time is required for laboratory work, the number of periods is increased. The total number of periods for all subjects reaches upto 40 per week. A term is of 15 weeks. There is one week's vacation in the month of April and 2 week's vacation on the occasion of Christmas Day.

**Methods of Teaching**

As regards of method of teaching, a teacher reads out his lecture to a crowd of about 200 or 300 students. This teaching method is not considered useful. The students do not like this method. In the second method, lecture is delivered before a class of 15 to 30 students and discussion is held on it. But this method is expensive. So a third method has been evolved as a viamedia. According to this method, the teacher reads out his lecture before a large number of students of his subject one or two times in a week. After that the students discuss the lecture in group with associate teachers who are themselves students holding Graduate Degree. This system is also found in affiliated colleges. In Liberal Arts Colleges, more attention is paid on the completion of the course. They do not care whether students have learnt anything or not. In American colleges laboratory method also prevails. In it even language teaching is done in laboratories and workshops, where taperecorders are used.

At the higher education level both college system and affiliated college system are popular. In colleges the number of students is less but the teachers are not quite efficient. Even then the students have sufficient contact with teachers and receive education. But in the university colleges the teachers are more efficient and the number of students is large due to which there is lack of student teacher contact. So the guardians are at a loss to decide where to admit their wards.

Even the standard of education in the above institutions is different. But every institution tries that the standard of its education does not deteriorate and the value of its degree is maintained. So students are put to disadvantage when they change the institution and migrate. In both the institutions, there is a minimum prescribed qualification for admission. The Degrees of both the institutions have Governmental and vocational recognition.

**Evaluation and Measurement**

The examination system at all places is almost the same. After the completion of half of the course, subject wise separate written examinations are held. At this stage, the question paper is of one hour only, but after the completion of the whole course, 3 hours question paper is given. The examination answer-books are of blue colour. Hence they are called Blue Books. To test specialisation in subjects, an additional general examination is held after 4 or 5 years. Even after sufficient precautions some students are found using unfair means for which they are punished.

Evaluation in examination is done both in the marks and grades *e. g.*, Grade A-90% or above marks obtained. Grade B-From 80% to 90% Grade C-From 70% to 80% Grade D-From 62% to 70% Grade E. -62% or less. But the student obtaining less than 60 per cent marks is declared failed. It maybe noted that these grades are very often determined on the basis of the performance of the whole group. If, by chance, at a test, most of the students do very badly, then it is just possible that the one scoring 50 per cent of marks may be given Grade A. Similarly, the grades may also be allocated.

**Education for Girls**

In the beginning, there was no co-education. Even now, in Wellesly, Sweet Briar, Vassar, Mount Holyoke, Mills, Brya Mawar and Smity colleges only women are admitted. Similarly, Williams, Amberst, Bowdin, Kenyon and Dart Mouth are colleges for male only. But, as a result of nationwide agitation, co-education has been started. In hostels, the male students have more facilities than female-students. The girl students are kept under full control in the early years and even in later years they are not allowed to move out after ten O'clock at night.

**Various Provisions**

The boarding and lodging fees in Government colleges is nearly 2,000 dollars annually, but in private colleges, it is 4,000 to 5,000 dollars per year. Thus the hostel provision is expensive. Poor students get scholarships. The scholarships are given on the basis of ability, character, physical and other efficiencies. Some students are paid remuneration for doing some extra work in the college.

To provide loan from different funds, a Higher Education Assistance Corporation has been established. Foreign students get loan for 12 months. Community colleges provide cheap education, The loan is repaid in instalments. Very nominal interest is charged on such loans.

For all round development, games-sports, gymnastics, clubs and various associations are organised. Co-curricular activities are run. Convocation is an interesting function of the year for the students.

***Fundamental Philosophy of University Education.*** In the beginning at the university and higher education stage, there was abundance of specialisation and research work. But after 1949, the higher education has been made useful for life, accessible and utilitarian and has been given statutory recognition.

***Sources of Income-***(1) Private Sources and (2) State Sources.

***Private Sources-***Endowment, tuition-fees, donation for immediate expenditure and gifts received in the form of scholarships and cash are main.

***State Sources of Income-***State grants, land grants, exemption from income-tax, nominal tuition-fees and private donations are the sources of income.

***Sources of Income of Private Universities***

***Endowment-***It is received in the form of movable and immovable properties and periodical donations from businessmen.

***Tutition fees*** are more than in the State institutions.

***Donation*** for Immediate Expenditure is received for the education of ward in memory and annual scholarships.

***Organisation of University.*** The representative elected by the Board of Trustees is the President of the University. All economic and organisational policies are determined under his chairmanship.

***Department System of University.*** Every subject has a faculty which is headed by a Dean. It has sub-departments and divisions. The activities of these are conducted by interdepartmental and inter-sub-departmental heads.

***University and College System.*** This system comprises of Liberal Arts Colleges, Undergraduate colleges, Degree or Graduate College.

***Administration and Students.*** In Liberal Arts colleges, the dean gives consideration to the report of students union. Old students are given details of expenditure on demand.

***Student Life.*** Student life is based on educational environment according to educational aims. Hostels are established for the sake of all round development of students.

***Curriculum and Vacation.*** Curriculum is expensive. There is freedom of choosing subjects. A term is of 15 weeks.

***Grades of Examination System.*** Evaluation is done on the basis of marks obtained but grades are also given on the basis of marks obtained as A, B, C, D, E.

***Women Education.*** No co-education prevailed earlier. Even now there are separate colleges for men and women. Co-education has started now.

***Fees Scholarships and other Facilities.*** In America, there is practice of giving scholarships, remunerative jobs and loans etc. The students are free to do extra remunerative work.

## QUESTIONS

1. What is the fundamental philosophy of higher education in U. S. A. ?
2. What are the problems that arise at the University level regarding organisation of courses ?
3. What are the sources of income for expenditure in the field of higher education in U. S. A.? Describe the sources of income for private universities.
4. How far is the organisation of University in U.S.A. worth following ?
5. What is the place of University President in its administration?
6. Describe the various organisational systems of universities.

# 19

# School Education

The organisation of secondary education in U. S. A. is a result of long continuous struggle. The Americans by nature are lovers of freedom and have faith in democracy. It was due to this spirit that primary education there could became compulsory and universal. Secondary education in U. S. A. developed because of the impact of industrial revolution and also because of primary education being made compulsory for children. After 17 years of age, the children had to face the problem of finding a suitable vocation. It was difficult to provide a vocation to every literate person. So the people decided to give further education to their children. Gradually secondary education developed due to collective public efforts. Since child labour was prohibitive, it was considered necessary to provide education till the children became adult. Consequently, provision of secondary education was considered necessary.

## Religious Schools

European immigrants in America were concerned lest their children were deprived of their old culture, civilization, literature and religion. So Latin Grammar Schools were established by religious leaders and priests. The expenditure of these schools was borne by religious communities and religious people. Because of high tuition fees and class dominated educational policy, children of rich families could receive education in them. The Latin Grammar Schools were established by Puritans with the desire of imparting education through religious curriculum. Such a school was established for the first time in 1635 in Bostan city. Upto the 19th century, the Latin Grammar School system was based an old traditions. Due to change in atmosphere, social awakening and educational interest, these Lattin Grammar Schools of secandary education were re-organised. People lost their faith in the leadership of priests and these schools were replaced by educational academies.

## Other Institutions

Benjamin Franklin is said to be the originator of American Educational Academies. In his leadership it was realized that secandary education should not be orthodox and traditional only rather it should be capable of preparing children for future life and should create vocational abilities. Thus it was planned to conduct education by giving it material scope. Consequently, first of all Educational Academy was established in Philadelphia in 1751. These Academies were very much liked by the people because those children who could not get further education due to some reasons, were able to get some vocation after receiving vocational education at the secondary level. So by 1830, about 500 academies were established in the whole country. The main feature of these academies was that they prepared children for future life from vocational point of view. That was the reason that then prevailing Latin Grammar Schools lost their attraction and Educational Academies with extensive utilitarian curriculum flourished day by day.

In the Academies, along with providing vocational education, political science, philosophy and military education were also included. Women education also found a place in this system. The management of these academies was democratic. The expenditure was met from donations and tuition fees paid by the students. Up to 1837, as is evident from the curriculum of the New York academies, along with English literature old classical languages, Greek, Hebrew, Roman etc. were also taught. Based on public needs and traditions, the Educational Academy system prepared students for higher education.

As a result of democratic spirit interest of the people was directed towards women education. It was realized that women too, have mental and physical potentialities like men. So, they should also get opportunities like men. Thus Educational Academy system got public support and it assumed a universal form. Thus education in U. S. A. developed in a democratic way.

**Public Schools**

Just at the beginning of the 19th century agitation started in U. S. A. against the colonial and conservative education. This agitation strengthened the view that secondary schools should not be conservative and should provide education different from the useless and expensive education of Latin Grammar Schools. So it was decided that in the new schools integrated curriculum of the Academies should be introduced. In 1924 and 1926, public secondary schools were opened in New York and Boston cities respectively. The Boston school was meant for women education. The aim of these schools was to provide college level education upto some minimum stage and to make education useful for catering to the needs of the people.

By the end of the 19th century, the need for providing graduation-level education was emphasised. So through higher and college level education, courses for awarding degrees were started. The aim now determined at the secondary level was that these schools should prepare an educational base for graduation level education. Till then, these schools were run from donations of the people. But they could not conduct programmes as desired. In 1827, in the Massachusetts State of U. S. A., it was enacted that a city consisting of more than 500 families should have universal education. As a result, there was a state-wide agitation for making secondary education free and universal. This led to significant improvement in the conditions of schools.

The Kalamazoo case in Micchigan State helped the case of making secondary education fees and shouldering of the responsibility of educational expenditure by the Government. It was decided in the Kalamazoo case that the Government should levy education-cities on people for making secondary education free in education-cities. The people opposed this decision and the matter was referred to the Supreme Court. But the Supreme Court confirmed the decision that if the local institutions and school Districts decided and if the majority was in favour, they could levy tax on people for the development of education above the primary level. Thus legal right could be obtained for making secondary education free and for levying tax for its development.

By the end of the 19th century, within the newly developed structure of secondary schools, integrated curriculum and methods of Latin Grammar Schools and Educational Academies were accepted. From Latin Grammar Schools, the ideal of social, religious, moral and intellectual development and from Educational Academies educational programmes of universal character and vocationalization were incorporated. Even after that the people could not get rid of individualistic bent of mind. The people still wanted that the schools should cater to the needs of every class of society. The Committee of Ten constituted in 1892, prescribed its Report- A-part of total population of students whose guardians are able to maintain them in schools and are desirous of higher education, should be provided all educational facilities upto 18 years of age. This report had its impact on education system. In some schools education was made compulsory upto 18 years of age. Generally, upto 16 years of age education could become compulsory unhindered.

With the beginning of 20th century, new awakening in U. S. A. changed the social, political and individual situation. Industrial Revolution led to national progress. A need for skilled labour was felt and the unskilled people had to face the problem of unemployment. The economic status of people improved and they began to weigh the contribution of secondary education on the scale of monetary gains. However, they wanted mental level training at the secondary level, with the development of spirit of freedom. So the secondary schools began to be considered as a means of producing worthy citizens in place of only leading to mental and intellectual development and providing a base of higher education. Now it began to be believed that the aim of secondary schools should be to teach citizenship, vocational training, control of fundamental processes, worthy home-membership, ethical character, health development, utilisation of leisure etc. Consequently, people were attracted towards vocational education with the desire of material gains. As soon as the demand for vocationally trained persons increased, the importance-of vocational training institutions increased. The number of students seeking admission at the college level came down from 75 per cent to 25 per cent.

**Room for Change**

The secondary education system began to change by the second half of the 20th century. Now the first 8 years of primary education began to be considered as lengthy and it was decided to frame 6 year curriclum. So the last years (classes 7th and 8th) of primary education were included in the 4 years (classes 9th to 12th) of secondary education. Thus, the curriculum of primary education was from 6 to 12 years and the age limit for secondary education was from 12 to 18 years. Along with this change, there was one more significant change. Now due to the need of vocational training, the first two years of college-level were included in the curriculum of secondary education and thus the duration of secondary education was extended from 12 years age to 20 years of age and the period of education was raised from 4 years to 8 years. Thus according to the first change, the education of 16 years comprised, primary level 6 years, secondary level 6 years and 4 years of college level education. But according to the second change, the 16 years of education were divided as 6 years, 8 years and 2 years at the three levels respectively.

According to the felt requirements, it began to be realized that the 6 year or 8 year period of secondary education had become lengthy. So it was divided into various grades. The first 6 years of secondary level curriculum were divided into two grades of 3 years each. They were named as Junior High School and Senior High School. But the second curriculum of 8 year secondary education was converted into curricula of 3, 3 and 2 years. The curriculum of the first 3 years was termed as Junior Secondary, second 3 years as Higher Secondary and final two years a Junior College curriculum. In 1902, the first Junior Secondary plan was implemented in Illinois State and in 1910, first junior secondary school was established in California State.

**Objectives and Purposes**

The immigrants from Europe in U. S. A. had established Latin Grammar Schools in order to maintain their basic source of religion intact and to maintain their traditional literacy and cultural atmosphere. The aim of these schools was to make the new generation devoted to religion and to prepare is fur college level studies. Thus the secondary education imparted by Latin Grammar Schools helped the people to obtain good posts and to exercise political, social and vocational leadership. From the management point of view, higher education was not suitable for every student. But the Educational Academics devised curriculum to cater to the rising needs.

Secondary education in U. S. A. has been influenced by the local atmosphere and it is generally controlled by the local people. But the pattern of secondary education is based on the recommendations of various national committees. In 1892, the National Education Association formed a committee of ten. This committee recommended some reforms of the programmes of secondary education with the view that the same should lay solid foundation for college level education and in order to give universal and general form to future education classical subjects and mathematics, etc. should also be included in the curriculum. After that in 1899 for the study of the suggestions of the committee of ten, a committee of thirteen was constituted. It was also called Committee on College Entrance Requirements. It proposed specific recommendations for secondary education programmes. Similarly, in 1911, a committee on the Articulation of High School and College was organised which presented various projects and recommendations for making the prevailing secondary education system more useful.

In 1912, the National Education Commission established a Commission on Reorganisation of Secondary Education. This commission after 6 years of deep study and observations, formulated cardinal principles of Secondary Education in 1918 for reconstruction of secondary education. According to these principles, the aim of providing education for complete and worthy giving to every citizen of the land after receiving this education, was accepted. The main aims for secondary education as recommended were seven as below:

***Health Education as an Aim.*** The commission recommended for the inclusion of health education in the curriculum of secondary education in order to develop a sound mind in a sound body. Suitable programmes from time to time should be organised for maintaining good health. Health education should motivate people to fulfil national domestic, social and personal duties devotedly.

***Command of Fundamental Processes.*** In order to make secondary education more utilitarian, the students should be helped to acquire finner grip over the tools of knowledge *i.e.,* their various senses should be adequately trained through the study of various subjects in the humanity and science groups.

***Worthy Home Membership.*** The secondary education should be such that the child after receiving it may become dutiful and a worthy home-member, by behaving ideally in home life. It should develop such qualities as co-operation, fellowship tolerance and sympathy in him.

***Vocational Education.*** At this stage, vocational learning and teaching should get prominence in the curriculum so that it may make the students vocationally capable and successful. Thus for future citizen so trained vocationally will be able to contribute to national progress and will be able to lead his life with high standard. This education should develop vocational interest, capacity and spirit of fellowship.

***Aim of Civic Education.*** Education should make the future citizens so worthy that they may prove helpful and useful for the Nation, World and society. The modern citizen should not only be able to solve national problems rather he should be capable of solving international problems also.

***Worthy Use of Leisure.*** Secondary education should create capacity for worthy use of leisure. The children should be able to utilise their leisure in developing their personality and improving their physical and mental abilities.

***Ethical Character.*** At the secondary education level those activities which could help in the character formation of citizens should be included in the curriculum.

In 1933, the need for reorganising secondary education was felt. For this reorganisation, Committee on Socio-Economic Goals of America was constituted. The committee formed in 1918 had emphasised individual development on the basis of development of individualistic education. But this committee laid stress on social development through social and cooperative educational programmes. This committee recommended to make American education more and more social, economic and universal. The following ten objectives were determined for this social and utilitarian educational organisation:

1. Physical security.

2. Equality of opportunity.

3. Economic Security.
4. Freedom.
5. Mental Security.
6. Fair Play.
7. Suitable Occupation.
8. Active and Flexible Personality.
9. The aim of Hereditary Strength.
10. Participation in Evolving Culture.

Similarly in 1932, the Department of Secondary School Principals presented two reports and suggestions to the Committee on the orientation of Secondary Education for the study of secondary education and for determination of suitable programme for it.

In its first report this Committee recommended to provide education for social ideals, their importance, development of abilities and character development. The committee defined this phase of process as education. In this kind of education, it was considered necessary to create capacity for motivation and guidance for the progress was possible only through secondary education. There was no possibility for this type of progress through primary education.

**Working System**

The committee on the orientation of secondary education constituted by Department of Secondary School Principals determined the following functions of secondary education:

***Development of Knowledge and Integration.*** It is the function of secondary education to develop and integrate knowledge of students (boys and girls) according to definite programmes, no matter even if those programmes are in diminishing degree and their practice should go on continuously till their growing intellectual level, desired general ideals, tendencies, appreciation, knowledge and training take a permanent shape.

***To Fulfil Probable Future Needs.*** It is necessary to reorganise secondary education in order to satisfy the probable future needs of students, keeping in view their capacity, interest and maturity while explaining to them the personal and social value of their needs.

***To Give Knowledge of Traditional, Cultural and Contemporary Social Duties.*** Modern secondary education should be such that it may create a spirit of progressiveness irrespective of existing creed, tradition and culture.

***Awakening for Specific Ability.*** Secondary education should be such as may create capacity and interest for specific studies and increasing specialization.

***Provision of New Knowledge Correlated with Previous Knowledge.*** The form of new knowledge based on previous knowledge should be so systematic that the child is able to achieve knowledge easily by knowing the theory, principles and importance of new knowledge, but he should not confine himself to that knowledge rather he should be curious to know more.

***To Create a Spirit of taking Interest in Human Activities.*** Secondary education should also create the spirit of taking interest in major field of human activities while generating a spirit of personal happiness along with social progress.

***Use of Progressive Teaching-methods, Independent Study and Research Principles.*** Through education at this level, programmes concerning demand in independent thoughts, execution of elementary principles of research, collective and, individual intelligence and self-directed practice etc. should be encouraged.

***Retention of Students in Schools till the stage of Diminishing Returns.*** The students should be retained in the school till they are prepared for self-study and it is realized that the school is no more useful for them. In such a situation, it is necessary to send the student in some other training institution or school where he is able to pursue studies himself.

In 1934, a Progressive Education Society was organized which did not give any solid suggestion till 1942 even after considerable deliberation and suggested to hand over the responsibility of secondary education to State Governments. It was also of the opinion that the State Government would be free in the determination of aims. Similarly, for determination of secondary education policy, Educational Policy Commission was formed in 1944 which considered it necessary to make secondary education free of all distinctions of sex, colour, atmosphere, place and State and suggested to make it well balanced. In 1947, again by appointing a Commission on Life Adjustment Education the educational aims were reviewed. This Commission gave certain suggestions for life adjustment and recommended to conduct education accordingly. The suggestions were as below:

(1) It should be the distinguished characteristic of Academy education to prepare worthy citizens.

(2) Education should familiarise students with daily behavioural activities.

(3) Education should lead to worthy home membership.

(4) Education should enable the citizen to utilize his leisure.

(5) Education should acquaint the citizen with basic tools of learning.

(6) This education should provide to the citizens proper vocational training.

(7) Education should create in the citizens a sense of appreciation of beauty so that they may understand art and nature.

(8) The education should enable the citizens to understand the significance and methods of science.

(9) This education should provide mental health and physical fitness.

(10) Such education should be provided to boys and girls which may create a sense off morality and create in them capacity for evaluating principles of moral conduct.

These new recommendations of the Commission on Life Adjustment guided the management of every secondary school to reconsider the secondary education programme. Gradually life adjustment was given importance in the curriculum, educational policies and aims. The policies prescribed by the commission were followed according to local environments, needs and tradition. By providing different subjects, attention was paid on the interest and-needs of boys and girls and the existing nature of school buildings, teaching and study facilities, aids and teaching methods. Inspite of several difficulties, curricular programmes to provide balances and useful adjustment were formulated.

### The Infrastructure

Because of the appointment of various Commissions and their recommendations, the nature and organisation of secondary education changed from time to time and ultimately secondary education assumed its present form.

### Different Kinds of Schools

The secondary schools based on previous system were comprehensive and expensive befitting the then plan and needs and their forms continued to develop till the end of the 19th century. But in the 20th century, the secondary education continued to be reorganized according to the recommendations of committees and commissions constituted from time to time. During the first half of the current century, special changes in the curriculums were brought about and specific courses were introduced. Besides the school for General Education, schools for specific subjects and vocational education were established-for example Practical Arts High Schools. High School of Commerce, Technical High School and Manual Training High Schools etc.

In U. S. A., the nature and organisation of reorganised schools are not the same everywhere. There is similarity only in graduation. General Secondary Schools are of 4 year curriculum in which education from class 9th to 12th is provided. Reorganised schools are those which run from classes 7th to 12th. The first three years of the secondary schools (*i.e.*. classes 7, 8 and 9) are called Junior High School classes and the last three years (classes 10, 11 and 12) are known as Senior High School classes. On the basis of re-organisation, the form of these types was adopted with very slow progress in 12-14 years. The following data make this thing clear:

| *Year* | *New System or Schools* |
|---|---|
| 1922 | 11 % |
| 1926 | 19 % |
| 1930 | 26% |
| 1934 | 29% |
| 1935 | 30% |

The number of students in 6 year secondary schools was more than that in the 4 year secondary school's. Upto 1935, the percentage of students in both the type of schools (of 4 year and 6 year curriculums) was 51 % while in reorganised secondary schools (of 6 year) alone was 49%. It is clear from this that even though reorganized schools were less in number yet they educated a large part of total population. Only 2% students received education in 4 year secondary schools. Even now it is noticed that if the number of students in reorganised schools is 266, in 4 year secondary schools only 85 boys and girls receive education. Thus in new secondary schools, the number of students is three times more than in pre-secondary schools. According to the data of 1983, the average of the number of students is as follows:

1. In Junior High School- 900 students per school.
2. Senior High School-800 students per school.
3. Junior/Senior High School classes-500 students per school.

In U. S. A., the education organisation (system) of secondary schools is not similar on the basis of gradation system. In some places, the curriculum is of six years and in other places it is of 4 years. The years of teaching of primary and college level are affected accordingly such as :

| *Primary Level* | *Secondary Level* | *College Level* |
|---|---|---|
| 1. 6 Year | 4 year (Class 7 to 10) | 4 Year |
| 2. 6 Year | 6 year (Class 7 to 12) | 2 Year |
| | (3 year Junior High School) 3 year Senior High School) | |
| | 4 Year (Class 9 to 12) | |
| 3. 8 Year | | 2 Year |

The recognized secondary level is like number 2 in which the primary level curriculum is of 6 years (at the secondary level 3 year Junior High School and 3 year Junior High School) and remaining 2 years are spent on college level education.

At the secondary level of American education, the Junior High School classes were started because In every sphere of life some skilled persons were needed. This need could be fulfilled only by reorganisation of the educational system. At that time, it was realized that the Junior classes generally classes VII and VIII which were included at the primary level should be combined with secondary classes and their curriculum should be different from primary classes. Thus by reorganising the curriculum, skilled persons could be prepared at the secondary level. The 6 year curriculum at the secondary level which is divided into 3 year Junior High School and 3 year Senior High School is not common. These provisions have been implemented in schools of big cities or those centres where in preconstructed school buildings all the secondary classes could not be held due to lack of space. Though Junior High School and Senior High School classes are held separately but they are complementary to each other. In some places, the Junior college level classes have been included in the college level while in some other places, they form a part of secondary level. Thus the nature of secondary education organization though extensive is not the same every where.

Secondary education organisation in U. S. A. is still at the experimental stage. The organisation of school has not totally changed the system but it has only introduced some changes from time to time according to the need and philosophy of life. To fulfil occasional requirements, education is organized on the basis of local environment. The data of types of schools after 1913 are as follows:

| Number of total secondary schools-52976 in which | |
|---|---|
| Junior High Schools | 8% |
| Senior High Schools | 12% |
| Senior and Junior High Schools | 30% |
| Secondary Schools | 50% |

The American educationists realized that the prevailing 8 years of primary education was not suitable for the mental and physical development of children. In last two years (classes 7 and 8) do not fulfil the needs of boys and girls. At the, same time, the 4 year curriculum of secondary level was altogether new for the students who came after finishing primary education and it took time for them to adjust accordingly. So it was advised that the problem could be solved by adding the last two classes of primary level with the secondary level classes. So by adding the last two classes of primary level with secondary classes, 3-3 yearly Junior High Schools and Senior High Schools were formed and the curriculum was continued according to their requirements.

In 1880, President Eliot of Harved University, enticising the 8 year curriculum of primary level suggested to reduce it. In 1888 with the start of Elementary Education Reorganisation trend, some efforts was made to reduce the 8 year curriculum. The committee of ten established in 1893 and the College Entrance Requirement Committee. In 1899 it suggested to change and reorganise the primary and secondary level education in 6 year curriculums. In the beginning, only classes 7th and 8th were considered as Junior High School. Later on, in was changed to 3 years. First of all, this reorganised system was introduced in educationally more developed areas like Masachussets and Springfield. Afterwards, in Columbus and Ohio in 1909 and in 1910, in California and Burkley, the new reorganised system was introduced for the first time.

The aim of starting this Junior High School level was to establish a link between the curriculums of primary stage and higher secondary stage. In the reorganisation of the curriculum, preference was given to the fact that this curriculum should help in understanding difficult subjects, being correlated with higher secondary curriculum after the primary stage and should prove suitable for physical, mental and social development of boys and girls. This curriculum was considered important because it was convenient for teaching and guidance for life, too. So, it was also called corner-stone because this curriculums, provides an opportunity to the students at junior high school level to understand their limitations and possibilities. The teacher is also able to understand individual interests and need of boys and girls. This curriculum may develop the natural tendencies of students and in teaching their individual differences might be kept in mind. By inclusion of pre- scientific and pre-vocational subjects vocationalisation has been brought about.

The Secondary Education Reorganization Committee had obtained official sanction for reorganising Junior High School classes recognised as intermediate educational unit between primary level and higher secondary level. This Junior High School level provides education to adolescents. So it may be called school for adolescents. This system has been less affected by academic interpretation of higher education or University education than the prevailing secondary education. At this level, education is given to students for their personal, social, civic, domestic and vocational adjustement. They are taught to adopt a healthy view of life by utilising their leisure properly. Thus the Junior High School system fulfils a great need of society and nation.

The adolescent age begins at Junior High School level. At this stage, the age of boys and girls is between 12 to 14 years. From the point of view of the curriculum, these classes are more developed extensive, liberal and cultural than the final classes of previously prevailing 8 year primary level classes. In this curriculum, provision for teaching is made in a systematic way by including combined subjects. Combined subjects are taught by one teacher for a long time. In subject combination, English, social studies and science are more common. In additional subjects home economics, industrial art, music are the main. In teaching, large unit method and correlated subject teaching are recognized more. Mostly the Junior High Schools are situated in separate building from Senior High Schools. According to National Survey of Secondary Education, the functions of Junior High School are as follows:

1. Progressive teaching system.
2. Supervision of studies.
3. Study-programme.
4. Admission and Promotion facilities.
5. Educational and vocational guidance.
6. Organising special subject combination.
7. Organisation of extra-curricular activities.
8. Separate school-buildings and teaching-aids.
9. Specially trained teachers.

According to new classification, classes X, Xl and XII are included at this level. Higher secondary organisation is a form of 6 (3 + 3) + 2 grading system. There is no entrance examination for higher secondary classes. But the individual interest, capacity, capability and age are taken into consideration and it is also considered whether this education will be useful for boys and girls seeking admission. Before admission the mental age of children is measured. Before this measurement their recorded scores, teachers judgment and intelligence tests data are looked into. For admission, in the process of measuring physical maturity, attention is paid to their weight, height and physical fitness records. In the measurement of their social age, available cumulative records connected with their social and cultural activities and background are studied.

In U. S. A., there are three types of this higher secondary organisation. One is 3 year lower and 3 year higher secondary grade. The second is 4 year lower and 4 year higher secondary grade. And in the third gradation, the lower secondary is of 4 year and the higher secondary is of 2 years. The four year lower and 4 year higher secondary schools are organised separately. Although 4 year higher secondary school organisation depends on local conditions, people's economic status and social outlook, still they are sufficiently widespread. In the States where higher secondary level educational system is of 3 years and lower secondary level too, is of 3 years, there the 3 year lower secondary schools, being a higher part of elementary education and because of the integration of higher secondary schools with them, are completely independent from the point of view of control and establishment. But they have to maintain contact and affiliation with Elementary school Districts. In Illinois, the higher secondary schools are not connected with elementary school districts, rather they are administered by a separate board of education. In this type of organisation, the 3 year system cannot be conducted.

From the point of view of curriculum, the 3 year and 4 year curriculum systems are sufficiently similar. Those secondary schools, too, where there is no question of higher-lower levels, are similar, advanced and liberal from the point of view of educational aims, methods, guidance, provision of teachers and students, behaviour. Apart from general education, secondary schools imparting education in specific subjects and speeialization have also been introduced. In these schools, Technical High School Miami, Florida and High School of Music and Arts and High School of Automotive Trade, New York are worth mentioning. Besides these many other secondary schools are being run.

According to the variety of curriculum, the secondary schools of U. S. A. may be classified in the following way :

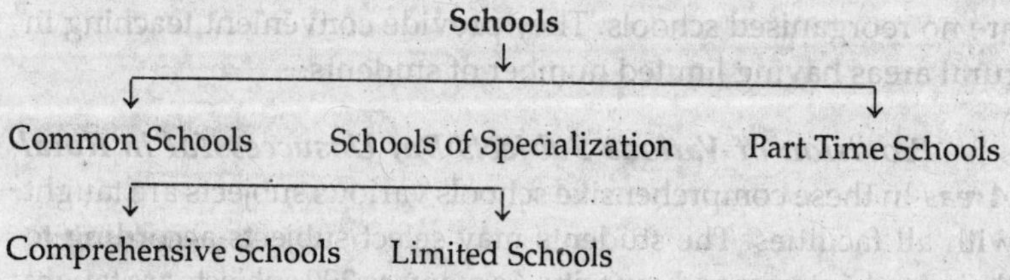


## Schools for All

***Comprehensive Schools.*** In the American educational organisation, the 4 year secondary schools prevailing in the grades

8-4-4 and 8-4 (2-2) and which are based on traditional methods are called Comprehensive Schools. Admission in these schools is given after completion of a year elementary education. These schools provide education from class 9th to 12th. Various subjects are taught in these schools. Therefore, they are called Comprehensive Schools. This education system tries to provide education for every phase of life. These schools have the following characteristics of universalness and comprehensiveness:

***These Schools are Public (Universal) and Democratic***-At the time of admission there is no consideration of sex, caste, class, colour and creed. Children of all communalities may receive education in these schools.

***Free Social Education***-The boys and girls of all communities and classes receive fee education through collective programmes. Thus the spirit of sociability is developed in them. Feeling of co-operation in created in the students.

***Consolidation of the Interests of all and Solidarity***- Then schools inculcate feelings of consolidation of interests of all democratisation and solidarity.

***Interesting Teaching-methods and Organisation***-Due to curriculum of these schools peculiar problems of teaching-methods and organisation do not arise and there are no diversities in them.

***Economical and Useful According to Rural Needs***-These schools are suitable and economical for rural areas where there are no reorganised schools. They provide convenient teaching in rural areas having limited number of students.

***Provision of Various Subjects But Unsuccessful in Rural Areas***-In these comprehensive schools various subjects are taught with all facilities. The students may select subjects according to their need, interest and capacity. As many as 200 subjects are taught here. Here art, commercial, vocational, agricultural subjects and subjects preparing for college level education are available. But evil then these schools are considered deficient as compared to urban schools. They prove more useful and comprehensive only in cities. The following deficiencies may be mentioned in rural areas:

***Shortage of Teachers***-Because of abundance of subjects, qualified teachers for every subject are not available.

***Lack of Student and Teacher Contact***-Due to shortage of teachers, the number of students is more than the number of teachers. As a result the teachers fail to establish contact with their students.

***Lack of Discipline and Control***-In rural areas, dedicational awakening in people is less than in urban areas. Consequently, there is a lack of discipline and control. Lack of sufficient facilities is also responsible for this indiscipline.

***Mutual Contact among Teachers Missing***-In re-organied schools, there is more of mutual contact among teachers. But in these schools, this contact is broken down because of too many subject departments.

***Sectarian View***-In these schools this characteristics may be noted.

***Classical Teaching***-In these schools classical teaching method is more important. The teaching is inclined towards this.

***Co-educational Defect***-Because of co-education, there is an attraction for opposite sex which creates many organisational problems.

***Education is Too Much Academic***-The educational organisation here has an impact of university education and hence it is full of too much academic tone.

***Limited Educational Aim***-These schools prepare students for college level education only. This should not be the only aim of education.

***Narrow Curriculum***-In these schools the curriculum is not connected with the needs of practical life of students. Hence it is narrow.

***Unsuitable for General Education***-These schools provide vocational and other specific training properly but they are unsuitable for general education.

***Unsuitable Individual Teaching***-Teaching is not provided to suit different mental levels capacity and abilities of students.

***Vocational and Co-curricular Activitie***s-Such activities do not receive attention. Modern languages science art and activities requiring manual labour are not given any special importance.

***Modern Teaching-Methods***-These are not adopted. Scientific methods are sparingly used.

***Lack of Similarity of Teaching-Methods like Other School***-The new useful teaching-methods that are used in other schools are not used in the same way in these schools. So there is no similarity of teaching methods. Consequently the teaching lags behind from other points of view except sociality.

***Lack of Recreation***-These schools do not provide healthy recreation and are not attractive and interesting.

***Limited Schools.*** These schools were established by the people for meeting their limited needs. Consequently these schools do not provide teaching in all the subjects and subject-specialization and opportunity for selection of subjects. The size of the schools depends on the limited needs and financial and other considerations. But as soon as the numher of students increases provision of teaching other subjects is made in these schools and the size of the school is increased. In the enlarged schools, provision is also made for the teaching of vocational subjects and other subjects-specialization. General education facilities are also provided. Such providing specific education are named as technical schools and vice-technical schools. In such technical schools. Technical High Schools and Oham is prominent.

## Model Schools

These schools were established for the sake of providing specialized vocational education. In these secondary schools introductory training in any specific vocation is given *e.g.*, subjects-specialisation technical, commercial art and trade etc. These schools have the following characteristics:

(1) Students having the same needs and interests relieve education in these schools.

(2) Teaching based on specific interest in quick.

(3) Qualified specialist teachers are available providing external knowledge and experimental practice.

(4) They create capacity for future life by providing full preparation for vocation.

But these schools are not free from drawbacks. All-round development of children is not possible in these schools. The main drawbacks are as follows:

(1) Premature vocation education is given.

(2) Education is not comprehensive, the subjects are not provided.

(3) Education system is not based on democratic conception rather subject in particular is paid more attention and that alone is considered important.

(4) They create a kind of class feeling.

(5) They are less important than the progressive reorganised schools, but even then their number is quite large.

**Technical Schools**

In 1906, some educationists and industrialists established a National Society for the promotion of industrial education. This society suggested to include industrial and vocational training subjects at the secondary level and demanded that plan should get Federal Appropriation. So in 1917, Smith Hughe's Act was passed which emphasised the provision of industrial and vocational education in the curriculum at the secondary level. Consequently, schools providing vocational and industrial education were established.

These industrial and vocational schools are generally run at vocational and industrial centres. This organisation is governed by some separate management. Three to four hours of education are fixed for industrial and vocational teaching. These schools fulfil industrial and vocational needs of the society and prepare students for present and future vocational life. Thus in these schools provision is made for the teaching of industrial and comrnercial subjects and training of vocations.

These schools are established with a view to provide education for some hours to those students who cannot receive education in schools because of being occupied in work throughout the day. These schools are of the following kinds:

***Continuation Schools.*** These schools are opened for 244 hours in a year for those students or adults who being occupied in work do not get education or who drop out before secondary level. In these schools teaching is done for 3 to 4 hours in a week on an average. These schools are organised and managed separately. They provide vocational and cultural education both. These schools are related with adult education system.

***Adult Evening Schools.*** Those persons who after receiving secondary education are engaged in some vocation and spend their whole day in that vocation, get education in Evening Schools. In these schools an effort is made to make adults efficient by giving them training in their related vocations. A feeling of worthy citizenship is created in them through general education.

**Junior Institutions**

Two kinds of views prevail in U. S. A. One of them is that secondary level education should be raised by two years and the classes at junior college level should he annexed with secondary schools. In accordance with this view, the first two years of junior college classes have been annexed with secondary schools and they are managed by management of local secondary school. The second view favours the annexation of two years of junior college with higher education or college education like the systems is England and Germany etc. These classes are governed by university administration and are considered as inseparable parts of higher education. The reason for this difference of opinion is independent local influence.

In United States of America, the idea of annexing first two years of junior college with secondary schools was propagated by Henry Happen of Michigan in 1852. But this view found a voice in the 20th century. In the beginning of-20th century, a movement was started saying that the 4 year college education did not fulfil the needs of the people and that education was not related to the life of-students and hence it was useless. If the first two years of junior college were combined with secondary level, these years would prove more beneficial because of being integrated with useful vocational education. It was further felt that the four year educational system was unnecessarily lengthy, because all the students could not complete that curriculum. Hence it was considered necessary to combine the two years of junior college with secondary education in order to make them more useful for society. By annexing the two years of junior college with secondary education, the knowledge gained at secondary level was systematised and reorganised in order to make it more developed, mature, useful, social and vocational. This system was first introduced in Illinois in 1902. The junior colleges were established in smaller number in the eastern states, but in Texas, western and middle-west States, this system developed faster.

These junior colleges could be established in greater number under State Educational Programme during the depression period which created trade deficiency. The third decade of the present century proved more important for the development of these colleges. After World War II, there was such a crowd of young men and women returning from war junior colleges failed to admit them all. Consequently, the municipalities and local education boards established new junior colleges. To meet the need of that time, many temporary junior colleges were opened whose curriculum had an impact of higher education. But even temporary junior colleges established in California and Illinois States were run with progressive courses.

California has been more forward in the establishment of junior colleges. Here the universities extended all co-operation in establishing junior colleges. The reason for this help was that there was apprehension of large scale admission of students at the university level. The history of Junior College Movement makes it evident that most of the junior colleges were established speedily about the year 1930. Private efforts helped a lot in this movement. By 1930, junior colleges had been established in 29 States of U. S. A. According to the date of 1950, the number of public Junior Colleges was 250 and the number of students receiving eduction in them was 1,87,659. At the same time the number of private junior college was 227 and the number of students there was about 55,045.

The financial position of private junior colleges and public junior colleges was different. So these institutions were classified according to their position. The public colleges received aid in the form of government grant and education tax. All the States do not have the same system. In California State, the Government grant is given on the basis of number of students. But in Taxas and other States financial help is provided through, Education Tax. The judgement of court on the controversy in North Carolina in 1930 that Local Education cities could enhance Education Tax to run junior colleges, gave them strength. The judgement of the court made it clear that necessary aid could be taken from Education Tax. In due course, sanction by special legislations to impose Education Tax and to take aid from it in most of the States was given.

In European countries, 8 year curriculum prevails from lower secondary level to junior colleges. The same curriculum is found in American education system. Here classes 13th and 14th are included in junior colleges. Pre-vocational education is provided in these colleges. Thus the needs of the local people are fulfilled. Higher colleges providing 4 year courses improved their educational standard with the establishing of junior colleges and most of them divided their courses in duration of 2 years each. Being situated in local areas, the junior colleges were near the 4 year higher colleges. So the guardians admitted their wards in junior colleges nearby instead of sending them to distant colleges. Thus the importance of junior colleges increased and they could develop easily.

The curriculum in junior colleges is very useful and modern. These colleges not only prepare the students for higher education through study of general subjects, but they also provide industrial and vocational education for earning a living. Because of terminal nature, these colleges have become more useful These colleges include all groups technical, scientific and arts. In the beginning the courses offered in these colleges were not much useful. But now these courses have become more flexible, developed and utilitarian because semi-professional and high skilled vocational subject have been included in them. The private junior colleges are more useful because they offer a better vocational atmosphere than public junior colleges. Adult education programme has been introduced in these colleges with the viewpoint of social welfare. These colleges provide complementary education to adult education and evening classes arrangement. At some places, in view of the importance of adult education, the junior colleges have been given the form of community colleges-where post-High School education is provided. The importance of junior colleges has increased due to following reasons :

(1) Those persons or young boys and girls who do not get any employment after completing secondary education and are unable to receive 4 year higher education, are benefited by these junior colleges.

(2) Those young boys and girls who cannot receive education in distant colleges or find that education inconvenient or find it difficult to get admission in them after secondary education or cannot bear the expenses of college education, are very much benefited by these junior colleges.

(3) These junior colleges by organising 2 year education provide educational opportunities to young boys and girls of all communities.

(4) The teachers teaching similar classes at the junior college level are more capable than the teachers teaching the similar classes at the college level because their method of instruction is better.

(5) These junior colleges have been made more useful for people by providing important programmes, complementary education and terminal nature of education.

Some critics criticise the junior colleges because the money meant for secondary education is spent on junior colleges and these colleges grasp most part of the aid from the education tax. These colleges are responsible for increase the education tax time and again and have rivalry with 4 year -colleges of higher education. But now these colleges are not rivals. Rather they are complementary to colleges and have become a part of higher education.

**The Syllabi and Time Table**

***Teaching Programme.*** At the elementary level all subjects are compulsory but at the secondary level, specific classes have been provided. The establishment of these classes depends on the needs of the local society, size of the school and region. In urban areas, the number of classes ranges from 20 to 30. But in rural areas one class secondary schools, too, are in sufficient number. Thus secondary schools are more liberal from the point of view of curriculum and programme. Thus these schools provide opportunity for the study of useful subjects.

Three groups of curriculums are found in secondary schools. One of them is compulsory for all students. The second group consists of semi-compulsory subjects which are not compulsory for all students but are compulsory only for those who want to be admited in specific group related to those subjects and the thira is of variable subjects which have free optional subjects. The students have to select subjects in prescribed number from the various subject groups. Thus in every secondary school, the number of subjects is made in the final year of secondary classes or in the very first year of secondary level education. In 4 years secondary level, the subject selection is required in the first year.

At the secondary level, the extension of curriculum has taken place due to reorganisation and need-based programmes. At this level almost 290 subjects are provided. A secondary school of a big city offers upto 100 subjects out of which the student select subjects according to their interests and needs. In American educational sphere it may be noted that most of the students leave their studies after secondary education. Hence efforts are made to make them fit for some vocation. So at this level basic training is provided in agriculture, industry and commerce etc. In the first year of this level, subjects such as sociology, experimental science, physical education, mathematics and English language are mostly selected. Other subjects of equal utility are selected from crafts, metal work, electrical skill, typewriter knowledge, animal husbandry, soil conservation, music, manufacturing, fashion-designing, drawing, painting and home science etc. These subjects are grouped according to utility and need.

***Vocational, Cultural and Co-curricular Activities.*** In most of the American schools, vocational and general education is given jointly. At some places, vocational and specific training colleges are different from general education schools. The merit of the joint system is that the students of literary, scientific and commercial groups too, get a means of earning a living by selecting utilitarian vocational subject or for becoming more skilful or getting specialization.

In secondary schools along with vocational and general education, co-curricular activities are also organised. These activities help in the development of qualities of citizenship. The students in order to acquire ability of mutual discussion, freedom of thought and expression and qualities of leadership get training through debates, student self-government and mock parliament etc.

The student administrative committee by trying to improve the teaching-methods of teachers provides opportunity to each others evaluation. Various institutions are formed for collective games and sports, literary programmes, recreation and utilisation of leisure where teachers acquire human virtues through constructive activities. The school provides teachers co-operation, rooms and other needed facilities for these activities. The students organize clubs according to their needs and interests. These co-curricular activities are very important at the secondary level. Schools, teachers, education department and administrators encourage these activities and after assessing the achievements of such activities, make other necessary provisions. All possible efforts are made in this direction.

***Latin Grammar School Organisation.*** In 1635, the Puritans in order to teach European languages, literature, political science and to maintain feeling of religious leadership, established these schools. These schools had their impact till the 19th century. Now they changed significantly and have been replaced by educational academies.

**Academic Institutions**

Industrial development affected education system since the middle of 18th century. Educational academies were established to help vocational and industrial life. In 1751, an educational academy was established for the first time in Philadelphia with the efforts of Benjamin Franklin. By 1830 the number of academies rose to 500. Women-education, naval education, vocational education, politics and philosophy etc. found place in them.

**High Schools**

Along with the industrial, social and political development, the demand for free, universal and public education had started in the 19th century. In 1821, the first public school in 1926, first Public Girls School, Boston and in 1924, Public School, New York were established. The judgement in the case of Kalamazoo case in 1874 and Committee of Ten in 1892, led to organisation of universal and free education.

**New Types of Institutions**

Finding the 8 year elementary education lengthy, the need for making an intermediate unit arrangement between primary and secondary education was felt. As a result, class 7th and 8th were joined with secondary education. At the same time, the first two year classes of higher education were also combined with secondary education. The secondary level was divided as-lower secondary 3 years, higher secondary 3 years and junior college system 2 years.

In the beginning Latin-Grammar Schools and educational academies were established to teach European religion, political science, literature and to fulfil vocational needs respectively. The nature of educational organisation changed from time to time according to recommendations of various education commissions and committees from time to time. According to the committee of

Ten of 1892, the aim of secondary education was to create general utility instead of preparation for college admission. Study of arithmetic along with classical subjects was also suggestion. In 1899, the Committee on College Entrance Requirements supported the suggestions of committee of ten. In 1912, the commission on reorganisation of secondary education determined seven aims of secondary education useful civic education, vocational education, command of fundamental processes, health education, worthy home-membership, education for good moral conduct and utilisation of leisure. Similarly in 1933, 1936, 1942, 1944 and 1947 various aspects of educational aims were stressed.

Development of education and adjustment, to fulfil possible needs, imparting knowledge of traditional, cultural and contemporary social obligations, create awakening for specialization, providing new knowledge, to create spirit of taking interest in human activities, use of progressive teaching-methods, independent study and research principles, to retain students till the stage of diminishing returns.

Kinds of Secondary school and classification. Two types of classification. In the first type, the secondary level is of 4 years (8 + 5 + 2 + 2) and in the second type of classification, it is of 6 years (6 + 3 + 3 + 2). In the first type, the secondary stage includes classes 9th to 12th. In the seclude classification from 7th to 9th lower secondary and 10th to 12th, higher secondary. Classes 13th and 14th are included in junior college.

**Various Systems**

At some places this lower secondary is included in higher secondary and at some other places it is separate from higher secondary.

It is complementary to lower secondary system. Classes 10th to 12th are included in this level. At this stage along with general education, vocational and industrial courses and specialization are also provided.

Classification of Secondary Schools according to Curriculum:

***Common Schools.*** (a) *Comprehensive Schools*-These schools are of 4 years. Various subjects are taught here. They are free and universal. Here the number of subjects may be 200. They lack modern methods. They are economic and convenient in rural areas. (b) *Limited Schools*-Vocational education and specialization is given importance for the local people. Facility of subject selection is limited.

***Specialized Schools***-Elementary training in vocational areas is given. More emphasis on vocational education then on general education.

***Vocational and Industrial Schools***-They are mostly established in industrial and vocational centres and are like specialized schools. They are useful for people.

***Part-time Schools.*** These schools are established to provide education to adult for some hours. *(a) Continuation Schools*-Education for 144 hours in a year and 3-4 hours education per week for adults. *(b) Adult Evening Schools*-Evening classes are held daily. Education is according to the needs of adults.

***Junior College System.*** First two years of college level (classes 13th and 14th) are included in the junior college. Mostly are considered part of college education but they are organised as part of secondary education.

Teaching Programme-Compulsory; semi-compulsory and selection of optional subjects-Three kinds of subjects. Semi-compulsory subjects are meant for students wanting skill in some specific vocation. Optional subjects are available in groups. Students select subjects according to their interest and need. Need of subject selection is felt either in the final year of lower secondary level or in the first year of higher secondary level.

**Extra Curricular Programmes**

Along with general education and vocational education, in order to create interest and spirit of worthy citizenship, creative, literary meetings, debating clubs, games and sports, recreational and swimming activities a reorganised under the supervision of teachers.

## QUESTIONS

1. Describe that present form of secondary education in U. S. A.
2. "The present nature of American secondary education is the result of following the recommendations of the committees and commissions appointed from time to time." Explain.
3. Why did secondary education system became important for the life of the American people? Describe the aims of the present secondary education in U. S. A.
4. "If the reorganized secondary education in U. S. A. is based on primary education, it is the foundation-stone of junior college system." How?
5. Explain the chief characteristics of curriculum of reorganised secondary education of U. S. A. and explain how it creates the feeling of adjustment in life.

# 20

# Elementary Education

Primary education makes an important contribution in the education of the child and his gradual formation of personality. While young, nervous system of the child is very delicate. However, he is eager for adjustment. Moral virtues may be created in the form of good habits at this stage. Discipline, hard-work, self-reliance, development of collective and cooperative spirit may be inculcated in him at this age. Future citizen of nation may develop qualities of citizenship on receiving proper primary education. The foundation of socialization is also laid at the primary stage.

In fact, the stage of primary education creates curiosities in those children who have not received education in an infant-education school before. Primary education is a form of compulsory education.

**Objectives and Purposes**

In U. S. A., primary education is an education imparted after Kindergarten schools. This education is a unit of fundamental education. Primary schools cannot be separated from Kindergarten education system. Generally, in primary schools education is provided after completing Kindergarten School education and Nursery School education. Some other teaching systems are similar to these systems in which the age of children and their level are taken as the basis.

The primary education in America is given with the aim of giving the children first lessons of citizenship for their socialization according to school needs and for fulfilment of basic teaching needs. This education is organized for developing democratic and social virtues in children. For socialization, they are taught to play collective games and sports, to study, to maintain mutual contact, to follow social ideals, and to practice ideal standard of behaviour. Through various programmes, efforts are made to teach the students proper utilization of time and opportunity, preventive measures for health, habit of work, exchange of good ideas, to hear and understand the views of others with patience and develop the quality of dutifulness. The education system of this level in U. S. A. has many similarities which are as under:

***Creation of Sociability and National Spirit.*** Man is a social animal. The child is a part of society. The spirit to work according to society and to follow its ideals should be created in the child. Nation, State, Community and classes etc. are social units. The world is a large society. So it is necessary to create the feeling of universal sociability in the child. The knowledge of social duties and rights should be given through primary education. These are the objectives of primary education in U.S.A.

***Consciousness for Good Health.*** Consciousness for health is developed in children at the primary education level through games and sports and physical exercises.

***Development of the Spirit of Freedom.*** In American primary schools, opportunity is provided to work freely and to understand freedom. Keeping in view the rights and duties, the use of freedom should be proper and acceptable. That the spirit of co-operation arises out of evaluation of freedom is also taught to the children in U. S. A.

***Harmony between Individualistic and Socialistic Ideas.*** If individualistic ideas are allowed to develop in children to the extreme, they cannot adjust themselves in modern social environment. So whereas the children are provided facilities and opportunities for individual development, they are also directed towards sociability. Individuality is developed in a social environment in U. S. A.

***Development of Self-Reliance.*** Primary education should be so imparted that the children may try to perform their daily activities themselves and become self reliant. In Kindergarten education such activities are encouraged which are developed further at the primary level. The aim of American Primary education is to provide opportunities to the child to solve his daily, personal, domestic and social problems himself.

***Development of Socialization.*** Socialization may be helped by adjust with the ideals of the society. So social ideals and virtues such as co-operation and feeling of fellowship etc. should be developed in children. Only then the spirit of socialization may be strengthened. Through literacy and knowledge of elementary mathematics, the child is lead towards social virtues and ideals. The spirit of socialization may be created by establishing contact with various persons of the society. These qualities are developed in children through co-operation and fellowship in various programmes.

***Development of Creativeness.*** In U. S. A. various equipments have been devised with the development of scientific knowledge. These equipments are means of material aids for teaching the child. Whenever the teacher or the child uses these implements, he not only gets pleasure but his creative faculties are also developed. In teaching, audio-visual sources help the development of creativeness. In these schools, creativeness is generally aroused through documentary films, news reels, magic lantern, photographs, radio programmes and newspapers.

The aim of primary education in U. S. A. is to provide opportunities of receiving developing knowledge through lecture programmes, debates and seminars.

**Basic Nature**

In U. S. A., the entire curriculum below the secondary level may be regarded as that of primary education. Here pre-secondary classes too, are included in the primary education. There is no junior secondary level here. After receiving this education, the children are admitted directly in secondary schools. These schools are called Graded Schools or Grammar Schools. They are called Graded Schools because the courses of study for the whole year are divided into grades in these schools and classes of different grades are formed for annual study. These schools have been named Grammar Schools because provision is made to extend literacy through three R's-Reading, writing and arithmetic.

Education systems in all the schools in U. S. A. are influenced by the people. This is true of primary education system as well. In the States, educational organization, duration, curriculum and programmes differ according to the traditions of people. In some States old traditions are followed, in some, new projects and old traditions and in some States both old and new traditions are followed in education systems. These differences may be expressed as follows:

**Courses and Examination**

American system of education was formed on old traditions, but with modern new researches and projects, the educational provisions too, are becoming modern. Although new schools also supplement local public needs yet difference is found in the gradation system according to the levels of education. There is no national or state-wide plan to formulate any particular educational policy and curriculum.

Generally, at the primary level, after admitting the students at the age of 6 to 8 years opportunity is provided to finish the studies of this level by the age of 12 to 14 years. But this primary education system has been changed at some places for starting new plans. Thus two types of schools are found there-the first type of schools are those where the child is taught from the age of 6 to, 14 years. These yearly classes of 8 years are called graded classes of primary level at some places and at other places, the first three years are included in Kindergarten education. Education from class 4th to 6th is considered primary level education and classes 7th to 8th are called junior secondary standard classes. These schools are considered as traditional school. The second type of schools are those where admission is given at 6 to 8 years of age and studies are finished at the age of 12 years. Thus six classes are included in primary level classes and 7th and 8th classes are joined with secondary classes and are termed classes of secondary stage. The first two or three classes out of the yearly classes of six years are considered of Kindergarten education and the remaining of primary level. These schools are based on new education plans.

In American schools, generally, two days in a week, *i.e.*, Saturday and Sunday are holidays and remaining five days are working days. The timetable of the day is of 5 hours or 5 hours which starts from 9 o'clock in the morning and remains upto 1 to 3 o'clock in the afternoon. In classes of junior school level, this duration is of 4 or 5 hours. The number of working days, too, is not the same in all the States. In Government schools also the number of working days is not same. The number of working days in a year varies from 152 to 187. In 1983, the average of working days in the whole of U. S. A. was 180. After that effort was made to bring uniformity in all the States. The duration of period, too, was changed. It was decided to fix the duration of a period from 15 minutes to 30 minutes and 25 to 30 periods per week were required to be taught and it was decided that the schools should remain open for 180 days in a year. The schools followed these prescribed days etc. But it has been noticed that according to the effect of local environment there are still many differences. There are fewer working days in rural schools as compared to urban schools and periods in lower classes are shorter than the periods in higher classes.

**Education for All**

Primary education in U. S. A. is universal compulsory and free. The data collected in 1930 reveal that 63.3% children of the age of 6 years, 95.3% or the age of 7 to 13 years were receiving education in primary schools. But because of continuous decrease in birth-rate, the number of students in primary schools decreased considerably from 1930 to 1936. This decrease was mainly noticed in classes of junior level whereas the number increased gradually in higher classes upto 1934. But from 1936 there was sufficient decrease. While in full six years *i.e.* from 1930 to 1936 the decrease was 4.2% in two years along (1934 to 1936) decrease was 1.8%. But as soon as the Second World War came to an end, the birth-rate increased suddenly which was so high that the Government and the local people had to work hard for providing education. To make up this deficiency single teacher schools were established and one-room schools were changed into complete primary schools.

Seeing that the number of students in schools was sufficiently less, compulsory Attendance Law was enacted and it was observed strictly. State and communities made efforts to provide educational and transport facilities. The result was that education became compulsory and universal. In the 8 classes of primary schools, attendance for all children between the age of 7 to 16 years is compulsory. This compulsion prevails in most of the States of U. S. A. According to the Judgement of Supreme Court in 1954, "There should be no distinction of class or colour in schools", the school education could become universal. Even now in West Virginia because of the distinction of Black and White, there are separate schools for the two.

**The Syllabi and Time Table**

In U. S. A. the general aim of primary education is to produce worthy citizens. In democratic States, creation of the feeling of citizenship is the main aim and with that aim the curriculum of the schools is constructed. Upto the nineteenth century, the aim of school education was teaching of 3 R's 'Reading, Writing and Arithmetic'. But since the beginning of 20th century, effort was made for the all-round development of children and new and elastic curriculums were devised. At that time with 3 R's the other subject were spelling, grammar, literature, composition, music, history , geography, elementary science, psychology and hygiene. Now 5 R's (Reading, Writing, Arithmetic, Relationship and Recreation) in place of 3 R's are included. Today, formation of social character is mainly emphasised.

For training of special character and development of worthy citizenship, new criteria of curriculum construction has been devised. Local people and State Governments both are engaged in the work of school administration and curriculum construction. Local institutions in urban areas enjoy more facilities than rural areas. The State Governments get the curriculum devised by Departments of education executed, in rural areas as well. In the construction of urban curriculum too, there is Government interference from the point of view of administration. As a result of modern psychological view point and development of research work etc., the curriculum of primary schools in U.S. A. is being refer.

The American educationists are making researches in the field of education. They have devised new bases of curriculum construction. The improvised curriculum has not been enforced in every School. Even then they help in lot of subject-matter of organization and it is being used properly for natural and desired progress.

The publishers of text-books also help in the development of curriculum. They prepare text-books according to revised and improvised plans. Their love of education is reflected in their publications.

The American people have great faith in secularism. They are not in favour of making religious education as part of curriculum. They are in favour of religious and moral instructions for the development of human vi tues.

**School Organisation**

In U. S. A. similarity is not found in the establishment and organisation of primary schools. The school organisations of every State, every region and local communities are not the same. The reason for this is the lack of a nation-wide organisation.

**Role of State**

This organisation includes those schools in which separate subject teachers are provided. These subject-teachers have separate teaching classes. These subjects rooms are equipped with related material aids and apparatuses. The teacher remains sitting in his room. Only the students go to the teacher in the subject-room at the change of period. First of all this system was started in the schools of New York in the 20th century. Now this system has come into vogue in all the schools run by Department of Education. This organisation is generally found in classes 7th, 8th and 9th. The higher classes of primary schools, too, are run according to this system.

**Old Fashioned Schools**

This school organisation is the old one-room system. These systems have changed according to modern developments. In one room schools one teacher taught all the subjects to all classes in one room. In rural areas and interior regions of States such schools are in vogue. Now according to changed conditions, keeping in view the number of students and classes of one-room schools, more teachers have been appointed in place of one teacher and more rooms have been built instead of one-room. A teacher teaches 2 or 3 classes in one room. So in this new revised system, in some places one teacher has been provided for one subject in one room. These teachers are appointed on the basis of classes and not on the basis of subjects and this provision depends on the number of students in a class. In one-room school, the teacher himself supervises the school. That teacher is known as Teacher Principal.

In those schools where separate teachers are appointed for different classes, there is a separate supervisor who is also a teacher. He is called supervising Principal. This organisation exists only where the number of students is sufficient.

**Various Types**

This type of organisation was recognised both at the primary and secondary levels, but now it is in vogue only at the primary level. First of all this organisation was implemented in Indian State, but it developed mostly in Detroit. This system of organisation started in the first decade of 20th century, but by the end of third decade it expanded sufficiently. At present, this system has been adopted by about 1500 schools in 400 cities of 45 States. The peculiarity of this organisation is that it solves the problem of paucity of funds, and shortage of buildings. This system, on the one hand is economical, useful and suitable for schools and on the other, it helps in the development of interest, capability and personality of children.

Under this system, all the students are divided in two or three groups. If one group studies in the class, the other group becomes busy in games and sports, physical exercises, excursion, experimental work, social service, gymnasium, laboratory, auditorium and school shops. When one group finishes its work, the other group takes its place.

## Management of Education

In. U. S. A. the school organisation is controlled and administered financially in two ways. One type of schools are those which are run by religious institutions and their expenditure too, is borne by the same institutions. These schools impart religious education, bible, Church-book, Church-Method and religious programmes find a place in these schools. The other type of schools are run by local groups and boards, The expenditure of these schools is met from donations by the public. These schools are not so much parochial as the above denominational schools which are run by Catholics. However, religious education and moral instructions are given in these schools, too. This type of religious schools and schools managed by local people are called private schools. Their number is not large. Besides donation, tuition fees are also a financial help. The second type of schools different from private schools are called public schools. The number of such schools is large and these schools are considered as the back-bone of education in U. S. A. Their expenditure is met from public taxation and they are controlled and managed by public representatives.

It is a peculiarity of schools in America, that parents, teachers, authorities and administrators all jointly help in school organisation. The authorities and principals provide such opportunities to parents, guardians, adults and public leaders that they can get a knowledge of students' progress, their interest, capacity and conditions and give useful suggestions. The parents, teachers, public and authorities all co-operate in making the schools helpful, strong, useful and modern.

The buildings and rooms of primary schools are equipped with modern facilities. There is a provision of transport for children. Interesting subjects such as painting, art, music and crafts etc. are also taught.

***Aims of Education at the Primary Level.*** The aim of American primary education is the development of worthy citizens. It also aims at inculcating the spirit of socialization, healthy temperament and creative and useful work. The tendencies of socialization and ideals are created through collective programmes, living, games and sports, recreation, health and physical training.

***Nature of Primary Education.*** The external form of primary education system is different due to social needs and variety of environment, but all the systems have internal similarities.

***Period of Teaching and Gradation.*** There are two types of schools in America. One of them impart teaching from the 1st to 8th class, The other types of schools are those in which classes 7th and 8th are combined with secondary level schools and first six classes are conducted at the primary level. In one the age-division is from 6 to 14 years and in the other from 6 to 12 years. Saturday and Sunday are holidays in a week. Daily teaching work is of 5 to 5 hours. Working days in a year are 152 to 187.

***Compulsory Education and Universalness.*** Education is compulsory for children from 7 to 14 or 16 years of age. There is no distinction in class, colour, religion or community. Education in universal. Schools based on colour distinction found only in Virginia. Curriculum and Education Programme.

Now there are courses of 5 R's in, place 3 R's of *e.g.*, Reading, writing, arithmetic, social relationship, and recreation. Religious education is secondary. Besides these, teaching in literature, history, geography, hygiene, agriculture, nature study, music painting, art and craft and home science is also provided.

From organisational point of view both one-room and multi-room schools are found where one or some classes in one or 2-3 rooms. Rural areas have more one-room schools than urban areas. In big cities, there is provision of separate teachers for different subjects, and rooms. From organisational point of view in some places, the students are divided into two groups. When one group becomes busy in academic-activities, the other group is engaged in extra-curricular activities. In the second shift, this turn is reversed.

The primary schools may be divided into two categories-private and public. The private schools are run by religious or social communities and religious education is given in them. The local public-schools are administered local by people and religious education is secondary there.

## QUESTIONS

1. Describe the nature of prevailing primary education in U. S. A. and explain the chief characteristics of its form.
2. In U. S. A., the supremacy and selection of curriculum, and educational programmes of primary education have been helpful in the success of teaching—how ? Explain.

# 21

# Initial Education

For the integrated personality of the child, the period from birth to 6-7 years of age is very important. Whatever tendencies the child acquires during early 6-7 years of his life, become his nature affecting later growth.

It is believed that even in the mother's womb, the child begins to acquire some impressions and after birth he starts learning one thing or the other from the environment. Although this process of learning is informal, yet because of its impact, the child gives some expression of his learning. Efforts have been made to educate children even before the, beginning of primary education at the age of 6-7 years. This education system is called infant education or pre-primary education. Froebel had laid emphasis of infant education. At the end of the eighteenth century Jean Oberin first of all established an infant school in Lumark. The infant education philosophy of Froebel had it's impact on all the countries of Europe and Ecols Maternells (Mother's schools) were established at several places in Europe. Several countries made various experiments in this direction. Germany originated a new infant education system. The school of this system was called Kindergarten. Such infant schools were established in England also. Nursery schools were opened in London and Manchestor cities. In U. S. A. kindergarten schools were opened in Wisconsin State for the first time.

Generally, nursery education is said to have began in U. S. A during the twentieth century. In 1919, first of all a nursery school was opened in New York city. The people of U. S. A. did not then encourage nursery school system very much because some people did not like to burden the mind of children at an early age. In 1920, infant education was provided in the Teachers' College of Columbia University. But from 1920 to 1930, there came a spell of depression in U. S. A. and the plan of Kindergarten schools and nursery schools remained blocked. But with the end of that crisis, according to New Deal Act, the Federal Government gave sufficient help to this education system. Consequently, from 1930 to 1940 the number of students in nursery schools rose to three lakh and that in Kindergarten became about seven lakh. Thus in the fourth decade of twentieth century infant education developed rapidly. Rapid industrial development here also led to the quick development of infant education. The establishing of these schools benefited those mothers particularly who were working in industrial or commercial establishments. They could become carefree at the time of their work after leaving their children in infant schools. Thus along with care of children, their character too could be formed in right direction. It was the reason that nursery schools were mainly established in important towns and industrial centres.

**The Organisation**

Pre-primary education of the infant may be divided into three age groups:

***First Group***-Education from conception to 1 year.

***Second Group***-Education from 1 to 3 years of age.

***Third Group***-Education from 3 to 5 or 6 years of age.

**Role of Parents**

Parents prepare environment and conditions for the future infant from its birth to life ahead. Education of the would-be child starts from the very coming in the mother's womb. So the parents should know their responsibility in this connection. Mere literacy, without the knowledge of child psychology does not make the parents successful in the fulfilment of their responsibility. So with a view to acquaint the parents with the psychology of the child and to give them necessary guidance in the direction of preparing proper environment, training schools and guidance centres are needed. The first year after the birth of the child has been considered very important for nourishment. This is the time when one becomes familiar with child psychology. For this guidance and training centres should be established.

In U. S. A. although the number of training and guidance centres for the training of parents in formation of proper environment for infants is quite insufficient, yet there are a number of guidance centres, clinics and research institutions under the Department of Education and Health Department which guide the parents for bearing the responsibility of infant's life properly. But only a few are being benefited by these institutions, not the whole people. Some local institutions also direct guide and provide psychological knowledge to the local people. Their knowledge needs to be universal.

**Nursery Level**

The life of the American people is very busy. The responsible members of the family remain engaged in some remunerative work. The parents cannot look after their children properly because of the load of work and shortage of time. So they feel the necessity of leaving their children to the care of some responsible person or institution so that their children may develop good habits and become skilful in doing their work. One year after its birth, the child begins to sit and move and begins to show some general tendencies. The child wants to play and do many things as other children do. His natural needs mainly are eating, easing natural calls, bath, cleaning of teeth and wearing of clothes etc. A small child is not able to do these things well. So in the beginning, be depends upon his parents for these things. So there should be some institution to guide children to do these things skilfully themselves. As a result; nursery schools, infant education centres and kindergartens have been established for the education and care of children. The parents become busy of their work freely after leaving their children in these institutions. In their absence, the children learn to eat, play and attend to their natural calls and other practical things and get behavioural education through play and recreational activities.

The age of admission cannot be fixed for nursery schools. In some places it is 2 to 3 years and in other places 4 years also. Children of 1 year to 18 months may, also get admission in these schools. The children of this age are admitted for protection because the parents cannot do their work properly with them. Thus in nursery centres and other such institutions the age of admission varies from 1 to 4 years. Such nursery schools are over 2,000 in number. They have not taken a universal form so far and are run by private efforts. These nursery centres have been established in big cities and industrial centres only although they are needed for every average family.

In U. S. A. there are three types of nursery schools. The first type of schools are those which are run by religious organizations, the second type of schools are organized by private effort and the third type of schools are either run by local institutions or State Government or Federal Government. But number of such schools is very small. To meet this shortage, the people have established infant schools at different places. Such schools are called co-operative nursery schools.

**Common Schools**

The Americans are so busy that they cannot look after their children. So enlightened families collectively establish such schools where their children can get home like atmosphere. These schools try to develop the personality of children. In those schools, education is imparted through collective programmes, functions, games and sports and recreation etc. Lively and practical study of external atmosphere outside school is done through excursions and tours etc. They are provided opportunities to visit local special places, playgrounds, museums and spacious buildings and big projects and organizations.

These schools are run by the co-operative efforts of combined families. The parents give financial help in the form of donations to these co-operative schools. The parents concerned co-operate in the programmes of these schools. Construction of curriculum, selection of books and arrangement of teachers are done by a committee elected by the people. The fathers utilise their leisure in decorating classes and preparing playgrounds and gardens of the schools. At times the mother co-operate with the teachers in preparing breakfast, dressing, games and recreation etc. The parents present useful programmes for the schools from time to time. They visit the Schools every month to know about the progress and future plans of their wards. At times, they also participate in the functions and collective progrmmes organized by the schools. Thus the parents get knowledge of infant's education and get satisfaction as well. These schools co-operate in the expansion of adult education by receiving help from the Adult Education Department as such.

**Kindergarten System**

In U. S. A., just as the nursery schools conduct education for children so also the kindergartens organize education for children. The only, difference is that this system is considered as a system after nursery school education. In these schools, the age limit for admission is from 3 to 6 years. In some schools, children below 3 years are also admitted. These schools have two main aims:

(1) To follow nursery education by including child-like qualities in children and to arouse curiosity for education in them.

(2) To impart subject-wise education and prepare the children for primary education.

In accordance with the first aim, the quality of gregariousness and co-operation are inculcated in these schools through games and sports and recreational activities. By working, living and playing together, the children on the one hand learn to lead a co-operative and collective life and on the other their health, too, improves and spirit of self-help is also created in them. These activities of children also develop in them feelings of self-reliance, curiosity and interest for knowledge. According to the second aim a basis for primary education is prepared. So programmes are devised for their physical, mental, social and cultural development according to their needs and stage of development. By giving them knowledge of simple words and numerical tables, they are prepared for primary classes. Kindergarten schools were established in U. S. A. as a result of too many mothers going outside home for work due to rising standard of living. The busy parent alive to the future of their children establishes these schools for their protection and education. This system though not compulsory is sufficiently popular.

Establishing of kindergartens in U. S. A. was started in the, nineteenth century. But they developed extensively in the present century. By the beginning of the current century, hundreds of such voluntary associations had been formed which established private kindergarten schools. Now with the establishing of public kindergartens not only the people but State Governments also help these schools financially. The educational standard of most of the Kindergarten schools is considered equivalent to the primary classes. The State Government sends necessary instructions to the Kindergarten schools. The Departmental officers and experts inspect these schools with a view to maintain educational standard and also motivate the teachers for maintaining the same. At some places, a specialist teacher has been appointed who not only supervises the school, but also approves educational programmes. About 40 lakh children receive education in private infant schools.

The infant schools of U. S. A. get aid from local public fund and State Governments, too, give additional grants. The Local Boards are empowered to expand and organise pre-primary education according to the local needs and have statutory provisions for establishing and patronizing Kindergartens. Insipite of all this, there is a scope for their further development.

In U. S. A. the development of pre-primary education is a result of the busy life of people. The parents are unable to keep their children with them during working hours: So there was need of such schools for the protection of children. Therefore, different schools of pre-primary education were established there. They are as follows:

***Intant-Education-Knowledge and Infant-Home-Education for Parents.*** If parents are ignorant of child-psychology, they cannot bring up their children as desired. For guiding parents guidance centres have been established by the Health Department of State Governments. Clinics also fulfil this need. There are other private institutions also which familiarise the parents with child psychology. Even then they need to be expanded.

***Nursery Education.*** To satisfy the instinct of gregariousness and development of cooperative spirit in children from 1 to 3 years of age, games and sports and other recreational activities are organized. The atmosphere of these schools is homely so that the children spend their time happily in the absence of their parents. These schools are organised by Local Boards, City Boards of Education, co-operative organizations, and private efforts in vocational and industrial centres. The most important infant schools are co-operative nursery schools. Their financial and other provisions are made by local people. State Governments also give grants. The parents take interest in the programmes of these schools and often visit the schools and extend co-operation.

***Kindergarten Education.*** Generally children from 3 to 6 years of age are admitted in these schools. These schools are responsible for education after nursery education and prepare children for primary education. They develop the personality of children. The State Governments and Local Boards give financial grants by giving them direction in educational programmes. Public infant Schools have been established at various places in large numbers. The public is responsible for their development and management. The Government tries to maintain standard of education through departmental experts. A specialist teacher is appointed for supervision and approval of programmes. The number of students in private and co-operative schools is above 40 lakh. They need to be made more popular.

## QUESTIONS

1. Describe the nature of Kindergarten education and its development in U.S.A.

2. What facilities have been include in the Infant Education system in U. S. A. ? How are the parents helpful in the provision for Infant education?

# 22

# Educational Administration

In U. S. A. development of education began due to immigrants from Europe. These immigrants imbibed various religious groups of European origin. Their religious beliefs made them persistent. They had to strive hard for their up-keep in a new land. So they developed a materialistic outlook and became more individualistic. So whenever there was a question of centralisation of administration, they opposed it. But in the year 1789, the people for and against centralisation reached a compromise. In 1789, the constitution of the land was formulated. According to this constitution, the powers of States and of Federal Government were clearly classified.

The American people adopted the European system of education in the beginning. Mostly the system had a great impact of British system: Although this system has gone through considerable reforms and changes according to the environment and new needs, yet it still appears to be influenced by the British system: In U. S. A. education is a private responsibility. Since there is no division of educational rights and responsibility between the

States and Centre, the educational organization has come mostly in the hands of the States. Most of the States have their independent system of education. The non-inclusion of educational responsibility in the constitution may be due to the existing conditions *i.e.*, before the drafting of the constitution, local public schools, Government schools, private schools, denominational schools had already been established and they were discharging their responsibility independently.

Even after the implementation of the constitution, the subsequent amendments of the constitution reveal no clarification of the division of educational responsibility. The 10th amendment of the constitution simply hints that the rights which the Federal Government did not reserve for itself and could be used freely by the States. They were not deprived of those rights. Thus the whole responsibility of educational organization was accepted by the States. However, it should not be concluded that the Federal Government had been apathetic to educational problems, it influences the education-organization indirectly though it may not control educational system directly.

The States could not utilise successfully the educational rights bestowed on them through amendments of constitution from time to time. The reason for this may be the mentality of the people for not devaluing from their traditional rights. The people while supporting the constitution considered educational responsibility reserved for themselves. Now the American schools are being managed by nearly one and half lakh Local Education Councils (Boards). Only in Labrador, education is administered and managed by the State Government and financial responsibility, too, rests, with the State Government.

### Role of Federal Government

It was explained above that the Federal Government influences and controls education indirectly although the State Governments may pursue their independent educational system. The Federal Government has provided land grants to the State governments from time to time and has given them financial grants for technical and industrial education. In the eighteenth century the land which was not in the hands of the people, was under the control of the Federal Government. The Federal Government give it to the State Governments as long grant for construction of schools under the condition that they would preserve it and use the income from the land for expansion of free education. The Federal Government continued to provide new land grants to State Governments for new schools from time to time. In 1830, the United States Congress increased the land grants and help further. At the end of second decade of the nineteenth century, according to the Smith Hughe's Act, the state governments were given financial grant for technical, industrial and agricultural education at the secondary level. In the last years of nineteenth century when Civil War broke out, the Federal Government gave sufficient land grants to state governments for technical and agricultural schools. At the time of the Second World War, the Land Grant System was handed over to the States by the Federal Government and gave by them the right of its preservation.

The Federal Government conducts its educational programmes through the education office. The education office has been established to control and conduct educational programmes. At the time of the Second World War in the year 1939, the education office which was independent so far, was attached to the Federal Security Agency. The different departments of the Federal Government, too, provided economic help for education of subjects concerning them. For example, in 1897, according to the Morell and Hatch Act, the Department of Agriculture gave land grant and financial help to State Government for improvement of Agriculture education in Agriculture schools. In 1917, the Federal Government by establishing Federal Board of Vocational Education, formulated programme for technical and vocational education and gave financial help. In 1920, the economic help given by the Board was left to the patronage of State Governments and the education of the retarded children was also attached to it. In the year 1912, the Department of Commerce and Labour of the Federal Government established Children's Bureau of Education. The main aim of this bureau was to study the problems of Civilian

Conservation Corps and to devise plans for child welfare. Thus the different departments gave economic help and grants to the State Governments for specialised education in their concerned subjects.

Whereas the Federal Government gave financial help and land grants to State Governments for specific programmes and educational projects, it also gave encouragement and financial help to private agencies and community agencies. During the depression period, some private and collective agencies organised some programmes for helping educational institutions. In 1933, when unemployment increased, the Government established a Civil Conservation Corps for employing unemployed persons and to provide vocational training. Similarly, another institution, National Youth Administration was organised in 1935. This institution heped the unemployed and offered part-time work to students during the period of their study. In the absence of public support this institution lost its existence within 8 or 9 years. The Federal Government realising the seriousness of the Second World War established two institutions-the Public Works Administration and Civil Aeronautic Authority. These institutions were attached to the Federal Government to compensate for the loss due to the depression and national defence. The National Defence Institution successfully helped in training defence workers and fulfilled its duty satisfactorily.

The problem of providing a living and vocation to unemployed persons returning from military services arose. So in 1944 to cope with the problem of unemployment and to train unemployed persons by giving them a vocation, Servicemen's Readjustment Act was passed. Through this act efforts were made to make the curriculum successful from the point of view of vocational training by providing scholarships and financial help. This provision made ex-servicemen and the persons returning from active service happy and they could conveniently earn a living. In 1948 the Federal Government increased the financial help given to this institution so that it might not suffer from scarcity of funds and might fulfil its duty successfully.

**Various Schemes**

The Federal Government has been providing sufficient economic help and land grants to State Government. The Educational programmes of the Federal Government may be classified as follows:

***Help to State-Government.*** The Federal Government gives financial help and land grant to State Governments. Financial help is given in various forms, *e.g.*, loan, percentage grant, grant-in-aid, Vocational Rehabilitation Grant, Forest Reserve and Mineral Royalty Grant. Similarly, land grants, too, are given to the State Governments in various forms, *e.g*.; Agricultural and Technical Education Land Grants, Saline Grant, Section Grant, Swamp Land Grant etc. The State Government provides grants to the schools according to their needs.

***Help to Regions Administered by the Federal Government.*** The Federal Government provides funds to schools situated in the region directly under its administration. This help is given to its employees, State Governments and private educational institutions for expansion of education.

***Partial Help by the Federal Government.*** Those places which are within the boundaries of U. S. A. and are under the Federal Government get full or partial help from the Federal Government.

***Fun Help for Education of American Indians.*** The Federal Government shoulders the entire responsibility of education native Indians in U. S. A.

***Responsibility of Training its Employees.*** The Federal Government bears the responsibility of training all those workers who serve the Federal Government.

***Co-operation in Foreign Educational Programmes.*** The Federal Government encourages and co-operates in all those educational programmes which are planned in collaboration with other nations of the world.

***Publication of Educational-Information of the States.*** The Federal Government collects informations regarding educational progress and work done in States and publishes reports and diffuses the same.

***To Bring Uniformity in the Education of the States.*** The Federal Government also endeavors to bring uniformity in the education of all the States. But it does not exert any pressure.

The Federal Government gives most of the grants and economic help without string attached but at the time of giving some grants, it tries to get the prescribed rules and conditions fulfilled.

**Role of Department**

The Federal Government has been eager to implement educational projects since the middle of the nineteenth century. It established a Central Department of Education in 1867. That Department began to be called as Education Office in 1930. Henry Benard became the first Education Commissioner of that office. In the beginning Education Office was an independent institution for implementing educational programmes but after the World War Second, it was included in the Federal Security Agency.

The President of the Federal Government appoints the chief of the office who is called the Education Commissioner. The Education Commissioner is appointed for an indefinite period. In the beginning the functions of the Education Office were as follows:

Functions concerning projects of educational improvement, functions of organizing education for non-European communities such as Negroes and American Indians, functions for providing education in regions like Alaska, functions of inter-state educational efforts and eliciting co-operation from different departments for educational facilities in States. But later on with vocational and industrial development, the programmes for the development of vocational and industrial education began to be taken up by the Education Office. Besides, to endeavour for the progress of education at the inter-state level, to collect data regarding progress of education in States and to publish and propagate them, functions concerning necessary reforms in the education system, functions increasing the number of training subjects, school organization and efforts to maintain the control of the Federal Government on them were also included in the duties of the Education Office.

The Education Office was attached to the Federal Security Agency at the time of the World War Second. Consequently, the scheme of the Federal Security Education was entrusted to it. The Education Office did remarkable work by completing all the functions entrusted to it under the scheme. The war-time security functions of the Office increased its importance. The Federal Security Education project included conduct and control of all types of education concerning war, expansion and progress of industrial education, organization of Civil-Defence Force, conducting of National Youth Organization and providing work for unemployed persons by giving them necessary vocational training. Inspite of its dutifulness, the Education Office did not fully succeed in its work. The reason for this was noncooperation of the States. The State Governments were suspicious and afraid of the Federal Government lest it should assume full control on them and they might lose their freedom. Because of this suspicious nature, the Constitution of U. S. A. and subsequent amendments could not mention anything regarding education. The people seeing that the Constitution has neither bestowed the rights of education to the Federal Government nor has it deprived the State Government from them, took it for granted that these rights were reserved for the people and the State-Governments. In such a situation, the State Governments began to establish direct contact with various federal departments in educational matters, without the consent of the Federal Government. Thus the importance of the Education Office was reduced. Today the work of the Education Office is limited. The Education Commissioner simply looks after the work of his office and after collecting data from the schools of States prepares a report for general information.

## Role of States

In the States, for formulation of educational projects and educational control, Education Boards are organized. The chairman of the State Education Board is called the Education Commissioner. To advise and co-operate with the Education Commissioner a State Education Department is established. Under the Education Department, there are Country Boards. The Country Boards function on district basis. The chief of the Country Board is called Superintendent of Schools. The Country Board looks after the work of Township, School Board and Local Board. In the beginning according to constitution, the State Government was responsible for providing education but for the sake of convenience, the State Governments delegated the right of providing education to local Boards. Thus even today the educational administration is run by Boards organised by the local people. But the American people also believe that Local Boards cannot bear the responsibility of education-reforms and educational progress properly. They also believe that the local boards have limited means and at the time of scarcity educational plans cannot be fulfilled successfully. As a result, the State Education Boards frame general education rules for the schools, determine educational programmes and exercise control on the schools. The State Education Boards prescribe rules for qualifications etc. and determine minimum standard of efficiency without interfering in the programmes of schools.

## Local Level Setup

Most of the immigrants from Europe were Catholics. They were very orthodox with regard to their social and religious sentiments. They strictly adhered to their religious and social traditions. Consequently, they established schools in their colonies according to their religious and social beliefs. These schools were controlled and managed by their religious leaders, preachers and missionaries. The expenditure of the schools too, was borne by themselves. With the change in conditions the administration of these schools also went in the hands of Local Boards. The Local Boards run the administration of these schools even today.

Local Boards are constituted by the elected members of the people. The members elect the administrative officer of the Local Education Board. This administrative officer is called Superintendent of Local School. The term of administrator and members is indefinite. But there cannot be more than nine members in this Board. Most of the administrative work is done by these Local School Boards. The number of these Boards throughout the country is about two lakhs. These Boards formulate curriculum to be taught in the schools on the basis of their social traditions and beliefs. The control of State Government on these is only for the sake of maintaining standard of education and for training in vocational subjects, otherwise regarding optional subjects, extra-curricular activities and religious subjects they are quite free. It has been noticed that at some places Bible is taught compulsorily with its comments and in some schools it is not allowed to he taught. Most of the schools in America are in the hands of Local Boards. The administration of the Federal Government is found only in regions administered by the Federal Government. In the Delaware State, the education is managed by the State Government. The feeling of patriotism being strong in America, subjects with patriotic feelings occupy an important place in the curriculum of schools.

**Liberal Setup**

According to the leader of the American Freedom, late-President Abraham Lincon, "democracy is a system of Government of the people, for the people and by the people." In America democracy was established on this basis. According to them man is not for the State, but the State is for helping and protecting the individual. If people are mentally and culturally well-developed, there will be no dearth of worthy citizens in a democracy. So it is the duty of the State that it should provide all educational facilitic to make a man capable and worthy citizen. Every person should get an opportunity to develop himself according to his need, capacity and interest and thus get an opportunity to add to the prosperity of the nation by becoming prosperous himself. This work can be done by the Government alone. In America, all the social units are free in developing national outlook. There is no social or political system determined by the State. The following are the three traditions of nation-wide education there:

(1) The medium of instruction should be one, *i.e.,* English.

(2) Educational literature should be national, *i. e.,* one.

(3) Education should be imbibed with democratic ideals.

The American Education is provided on graded stages. There are the following four stages of education:

(1) Primary Stage.

(2) Secondary Stage.

(3) College or Higher Education.

(4) Vocational Stage.

Educational institutions from primary stage to secondary and college stage are run by the Local School Boards under the responsibility of the State Government. Teaching of vocational stage begins after secondary and college stage. Vocational training is not given in public schools. Vocational education and training schools are quite separate from public schools which are run by the Federal Government and State Governments. Apart from the above four stages, general course, industrial course, vocational course and the professional specialization are also available.

The public schools run by the Local School Boards are the pillars of American education. These schools remain affected by the related people and environment. The competency and success with which these schools had overcome the shortage of scientific and vocational education, could not be seen even in the schools administered by the federal Government. The importance of these schools lies in the fact that their form changes with the change in needs and ideals. That is the reason that these schools could provide education and training facilities as soon as the outline of the new education was received and need of new education was felt. These schools provide commercial, professional and specialized training according to the need and interest of students, as far as possible.

**Basic Ideology**

Although education systems in U. S. A. are based on their independent systems, yet in the diversity of systems, there are some similarities also. These similarities may be considered as the fundamental tendencies of American education. The following fundamental tendencies are worth mentioning:

(a) Universal and Free Education-The provision of education in U. S. A. is classless, secular and free. Every child, belonging to any religion, community, class, sex and colour receives education with all facilities free. The education is imbibed with feelings of patriotism and devotion to the Nation which make the American citizen capable and nationalist.

(b) Education with Democratic Ideal-The American schools are run by a Board constituted with elected members of the people and these schools are also established by the people and for the people. Thus education there is fully democratic and presents democratic ideal. Equality of educational opportunity is available to the people. The responsibility of education rests with the State Governments but the local units fulfil the duty sufficiently with ease.

(c) Single Ladder System of Education in the States, the system of education is that of single ladder. So the education system may be called a single ladder system. An the States provide education of primary, secondary, higher and vocational stages. Technical and vocational education in all the States is provided after the secondary stage. The lower stages prepare able students for higher stages.

(d) Similarity of Economic Management-Most of the educational expenditure is borne by the local people. The State Governments and the Federal Government give only partial aid.

(e) Dynamic Tread and Experimental Facilities-The ideals of a country provide base to the education is for formulating education systems. The same is true of American system. The facilities for scientific inventions could be made available due to change of ideals and guidance from the educationists. Education there is most recent and new. The American education prepares the citizen not only for life but also makes him capable of contributing in living itself.

The American people believe in their rights due to which education could not be centralised. That is the reason why the Constitution does not' clarify the rights of the States and Federal Government. Till now, the responsibility of education rests with the States and through them it has been delegated to the local units which are free to implement it.

***Contribution of the Federal Government in Education.*** Although the Federal Government has no direct control over the educational sphere, but it influences education through the projects of Education office and by giving land grants and various other grants. In the year 1920, the Federal Government left the grants to the patronage of State Governments. It gave financial help to private and collective organisations from time to time. During the depression period, to overcome the problem of unemployment, it provided financial help to various organizations and also gave financial help to unemployed military personnel during the World War Second.

***Education Programme of the Federal Government for Giving Encouragement.*** The Federal Government gives land grants and grant-in-aid to State Governments. It conducts education in the regions administered by it itself and also looks after the education of American Indians. It provides training to its employees and helps in the foreign educational projects.

***Education Office.*** Education Office conducts the educational programmes of the Federal Government. Its chairman is called Education Commissioner. At present, the function of the Education Office is to collect data from State Government and publish its report on that basis for publicity.

***State Education Administration.*** Except Delaware, educational administration was handed over to Local Boards in all the States. The State Government simply tries to maintain the minimum standard of education, determines curriculum and frames general rules, controls schools, executes educational plans and provides for vocational and scientific training. State Education Boards are established in the States for this purpose. The chairman of the Board is called State Educational Commissioner. Country-Boards, Education Township and Education Districts work under it.

***Local Educational Administration.*** Most of the schools in the States are managed by Local Education Boards. It is an independent and complete unit from administration point of view. The Federal and State Governments have very little control on it. The number of Local Boards in U. S. A. is about two lakh. A board is constituted by 9 members who are elected by the people concerned. Its chairman is Superintendent of education who is elected by the members. He is the chief administrative officer. These Boards are free to organise education according to the need and interest of the people.

***Democratic American Education.*** Here the schools are of the people and for the people. They are responsible to provide equality of educational opportunity to an irrespective of caste, colour or creed. The schools change their educational system according to the need.

***Functional Tendencies of American Education.*** Education in U. S. A. differs from State to State yet it is similar in some respects.

These similarities may be called Fundamental Tendencies of Education here *e.g.*, universalness, free education, democratic outlook, one ladder based education system, similarity of financial arrangement, dynamic tendency and experimental facility.

## QUESTIONS

1. Education system in U. S. A. is democratic. How far do you agree with this statement?
2. "The Federal Government of U. S. A. even without having full control on education is not indifferent to its duties in relation to education." How far is this statement true ? Explain.
3. The educational administration in U. S. A. is a result of gradual development. Explain.
4. The schools in U. S. A. prepare worthy citizens. How?
5. "American school and their organization enjoy full freedom; the Government interference is limited." Explain.
6. Write short notes on :

   (a) Education Office

   (b) State Education Board

   (c) Local Administration

   (d) Democratic Tendency in American Education

# PART-FIVE

# EDUCATION IN RUSSIA

# 23

# University Education

Higher education means that education which is imparted by universities and higher schools or institutes. In Russia, all higher schools and universities are controlled by the government and they are wholly State Governed. All those training institutions which train specialists, are controlled by Commission of Education. Before 1946, the higher schools were controlled by those universities to which the persons receiving education belonged. But due to administrative difficulty the general guidance of all higher schools was put under the control of committee on higher education. This committee was converted into Ministry of Higher Education. Later on in 1953, the Ministry of Higher Education was combined with Ministry of Culture which look the form of Central Administration of Higher Education. From the view point of local administration, an academic council is formed of members' of able professors and this council contributes in the development of higher education by helping in the selection of teachers, educational arid research problems.

## Criteria of Admission

After passing secondary education, all citizens within (7 to 35 year of age can take admission in higher education schools after getting through an entrance examination. The student of literary group is examined in Russian language, national history, one of the foreign language, *i.e.,* English German or French. And for technical higher education, examination is held in mathematics, science, Russian language literatures and one foreign language. The examination's both oral and written. Students getting gold and silver medals do not have to appear at the entrance examination.

## System at Work

The Russian Universities are divided into concerned departments or divisions according to specific curriculum. Here, there are different departments like Agriculture, Education, Fine Arts and emphasis is laid on the study of specific industrial practice, social and economics.

## Technical Courses

A student can select any vocation of his choice before taking admission in any institution of higher education. However, a vocation can be chosen even after completing higher education, but the government does not encourage such a choice for it does not determine the direction of education. So before admission to any university, not only the vocation has to be chosen but also the specialised area of that vocation.

## The Administration

Rector who is also called Chairman is the highest authority of the university. For his assistance he has two colleagues—one for bearing the responsibility of educational programmes and the other for administration and looking after financial matters. Different subjects have different faculties chaired by Deans of Faculties. In all higher education schools and universities, there is a learned council, known as Senate. This council or senate includes Rector, his two assistants, Dean of Faculties and elected representatives of students. Under every Dean of the university, there are 4 to 9 faculties. Every professor does research work along with teaching for which he gets periodical promotion.

### The Syllabi

The curriculum prescribed at different stages of higher education is approved by the Cultural Ministry of Russia. The teachers and students work according to the prescribed curriculum and programme schedule. This curriculum includes laboratory work, general lecture, workshop practice, seminars and studies. A copy of the curriculum is given to each student and teacher in the beginning of the session. The same subject and curriculum commence in all the departments of a faculty simultaneously. But in the final years different branches of science subjects are taught and different constructive activities have to be performed by the students.

### The Time Table

Ordinarily there are two terms of higher education, which make the academic session. The first term, generally, is from September 1 to January 23. After that they have winter vacation of two weeks. The second terms is from February 7 to July 1 and after that there is summer vacation of two months. The examinations are held at the end of each session. A student is admitted to the new curriculum of the next session after he had passed the examinations in each term. He is declared to have passed in practical on the basis of his attendance in the practical work. Then he gets further education.

The duration of higher education is generally from 4 to 6 years. The duration is determined according to the education field. Generally, the curriculum of Pedagogical schools and Agriculture schools is of 4 years and duration of higher technical school is of 5 years and medical institutes is of 6 years.

The planning bodies determine the annual number of boys and girls passing the examinations and government approves and treat them that as a part of Annual Plan. The students are familiar with the field of their work. So they do their practical work in factories as engineers and foreman. For example, the St. Petersburg Ship Building Institute sends its students to the ship-building factory for practical work and during that very period they are made responsible for production-tasks. After the completion of practical work, as soon as they pass the examination, they are divided into different sections and they have to give direction in those very sections. After the award of degree the state service commission places them according to their inclinations.

**The Stipends**

The state awards scholarships to progressive students. The scholarships' are given by Education Directors. The students of excellent category is given 25 per cent additional money in addition to regular stipend which is sufficient to meet his minimum requirements. Thus the student studies free of any worry. The above stipend generally, is of 500 to *800* roubles which is based on type of higher education and years of study. For the students, specialising in research or study, the scholarships are reserved in the name of important politicians or scientists.

The wards of parents who are killed in war or rendered invalid, are given free education. The higher education fee is *500* to 600 roubles annually. Physcial education is a compulsory part of general education. Every student is given facilities for boarding and lodging and medical aid.

**Role of Library**

In Russia, the library facilities are provided without any fee. The libraries are equipped with various courses, study material and text-books. Every subject faculty has branches of library. *For* professors, teachers and older students, help book for research work and study are made available in the library Reference books are available for different departments of a faculty. The libraries of universities like that of Mascow occupy important place throughout the world.

**Education at Doorstep**

Education through correspondence has been prevailing in Russia for the last thirty-five years. At present almost 35 correspondence course institutes are at work. Admission rules, examination system and curriculum are like regular students. After passing the examination, they are awarded degrees like regular students. The government recognises this education system like formal education.

***Administration and Admission System of Higher Education***-The students after passing secondary examination choose some vocation and appear at the entrance examination. The student who are medal holders do not have to appear at the entrance examination. The admission age is 17 to 35 years.

***University System***-The different classes at this stage are agriculture, military education, fine arts, technical, industrial, social and economic. The student is entitled to choose his vocation before admission. University system is conducted by Rector and his two colleagues. Recor, Professor, Dean, student-representative and two colleagues of the Rector constitute the Senate.

***Higher Education Curriculum***-Laboratory and workshop practical is compulsory along with studies. The planning commission controls the curriculum of the whole year and the cultural ministry approves it.

***Two Terms***-First term is from September 1 to 23rd January, and the second term is from February 7 to July 1. Examination is held after each term. The duration of education is 4 to 6 years.

***Scholarship, Library and Correspondence Education System***-The excellent student gets scholarship and 25 percent additional money. Library faculties are free. Teachers, students and research scholars get all facilities. Now education is given through correspondence like regular students. The curriculum and degrees are treated equivalent to degrees given by other regular universities.

## QUESTIONS

1. Describe the system of higher education in Russia and explain how the students are made care-free for research work and higher studies.
2. Write short notes on :

   (1) Russian-Higher Education Libraries.

   (2) Technical Practical Work in Russia.

   (3) University System.

   (4) Higher Education through Correspondence in Russia.

# 24

# School Education

In the beginning the Government of Russia had started a ten years School Plan for children of 7 to 17 years of age. In this plan the main consideration was centralisation of schools. Provision was made for education from the primary to secondary stage in such schools. Many such schools were started. After the World War II, this plan failed and the ten year education was divided into three groups. First four years for primary education and last six years were set for lower and upper secondary education. The secondary education was further divided into lower secondary and upper secondary stages. Thus from Class 1 to 4 was primary classes, from class 5 to 7 lower secondary classes and from class 8 to 10 secondary classes were fixed. The lower secondary stage was meant for children between 11 to 14 years of age and the secondary classes were for children between 15 to 18 years of age.

In Russia the seven-year system and six-year system prevail. In the seven year system, with four years primary education, 3 years secondary education has also been included. Later 3 years secondary education is imparted either in the same building or some other building nearby. In the six years system, 3 year lower secondary curriculum are taught. Mostly seven year schools are run which enable the maximum utilisation of school building.

**Combined Classes**

According to the policy of the Government upto 1943, the education of boys and girls continued together at every stage and the administration felt happy at their success. But after 1943, some disciplinary problems arose and in the schools of secondary stage, separate arrangement for boys and girls had to be made. Gradually, this change came down to lower secondary stage also. Only in the vocational and rural spheres, co-education prevailed upto the lower secondary and secondary stage. Now co-education is limited upto primary stage and in some rural areas and vocational sphereas, it continues at the secondary stage also.

Some did not consider the co-education system as good. But some people considered co-education proper. From 10 to 17 years of age, education has been made separate. But now co-education is being extended at the secondary stage again.

**The Syllabi**

In classes sixth and seventh general science, mathematics, history, geography, art or mechnical drawing and Russian or mother.tongue are taught. If the institutions is in Russian language region, Russian language is taught in the third class, otherwise mother-tongue is taught from class V. For boys physical education, social studies, modern politics are also compulsorily taught. In classes VI and VII the teaching of physics and chemistry is started.

Realising the need of higher academic education, in class VII to X curriculum was made different from the previous classes. Now more emphasis is laid on the teaching of mathematics and science. From 1947 logic is also being taught. Russian literature in place of Russian language and mechanical art instead of general art have been included. The entire curriculum is formulated by the Education Ministry of the region concerned.

**In Classroom**

Keeping the last day of the week as holiday, 6 days week in Cities and 7 days week in rural areas are in vogue. Academic session or year is from September to June. The opening day for every class is September 1, but closing dates in June are different. The closing date for class I, for classes 4 to 7 June 10; for classes VIII to X is June 20. During the session from December 30 to January 10, there is winter vacation and spring vacation from March 26 to 31. In some places the spring vacation is from March 26 to April 26, that is, for full one month. This difference is due to climate. The weekly hours for class V are 26 and for remaining clasees 27. In rural areas, the periods are 31 in Class V and in the remaining classes they are 32. A period is of 45 minutes duration and the schools start work at 8 to 9 o'clock in the morning. Subject teacher system prevails and there is class teaching. But for backward children,' individual teaching is also provided. Classification is done according to the age of students Transfer examination is held at the age of 11, 14 and 17.

**Teaching of Theology**

Although some teachers are religious by nature, but they cannot give religious instructions ,anywhere. Secondary Education is religionless and science based. Teaching is done without having any religious base. Science teaching at the secondary level also helps in removing any religious superstitions. Hence because of scientific teaching no religious education can be imparted at the secondary level.

**Foreign Languages Taught**

Amongst the foreign languages, French, German and English have been recognized as optional subjects which the students can study upto a prescribed limit. Social Studies Teaching After acquainting the students with social, economic and political systems of the world, they are made familiar with the national, social, economic ideology of Russia. Although the student can study social and other systems of the world fully, yet he can neither study nor be taught social studies beyound the limit prescribed in the curriculum by the Education Ministry. The social studies of the world are taught with the objective at it may help them to solve the problems of poverty in their own country.

## Education for Health

In view of the military importance, physical education has been made compulsory since 1944. It is compulsory for all classes at the secondary stage. In the last final three classes, *i.e.*, 8, 9 and 10 the physical education takes the form of formal military training. The drill sergeant marking attendance of student, gives physical training for about 15 minutes before teaching begins. The girl students are given knowledge of nursing, art, telephone and radio in place of physical education.

## The Expenses

From primary classes to class VIII no fee is charged. In the remaining classes ninth and higher vocational and technical institutions fee is charged. The fee is 3 per cent of the total expenditure. Orphans, disabled parents and sons and daughters of military personnel are exempted from payment of fees. Excellent students, besides being free from payment of fees, are paid scholarships also.

## Evaluation and Measurement

In Russia, at the time of examination, the disciplined behaviour of the student during the session, completion of work and his regularity are given special consideration. Generally, the examinations are oral. Except for class seventh and class tenth examinations of remaining classes are held in the month of June. At the time of examinations, question-papers are given like primary examination, out of which the student selects the question paper of his choice and appears at the examination. This examination is secondary.

The main examination is of work and behaviour during the whole year. The medium of examination in classes VII and X is Russian language and except in mathematics, tests in all subjects are oral. With the co-operation of education officer, principal, class teacher and two other teachers, a Council of Examinations is constituted which makes arrangement for the examinations, prepares question papers and evaluates the work, conduct and discipline of the student during the whole year. As soon as the students select the question-papers, fifteen minutes time is given for thinking. And then they give oral answers. Students passing the examinations are awarded medals on the basis of their achievements. Students who fail, appear at the examination again in the month of August. Gifted students are allowed admission in the university without passing matric.

## Technical Options

According to the law of compulsory education, a child should compulsorily attend school upto the age of 14 years, *i.e.* upto the seventh class, because the law applies to the children up to 15 years of age and those upto 14 years of age cannot be employed by any industry. Thus class VII is the turning point. It is, therefore, necessary that the child should almost determine his vocation when he leaves class VII. According to this system, the student getting the highest marks is sent for higher studies and technical training after class VII, the student getting average marks for training in average class professions and the ordinary student is selected for industrial centres.

To say that the Government forces the students to choose such professions is not true, because almost in all countries of the world the brilliant students are selected for technical and higher posts training. The remaining students get ordinary workers' points automatically. Counselling is given to the students according to their interests and aptitudes. Vocational informations are given to the student through news-papers, magazines, transport vehicles and building posters. For military and scientific posts, the best students are selected. The students reading in classes 8th, 9th and 10th are prepared for higher education. The higher education representatives attract the 10th class passed students for higher education after meeting them personally.

There are nearly 8000 Technicums in Russia for preparing middle grade specialists through technical and industrial education. These institutions organize 3 to 5 years courses in industry, agriculture, health-services, legal practice, economics, teaching etc. for those boys and girls who have passed class VIII. The training-programme of these technical and industrial vocation is devised by the Education Ministry. But expenditure on buildings, equipment and general management is borne by the concerned Ministry which intends to have trainees for the concerned industry. Different vocations have different training centres.

After imparting training in different vocations, these institutions make arrangement for teaching of higher secondary classes. This enables the trainees to get full secondary education in the same school. The students of exceptional abilities are admitted to universities without matriculation.

For ordinary students, *i.e.* students, who pass class VII with average marks, factory schools have been organized. These students become workers after training these schools. These factory schools are of 3 types. In the schools of first type, semi-skilled labourers who receive training for mining centres, constructive projects and other industries are prepared. The second type of schools prepare mechanics after two years' training course in all types of transport, machines and industries etc. And in the third type of schools, training in rails and tele-communications is given.

All these training schools are free. The trainees live in an atmosphere of military preparation and receive training. No trainee can leave the school without completing and prescribed discipline and rules have to be followed for some time even after training. After the completion of the training, service has to be rendered for 4-5 years in the field of the concerned Ministry of Industry. The entire expenditure on boarding and lodging of students is met by the Government.

***Secondary Education and Co-education-***10 years education has now been divided into primary, lower secondary classes. Seven year schools have been established by joining lower secondary 5th, 6th and 7th with primary classes. There are some pre-secondary schools of 3 year each.

Co-education is only at the primary and lower secondary stage. Now there are separate secondary schools and universities.

***Curriculum and Time-Table-***The first group is the lower secondary and the second group is secondary. Their curriculum is separate. Russian language is taught with the mother tongue from the class 5th. All subjects are taught 6 days week in cities and 7 days week in rural areas. Last day is a holiday. City secondary schools have 27 periods a week and rural schools have 32. Class teaching prevails. Individual teaching is also done.

***Secondary School Fees and Teaching of Different Subjects-*** Religious education is prohibited. French, German and English languages are taught upto a limited extent. In teaching social studies information regarding social, economic and political system of the world is given. Physical education is compulsory. At the higher secondary stage training is like military training. No fees at the lower secondary stage are charged. Orphans, sons and daughters of military personnel and disabled parents do not have to pay any fees. Brilliant students get scholarship. Examination System and Choice of Vocation Only oral examination is held. Work, conduct and discipline are mainly considered. Vocation is chosen after the class 7th. Brilliant students admitted for higher technical training. Ordinary students get training for workers' post. Selection for a profession is based on ability.

***Technical and Industrial Training***-First type of schools are technical and higher vocationalInstitutions to which exceptionally brilliant students are admitted. The second type of schools are Factory schools in which ordinary students get workers' training. Education is free. The Government bears the expenditure.

## QUESTIONS

1. Explain the prevailing secondary education in Russia.
2. Why is the examination system in Russia different from our examination system? Describe the Russian examination system and choice of vocation system.
3. Describe the prevailing curriculum, grading and other systems in the Russian secondary education.
4. Describe the technical and industrial training system of Russia.

# 25

# Basic Education

In the Republic of Russia sufficient attention has been paid to the development of primary education. Effort was made in the trust Five Year Plan to provide free, compulsory and universal and extensive education to children between 8 to 12 years of age. Four-graded schools were established. Among the four-graded schools some were one room schools. The responsibility of primary education is on the Education Ministry. For children between 7 to 15 years of age universal, free and compulsory education is provided.

Due to the Second World War, the education system for children between 7 to 15 years of age was shattered and the teachers, students and employees were recruited for military services. The school-system failed. Due to shortage of workers in industrial concerns, children between 14 to 15 years of age were engaged. In the final classes, the number of students came down to 5 per cent. After the end of the war, the primary education was reorganised but the prevailing four-graded schools continued to run.

Russian educational system is psychological. Class-teaching method is emphasised there. From psychological point of view the educational programme does not exceed for 20 minutes and effort is made to arrange individual-teaching, but the children get opportunities for self-activities they are also to take up activities as directed by the teacher. The duration of a period for older children is 45 minutes and that for younger children is a little less. Effort is made to maintain the feeling of respect for the teacher. The school timings change according to weather, but generally the school hours are from 9 o'clock in the morning to 2.30 or. 3 p. m. The teaching work comes to an end when the hell rings. Small children are relieved at 10 o'clock. The teacher work there for a minimum of 4 hours and maximum of 6 hours in Four-Grade schools. Where there is shortage or teachers remuneration is paid for work done in extra hours.

The school are run in strong buildings as well as in lents. One-teacher, one-room and four-graded schools are prevalent. The provision of tents is made in backward areas due to nomadic nature of people there. Though the schools may run in tents, yet they are neat and clean. Now a plan is being prepared to make the schools in large and spacious buildings.

**School Organisation**

The educational system in Russia is quite progressive. In the beginning, the discipline is not imposed strictly,. But later on it is obligatory on every institution to follow some disciplinary rules.

At the end of the Second World War, the Russian educationists laid emphasis on making the atmosphere in schools more orderly and suggested that tendency of self-discipline and regularity in children should be created only through such an atmosphere. Only adults can determine their future becasue the minors are not much experienced, capable and wise. So through a disciplined atmosphere young children are made conscious of their future course of life.

Certain rules are taught in schools through language teaching. Efforts are made that the rules are followed by children and they maintain personal cleanliness. No child below the age of 16 years is encouraged to see any drama or movie without permission and cannot walk on the road after 10 o'clock at night. These rules are followed by the child even in domestic and social spheres.

If any child behaves in a way that is abnormal or undesirable he is shown to some psychiatrist or doctor. After ascertaining his physical or mental ailment, his home-atmosphere is also looked into. Thus the reason of his abnormal behaviour is ascertained. After this the school authorities are informed regarding such children and efforts are made to improve them.

**The Syllabi**

The responsibility of determining primary education curriculum rests with the Education Ministry. In this system, pronunciation, into nation and use of words are taught. In consulatation with the Education Minister of the Republic curriculum is formulated. At the primary stage each subject is compulsory and there are no electives.

In the first three years of education at this stage, supplementary programme, experiments demonstration field trips, dramatisation and fine arts are included. In teaching these means are used to the maximum extent. At times the children are taken to opera or professional theatres for recreation.

At the primary stage the children are taught language, mathematics, geography, history, arithmetic, music, nature study and physical education. In the four years of primary education, reading, writing speaking and use of grammar are taught. In the teaching of geography, national level geography and local geography are taught. Historical events of the country are also taught. Economic aspect of geography is to be compulsorily reflected in teaching. These subjects are taught by using suitable material aids and equipments Charts, models, maps and pictures (movies) are mainly used. The writing and publication of text-books is also the responsibility of the Education Ministry. The text-books are first sent in schools on experimental basis and then they are published in different regional languages and after translation are sent to different language schools. The text-books are prepared according to the interests, aptitudes, need and capability of the children. The teachers are authorised to suggest inclusion of educational apparatus and material aids in the text-books. Different text-books and courses are revised and amended accordingly.

The gradation of lessons to be taught in six days of the week is decided in advance. In the first and second classes 24 lessons, in the third class 25 lessons and in the fourth class 27 lessons per week are taught. One teacher teaches all the subjects in one class. At some places, the same teacher teaches his class for four years. After a period of 45 minutes, there is a recess of 10 minutes. At mid-day recess of 15 minutes is given for refreshment. Mid-day - meal is provided at about 2 or 3 o'clock and before that refreshment is given. At some places, only refreshment is provided and the students make separate arrangement for food by making payment. In cities, the schools have kitchens and restaurants where the students take their lunch.

**Measurement and Evaluation**

At the primary stage, for conducting examinations, an examination committee consisting of the headmaster and two teachers is constituted. A member of the education region or the inspector of schools remains present at the time of examination. The examination is oral. At the end of the fourth year, there is a Transfer Examination which is the last examination of the primary stage. On passing this examination, the child is admited to class 5. 5th class is the first year of lower secondary stage.

The Education Ministry issues an examination card which gives a short description of the related subjects. On the basis of this statement, the teachers select question papers and make amendments in the curriculum. At the time of oral examination, the examinee remains careful about correct pronunciation and way of answering questions. Efforts are made to establish rapport between the examiner and the examinee. The evaluation is so made that the students feel no bias in evaluation on the part of the examiner.

***Primary Education System, Time and Classes***-In the early years, 4 years primary education was conducted for children of 8-to 12 years of age on one class one teacher basis. In the post-war period, it was made compulsory for children from 7 to 15 years of age. The period is of 45 minutes duration for elderly children and of 20 minutes duration for young children. The school runs from 9 o' clock to 2;30 hours in the afternoon. Young children are relieved earlier. There is a 10 minutes' recess after every period. In the middle, there is 15 minutes' recess for refreshment or lunch.

***Discipline System in Primary Schools***-With the social view-point, the child is induced to behave properly with teachers and others in the society. In case of abonormal behaviour, a psychiatrist or doctor and authorities try to reform him.

***Curriculum and Examination Systems***-Langauge, mathematics, geography, history and art are taught through dramatics, excursions and material aids. Pronunciation, intonation and their use are emphasised. 25 to 27 graded lessons are taught in a week.

Examination is oral. An examination committee consisting of the headmaster and two teachers conduct the examinations. Transfer Examination is held at the end of 4 years.

## QUESTIONS

1. Explain dearly the primary education system prevailing in Russia.
2. Describe the examination-system at the primary level in Russia.

# 26

# Initial Education

The present pre-primary education is meant for children between 3 to 7 years of age. The pre-primary education prepares the child for primary education and educational atmosphere is provided. There is no artificiality in the educational atmosphere of young children. Their natural tendencies are made significant by laying emphasis on the development of their, cognitive senses.

It is preseumed that the home-atmosphere of children does not provide them, opportunities for proper education. It is felt that the young children need pre-primary education. The Government intends to create a system that enables females may not be required to earn a living rather they may be free to preserve the natural development of their children at the pre-primary stage. So long as mothers go to work or are in some service leaving their home, their infants need pre-primary schools. By doing so, the mothers become carefree and become ready to work.

**The Setup**

The Russian Government has entrusted the responsibility of providing pre-primary education to Health Ministry. The Education Ministry encourages various industrial concerns, mills and factories to open nursery schools and kindergartens in their areas. Accordingly, the school are run by the institutions in their respective areas. These industrial centres make arrangement for the meals etc. of their wards. The arrangements are, made from the funds of industrial organization.

**Nursery Level**

In Russian Education, educational environment is paid great attention because the child develops according to the environment. The child may be moulded according to the environment. The health of the child and, his physical development help a jot in the educational process. So before leaving the physical development to nature, the school physicians in the schools give practice in exercises to develop the health of the child. As soon as the child is of about 10 years of age, by controlling his habits and tendencies, he is guided in the desired direction.

The health of children is given special attention in pre-primary education because health helps in acquiring good habits and brings neutrality in their social development and becomes a good means of other types of development. The children are helped to develop good health by conducting scientific programme of physical exercises through various equipments. The feeling of co-operation is helpful in giving the right direction to the spontaneous tendencies of children which lead to their social development. In the nursery education system such toys and equipments of games are used with which they cannot play alone and mutual help is necessary.

Nursery schools also try to improve home-environment of the child. The health visitors guide the mothers at home and at the state-milk distribution centres the parents get such informations which guide the mothers regarding health and nourishment of the child. The teachers of kindergarten visit the houses of children and advise the parents as to how they should prepare their children bofore admitting them to kindergartens. Kindergarten schools and nursery schools are very co-operative mutually. The nursery schools prepare the children for Kindergartens. The government tries to induce people to open nursery schools in their respective areas. It provides them some monetary help also. The burden of village schools is on the Housing Committee which bear their expenditure.

**Kindergarten Schools**

The kindergarten system is slightly different from the nursery system. The kirtdergartens are very useful for female workers. The female-workers engage themselves in their work freely after admitting their children in these schools. In rural areas, for ladies engaged in cultivation, summer kindergartens are arranged. Their working hours are like nursery schools and the time is almost the same which is required of the female workers for work.

Industrial centres and commercial centres look after, manage and bear the expenditure of the kindergartens established in their areas. But they are run according to the instruction of the Government. The parents bear the expenses or-their wards themselves, but pension holders, war sufferer families and unmarried mothers have to pay only a prescribed part of the expenses.

The teachers create proper atmosphere for admission before hand. They advise the mothers for creating the atmosphere of kindergarten education, by visiting their houses and nursery schools and influence them with their contact. The children who are very sensitive, are kept in the contact of nursery teachers for 6 or 7 days so that they may be made familiar with the new atmosphere of kindergarten schools.

In the Russian kindergarten practice is given in dance, music, various exercises and physical education. Various equipment which inculcate the feeling of co-operation are used for their games, recreation and learning. These kindergartens, in principle, prepare the children for primary education. They are provided opportunities to learn through excursions. Descriptive practice of agricultural areas, industrial areas and other lovely places is given to them by taking them to such areas. To conduct literary activities, various literary personalities, poets and authrors are invited to recite their compositions and make them happy through the introduction of such personalities. A democratic outlook is adopted in these schools. The lady teachers teach them reading, writing and arithmetic, giving them motherly treatment. They develop the personality of the child. They work only for the prescribed six hours. For convenience sake they fulfil their responsibility in shifts.

***Pre-primary Education System and It Organisation***-In Russia pre-primary education is organised to look after the children of female workers during the time of their work. It is directed by the Education Ministry but these schools are managed and supported by the concerned industrial units. Health and physical development of the child are carefully looked after.

***Nursery Education***-These schools are established to form good habits in the children upto 3 years of age and to keep them healthy. These schools also enable the working ladies to remain carefree during their work. Health visitors try to adapt the children to physical labour and exercises. The feelings of co-operation and help are inculcated through games.

***Kindergarten***-After nursery education, children between 3 to 7 years of age receive education in them. Their aim too is to keep the working ladies carefree during working hours. Before admission in the kindergartens, proper atmosphere is created at their homes and nursery schools. Reading, writing and arithmetic are taught. Effort is made to develop healthy and good health through physical exercises. The lady teachers given motherly treatment. The parents pay fees but war sufferers, pension-holders and unmarried mothers pay minimum fees.

## QUESTIONS

1. Give a general description of the pre-primary education system in Russia. Explain how they are helpful in forming healthy habits.
2. Describe the aims and nature of nursery education in Russia.
3. How are the kindergartens in Russia helpful in developing the personality of the child?

# PART–SIX

# EDUCATION IN INDIA

# 27

# Teacher Training

About a hundred years ago much importance was not attached to teachers' training. But now this has become so important that no untrained person is appointed to teach in a school recognised by the government.

In anceint India, the *Guru* (the teather) used to entrust the teaching work to the brilliant student in his *Gurukul* (school). The students were divided in groups and each group was placed under the charge of a brilliant student for guidance and teaching. This is known as the monitorial system. We shall understand this system below. In 1787, Andrew Bell in Madras recognised the merits of this system. Gradually this system led to the understanding of importance of teachers' training in India. We shall understand the Monitorial system and the other aspects of teachers training in this chapter.

**The Background**

In the beginning individual efforts played a major role in the development of teachers' training in our country. At first, attention was given to the training of primary school teachers. For this purpose Dr. Kare established a normal school at Srirampur. After this the Local School Committee of Calcutta opened a teachers' training centre in 1819. In 1825 Thomas Munroe opened a central school in Madras for training of teachers. The same year in 1826, an education committee in Bombay trained 28 managers of primary schools and entrusted to them the responsibility of supervising primary schools. The women committee of Calcutta opened a training centre for training lady teachers.

The Government also made some efforts for training of teachers. Woods' despatch of 1854 also emphasised the importance of teachers' training. The Despatch of 1859 again emphasised the importance of teachers' training and recommended the allocation of separate sums for the salary of trained teachers while giving grants to schools. The government opened normal schools at Calcutta, Bombay, Poona, Surat, Agra, Meerut and Benaras. Three additional normal schools were opened at Calcutta.

So far no arrangement was made for training of teachers of secondary schools. In 1856 in Madras and in 1881 in Lahore, training colleges were opened for training of secondary school and primary school teachers. In the training of primary and secondary school teachers, the monitorial system was adopted. In the training of primary school teachers the contents of the curriculum were emphasised and for the secondary school teachers extra-curricular activities were given greater importance.

During the period between 1882 and 1947, the training of secondary school teachers was emphasised, there were about 34 teachers' training colleges in the country by 1947 for the training of secondary school teachers. By 1947, 339 normal schools for training of lady teachers and 189 normal schools for training of male teachers were established. At these training centres 2,493 graduates, 23,754 primary school teachers and 10,193 lady teachers were trained.

According to the recommendation of the Education Commission of 1882 and the educational policy decided in 1904 an effort was made to effect improvement in the curriculum of teachers' training colleges. According to the educational policy of 1904 the graduate training was prescribed for one year and the undergraduate for two years. According to the educational policy decided in 1913 the untrained teachers were to be removed from schools. This increased the importance of teachers' training. After this the Hartog Committee of 1919 and the Calcutta University Commission of 1918-19 further emphasised the importance of teachers training in their reports.

## Development in Free India

After independence the all-round development of the child was accepted as the aim of education. It was decided that the Basic Education Scheme as started in 1937 should be incorporated in the curriculum of the schools. For this it was realised that able and trained teachers were necessary. So many types of teachers' training were emphasised for various levels of education. In short, the following types have been current during the post independent period:

1. Teachers' Training for pre-primary schools.
2. Teachers' Training for primary schools.
3. Teachers' Training for Junior High Schools.
4. Graduate Teachers' Training for Secondary Schools.
5. Training of specialists.
6. Post Graduate Training and Research Work in subjects allied with Teachers' Training.
7. Training for lady teachers.

Below we shall look into the nature of all these: Teachers' Training for Pre-primary Schools.

In this type, high school or junior high school passed persons are trained for teaching in pre-primary schools such as-nursery,

Kindergarten and Monstessori. Regional differences are found in the curriculum of these training centres. The M. S. University of Baroda is running a post graduate training institution for training pre-primary school teachers. For the training of pre-primary school teachers, the Central Government has established Indian Infant Education Committee. Since 1953-54, this committee is working in the area of pre-primary school teachers' training. By now there are about 10 government and 40 private training centres preparing teachers' for pre-primary schools.

***Training for Primary Schools-***After the achievement of independence, as we have already stated earlier, basic education pattern was accepted as national policy for primary education. But all the primary schools in the country could not converted into Basic Schools. Hence two types of primary schools have been current in each State in the country basic and non-basic. Hence for the training of teachers as well two types of training system had to be arranged-one for basic schools and another for non-basic ones. Two years' course has been accepted for these training schools. In one high school passed persons were admitted and these were given an upper certificate and in another middle or junior high school passed students were admitted and they were given a lower certificate.

There is a great deal of difference in the curriculum of the basic and non-basic schools. The basic curriculum has been divided into four groups-handicrafts, education, social experiences and literary groups. In certain States some new elements have introduced in the basic curriculum according to the regional needs and they have been accepted exactly as such. In the non-basic school no importance is now attached to handicrafts. According to the varying aspects of the curriculum of the basic and non-basic schools, the teachers are trained for suiting the needs of the two.

***Training for Junior High School-***For junior high school teachers' training intermediate passed persons are admitted. Each State has its own system for this type of training, but the curriculum remains almost the same. Its curriculum has two main parts theoretical and practical. In Jabalpur, Sagar and Nagpur Universities there is one year Dip. Training Course and in Baroda, Gujarat, Bombay, Karnataka and Poona this course is known as Training Diploma and it is of one year. In U. P. it is one year and is known as B. T. C. C. T. or J. T. C.

***Training for Secondary Schools***-In the various States of the country many training colleges are run for preparing teachers of secondary schools and inspectors of schools. Most of the universities in the country are offering B. Ed. Courses for this purpose. Certain Government and Private Training Colleges are offering courses for this purpose. Hundreds of affiliated colleges allover the country are training teachers for secondary schools. Some of these colleges are having courses on the pattern. Other colleges and universities are offering almost identical B. Ed. courses.

**Efficient Trainers**

Under this programme, the teachers are trained for particular subjects, such as music, fine arts, home sciences, physical education, handicrafts etc. In 1957 the Laxshmibai Training College was opened at Gwalior for physical education. There are about 12 institutions training in fine arts. Research facilities are also available in these training centres.

**Research in Area**

This programme is one year after the B. Ed. course. This is called M. Ed. Aligarh, Lucknow and Kanpur universities are running M. A. (Education) courses of two years, for persons who have passed B. A. with education as an optional subject. Some universities have started M. Phil. (Education) courses of one year after M. Ed. This is like a pre-Ph. D. course. On getting M. Phil one may submit Ph. D. thesis after doing research at least for two years. This provision for Ph. D. research is available only in the non-basic training colleges. There is a need of research work of the Ph. D. level in the basic pattern as well.

**Female Teachers**

Both men and women receive training in the same college. There are some separate colleges for lady teachers only and in other training colleges some scats are specially reserved for girl candidates.

**On the Job Training**

In certain States in our country, there are some men and women teaching in schools but have not been able to receive training because of their adverse circumstances. Besides, there are many such trained teachers who received training decades ago. Since then there have been many innovations in the field of education and they are not aware of the same. For these trained teachers, we need refresher courses for acquainting them with the latest developments. For this purpose, we shall have to run the following programs :

1. Part-time courses
2. Correspondence Courses
3. Summer Vacation Courses
4. Refresher Courses and
5. Seminar.

Some universities and teachers training colleges in our country are running some of the above courses. Some Extension Centres are offering Short Term and Long Term courses for the benefit of in-service teachers. The Ford Foundation and U. S. Technical Co-operation Mission give some grant for such programmes and they also organise some teaching materials.

**The Remedies**

Efforts are being made for reforms in teachers' training in our country, but so far satisfactory progress has not been achieved due to certain reasons.

***The Problem of Making Training Useful to life.*** The purpose of our education is to effect an all-round development of the individual. So we need some teachers who may help in achieving this goal. This is possible only when the teachers' training is useful to life. The Basic education curriculum appears to be so. For the multipurpose schools we need teachers who are trained on the Basic education pattern. Similarly, the training programme should be made useful for each level of education, in other words it should be job oriented.

***The Problem of Difference between the Basic and Non-basic Training.*** So far education had been generally non-basic. Therefore the teachers are being trained on the non-basic pattern. There is a great deal of difference between the basic and non-basic curriculum. In the basic curriculum sufficient emphasis is laid on social life and practice. An opportunity is also given for thinking on village problems. In the non-basic curriculum, these features are absent and the emphasis is generally laid on teaching methods and on urban life. It will be better if we do away with the difference in the basic and non-basic curriculum and forged out an integrated curriculum

***The Narrowness of the Training Programme.*** Teachers' training programme in our country was organised at the time when there was no basic education curriculum. The university has made the B. Ed. curriculum more comprehensive. But the Secondary Education Commission (1952-53) has considered this programme as inadequate and has suggested that it should be made of two years duration and should be made so comprehensive as to meet the needs of multipurpose schools by producing the teachers of the required qualifications. It has also been suggested that the training colleges should be established in rural areas in order that he trainees may get acquainted with various village problems. During the training period the trainees should be given opportunities for rendering some social service to the people of the adjoining vicinity. Such changes should be incorporated in the curriculum of the normal schools also.

***The Need of Training for University and Degree College Teachers.*** It has been felt by some that the University and degree college teachers should also get some sort of training in order that they may understand how to present a certain subject before the students for meeting their curiosity or generating curiosity in them for new knowledge. This idea of training is naturally repugnant to most of the university and degree college teacher as they think that they are past masters in their area and they do not need any instruction regarding methodology of teaching. In fact, the problem of devising some training programme for university and Degree college teachers is controversial. However, it will be beneficial to produce some good books on methods of teaching for university and degree college teachers, and those interested may choose to benefit themselves by the same. The universities and the Government owe special attention and responsibility in this context.

***The Narrowness of the Post-Graduate Teachers Training Programme.*** Under the post-graduate teachers' training programme, we have M. Ed. and M. A. (Education) courses running by some universities and affiliated colleges. The purpose of these courses is to produce persons with administrative abilities and teachers of training colleges and inspectors of schools. It is felt that the M. Ed. programmes should be made more comprehensive and liberal for producing all sorts of specialists in the area of education.

***The Problem of Research in Education.*** The purpose of teachers' training centres is not only to train teachers but also to make investigations in various educational problems. The aim of research should not be only to get a dectorate degree, but also to do work of creative nature. Hence in the selection of the topic of research, great care is needed in order that the outcome of the research may be thrilling to the readers and may also point out to further researches in the allied area.

**Teacher Education**

The teacher is the maker of the nation. He produces administrators, statesmen, physicians, engineers, lawyers and other types of worthy citizens. Therefore the teacher should enjoy a very respectable position in society. But the condition of teachers is not happy in view of the ever-rising prices and other problems associated with the present-day demands of life. Our teachers should be so handsomely paid that they may devote themselves entirely to the job under their care. The necessary medical facilities should be easily made available to them on nominal charges. Residential and further education facilities should also be given to them in order that they may live a respectable life. Unless we respect our teachers, they will not respect themselves and they will fail in their sacred duty of producing worthy citizens for the nation.

***Development of Teachers' Training.*** Monitorial System before 1882. Training before 1947 and after.

***Training during the Post-Independencies Era.*** 1. Pre-primary teachers' training, 2. Primary school teachers' training, 3. Junior High School Teachers' Training, 4. Secondary School Teachers' Training. 5. Training of Specialists, 6. Post-Graduate Training and Research work, 7. Training of women teachers.

***In-service Teachers' Training.*** Part-time, Refresher Courses, Correspondence Courses, Summer Courses, Seminars.

***Problems of Teachers Training.*** 1. Training should be useful to life, 2. The difference between the basic and non-basic teachers' training, 3. Narrowness of the curriculum 4. Training for University and Degree College Teachers, 5. Post-Graduate Training, 6. Research Work.

***Condition of Teachers.*** Teachers must enjoy a respectable position in society. The Government should make the position of teachers strong by giving them handsome salaries and other necessary facilities. The teachers should consider themselves as social workers.

## QUESTIONS

1. Describe the current teachers' training programme in India.
2. What are the major problems of teachers' training in our country ? Suggest measures for their solution.
3. Suggest measures for the reforms of teachers' training programme in our country.

# 28

# Social Education

Democracy can succeed only when the general public is adequately educated in the principles and implications of the same. This is possible only when the people are literate. So after the achievement of independence, our leaders planned to promote education of the illiterate adults who were entitled to vote.

## The Perception

Adult education does not imply only to make adults literate. In fact, it means to educate the total personality of the adult and as a first step towards the achievement of this objective we make them literate, *i.e.,* in other words we help them to acquire command over the tools of knowledge or reading, writing and arithmetic. When they succeed in acquiring this command, we strive to educate them into economic, social and political problems of the day in order that they may become intelligent citizens for taking right decisions when they are faced with a number of alternatives. If they fail to acquire this skill the mean and self-centred people will exploit them for their own interests. Consequently, democracy will fail and will yield place to dictatorship.

From the above, it is clear that the purpose of adult education is not merely to impart bookish knowledge. In fact, as we have said above, philosophy of adult education aims at the education of the total personality of the adult. This will be possible only when we try to develop in them various types of skills with a view to make them successful and socially useful members of the society. We cannot prescribe any limit to adult education. We have to help the adults to acquire useful knowledge in professional, political, economic and social spheres. This is what philosophy of adult education stands for.

So far in our country in the Held of adult education our main emphasis has been to make the adults literate. Only that adult education is worth the name which help the adult to understand all the social, economic, cultural and political problems and their solutions. For this a well-planned programme has to be thought of and executed.

**Current Position**

Much has been done in the area of adult education in many Western countries. In their comparison, we have done very little in this field. In the Western countries adult education has been made available to labourers, women and many service-class people. Through adult education these have not been made only literate, but, they have also further developed their professional skills in commerce, industry, technology and science. They are given free education. Evening and part-time day classes and university extension classes have been arranged for the benefit of these people. So far we have been able to do a little in this field. Below we are giving a brief summary of the growth of adult education in our country:

**The Background**

Adult education was begun in our country with the beginning of the current century. But for the first 20 years nothing remarkable could be done. In fact, then the people did not exactly understand the correct meaning and purpose of adult education. In the provinces of Madras, Bombay and Bengal some night-schools were started for those boys who, due to working in the day in offices and factories, were not able to get education. In 1909 there were 775 such night schools in Madras, 1028 in Bengal and 167 in Bombay. During the coming years, the number of these schools came down. This situation continued till 1920. In 1921 some representatives of the people went to legislative councils and these representatives raised their voice against the prevailing illiteracy and tried to do something for adult education and established some libraries and reading rooms for adults.

**Growth and Development**

Upto 1927 adult education work has especially been done in Madras, Bombay Punjab and Bengal. In 1927, there were 5,604 adults schools in Madras, 193 in Bombay. 3,784 in Punjab and 1,519 in Bengal. Uttar Pradesh also did something in this field.

Due to financial stringency in 1927, many adult schools were closed, but certain missionaries continued their efforts in this direction and did commendable work.

Bombay alone continued its efforts for adult education and its progress was maintained till 1937. Many social organisations of Bombay promoted an expansion of adult education. In these organisation, Adult Education League of Poona Social Leauge and Bombay City Literacy Committee of Bombay are worthy of mention. In 1932-33, there were 143 adult schools in Bombay-The number became 180 in 1937. The number of students in these schools were 5,660 in 1932-33 and in 1937 the number rose to 6,299. In Baroda and Travancore adult education was encouraged and many libraries were opened for adults. But in 1937 the efforts for adult education were slackened.

In 1937, in 8 of the provinces of the country, Congress Ministries were worn in according to the Government of India Act of 1935. The Congress Ministries in all the provinces showed immense interest for adult education and it was promoted unprecedentally. The popular ministries widened the scope of adult education and it was not limited to literacy alone. Now adult education was understood as social education and accordingly the programmes were planned. Audio-visual materials such as Magic Lanterns and Cinemas were also used along with suitable books especially prepared for the purpose.

Under the adult education programme "let an educated one make another literate" scheme was started in 1937. Due to this by 1939-40 adult education progressed in various provinces. Below we are hinting at the progress made in various provinces under this new scheme.

***Uttar Pradesh.*** In population U. P. is biggest in the country, but educationally it is one of the most backward States. Education Department was first established in this State in 1930. The popular Congress Ministry in 1937 gave a special impetus to the adult education programme. For this purpose several night schools, libraries, reading rooms and training centres were opened under the supervision of the Government. In order to generate interest in the public for adult education every year "literacy day" and "literacy week" used to be organised. On the first literacy day in U. P. 768 libraries and 2,600 reading rooms were opened. Fort libraries were started for only women in 1940. About 272 additional libraries were opened in 1941.42. Many books in Hindi, Urdu, geography, history, mathematics and handicrafts for adults were published by the Government. In the district of Faizabad, 500 rupees per centre were distributed to fifty Women Welfare Centres. Thus, during a short period commendable work was done by the U. P. Government for adult education.

***Punjab.*** In Punjab Learn and Educate movement was started and Rs. 28,800 were given as a grant for adult education in the First Five Year Plan. This money was utilized in opening some new adult schools and helping some old ones.

***Orissa.*** 425 centres of adult education were opened in Orissa in 1940-41. 8,147 adults were educated by these centres.

***Bihar.*** In Bihar Make your Home Literate Movement, was started with great enthusiasm. Dr. Saiyad Mahamud led this movement. 24,289 adults were made Iterate during 1941-42. This work was continued even during the Second World War period and a Provincial Public Education Committee was established for looking after this work. During the period every year at least tow lakh adults were educated in Bihar. In 1942-43 in the Adult Post Literacy Examination 1,11 ,000, adults passed this examination. In 1946 when the Congress Ministry was again sworn in, the adult education programme was again started with great zeal.

***Bengal.*** Adult education programme was quite smooth in Bengal amongst farmers, because this was entrusted to the Adult Education Rural Reconstruction Department. Under the adult education curriculum agriculture, animal husbandry, cooperative work, health and other useful subjects for the villagers were included.

***Assam.*** In Assam a separate department was started for adult education under a mass literacy officer. About 1,200 centres were opened for adult education. In 1941 libraries were opened for further education of those adults who had received some education.

***Bombay.*** In 1927 adult education programme was started in Bombay along with the establishment of provincial education board. In 1937 the Congress Ministry took active interest in the adult education programme. During 1942-43, the Bombay Government granted Rs. 50,000 for adult education in villages. In 1945 a number of centres were opened for adult education and each centre was to educate 1000 adults. On this programme Rs. 9400 were allocated for each year.

***Princely States.*** Baroda, Travancore and Mysore did good work in the field of adult education. In Baroda and Travancore the progress was better than in the British India. The Mysore University and the Mysore State Literacy Board did good work. In 1942-43 in Jammu and Kashmir 4,050 centres were opened for adult education. In the hilly areas and in Sind as well some work was done for education of adults. An attempt was made to educate Harijans and tribal people.

The scope of adult education was widened after independence and it was decided that adult education should be termed as social education, because it was thought that adult literacy should aim at educating the total personality of the adults. Accordingly some literature was prepared for education of adults and new methods of teaching were also adopted.

**An Overview**

After independence social education was divided into the following three parts :

1. To make the illiterate literate.
2. To encourage writers for writing books for social education
3. To acquaint the adults with their social rights and duties. Accordingly, the following points were specially emphasized in social education:

   (i) To impart the knowledge of civic rights and duties in order that the necessary ability may be developed for running a democracy.

   (ii) To give a knowledge of historical and geographical background of the country.

   (iii) To acquaint with the current social traditions and circumstances.

   (iv) To impart knowledge of the things that promote good health.

   (v) To develop ability for helping in the economic growth of the country.

(vi) To foster the feeling of co-operativeness and internationalism.

(vii) To develop aesthetic sense.

The following twelve point programme was chalked out in 1948 for fulfilling the above objectives:

1. To make the village school a centre of education, recreation, sports and social service.
2. To fix up different time for education of different age groups.
3. To fix certain days in the week for ladies and girls.
4. To utilize audio visual aids at least once a week.
5. To provide Radio-sets to schools and to organise special programmes for school children.
6. To stage dramas of educational value in schools and to award prizes to participants.
7. To organise national and folk-song programme.
8. To give training in handicrafts according to local needs.
9. To impart knowledge about agriculture and health through departmental government officers.
10. To organise lectures of leaders on national problems and to stage cinema shows by the Information Department.
11. To organise group sports and games.
12. To organise exhibitions and fairs.

To implement the above twelve point programme a conference was organised of Education Ministers of various States in 1949. This conference decided that within three years 50 per cent of the persons within the age group of 12 and 50 years of age would be educated. Due to financial difficulty this objective could not be achieved although the Centre Government gave a grant of one lakh rupees for this purpose. The Central Government established the Mohan Lal Saxena Committee for educating persons within the age group of 12 and 40 years this committee recommended that both the Central and State government should equally share the financial burden involved in adult education. Under this plan some work was done in adult education in some States. We are hinting at below the progress made by some States:

***Delhi***-Around 1950, a number of adult education centres were opened. Sixty centres were opened in the adjoining rural areas for which 62 teachers were trained in the methods of adult education.

***Madras***-In 1949-50 six rural colleges and 100 schools were opened for adult education. Some centres were also opened for training teachers for teaching Tamil, Telagu, Kannara and Malyalam languages.

***Bombay***-In this province, there were many labourers in various cities. In Ahmedabad Sholapur Khandesh and Hubali good work was done in adult education. For experimental work in social education 80 centres of rural areas were chosen. Adult education officers were appointed. Each officer was entrusted with the responsibility of educating atleast 1000 adults. In Bombay city also good work in adult education was done. Labour Welfare Centres were opened in labour colonies.

***Madhya Pradesh***-Adult Education Camps organised at various places in this State. In 1948-49,451 such camps were opened and 41,274 men and 20.924 women were educated in these centres during the year. To encourage the expansion of adult education every adult was given an allowance of Rs. 2.00, women Rs. 5.00 and teachers Rs. 20. 1,000 Radio sets were given to village centres of adult education.

***Uttar Pradesh***-A separate department was established for adult education in U. P. This department opened 62 schools for women and a number of schools for men for imparting adult education. In 1948-49, 49,382 adults were educated. In 1951,-52 there were 2,200 adult schools and 3,600 reading rooms for men and 435 for women were established. Besides there were 1,518 libraries. Within 1948 and 1952. 13,50,000 adults were educated and 1,75,000 books were distributed to adults.

Some work in adult education was also done in Rajasthan, Hyderabad, Jammu-Kashmir and West Bengal after independence. Some work for educating the handicapped and blind was also done and for training the blind a school was opened in Dehradun.

Our Indian Government accepted the UNESCO plan for adult education with a little necessary modification. Accordingly, a number of camps were organised in villages for adult education. An attempt was also made to educate lakhs of refugees who fled from Pakistan.

Under the Camp programme three objective had to be achieved. These objectives were:

1. To spread literacy.
2. To generate the sense of civic rights and duties and,
3. To develop thinking power through recreational programmes.

***Under Literacy***-The adult was enabled to write his name and names of his relations, mohalla, village tahsil, block, district, State and country etc. and to write simple letters.

***Under Civic Rights and Duties***-To enable the adults to read and understand the related books, newspapers.

***Under Developing Thinking Power***-To teach to count upto 100 and do simple additions, subtractions multiplications and divisions and to measure weight length and to understand values of coins.

For the above objectives cultural functions, sports, games and exhibitions were to be organised.

It was decided that the Adult Education Camps will be established throughout the whole country. A scheme was made in Madhya Pradesh to train volunteers. The volunteers were to be of at least 16 years of age and at least seventh class passed. A director was also to be appointed to supervise the work of these volunteers. A camp was to be run for five weeks. This scheme of running camps went on very well in Madhya Pradesh.

In other States also the above scheme was started and in some of them the duration of a camp was made of eight weeks. The college and school teachers were encouraged to work in these camps during their leave or leisure period.

Under the social education scheme it was aimed to educate the villagers in civic duties and responsibilities and to educate their total personality. Some arrangements were also made for their recreation and also to impart them general knowledge. Some pilot projects were also opened in some States for giving social education. In various Five Year Plans much work was done towards the achievement of the objectives of social education. However, the expected success could not be achieved. For social education, Janta Colleges. Libraries and social centres were opened. A programme for producing social education literature and its distribution amongst adults was chalked out. We are hinting below at the nature of these:

***Social Centres***-The purpose of asocial centre was to impart social and cultural education to adults. In it there was an arrangement for healthy recreation. It was generally opened in the Panchayat Centre school and other places of social gathering.

***Libraries***-For these such places were selected where there could be good gathering. Books relating to agriculture industries civic principles literature, business and trade, health and domestic science were kept in these libraries in order that the adults could benefit themselves by these.

***Janta Colleges***-The purpose of these colleges was to train workers for working at the social centres in villages. These workers were to function as leaders in social and public work. Simplicity and utility was emphasised in these colleges with a view to give cultural and social education to trainees who will guide the adults for achieving the purposes of social education.

For framing the curriculum for Janta Colleges, a conference was arranged in Mysore for seven days in 1956. This conference made the following recommendations:

1. The Janta Colleges should be run in such a way that the teacher and taught may live together. Sufficient land should be given to each Janta College for agricultural work.

2. The Government should take its entire responsibility or it should be entrusted to good voluntary organisations.

3. The Government should give adequate financial aid and other facilities to Janta colleges.

4. Persons within the age group of 15 and 40 years alone should be admitted in them. There should be separate colleges for men and women.

The Government of India has produced more than 300 books for social education in different Indian languages. Literature for children has also been published under the supervision of the government. The Central Government has introduced a scheme of giving 15 prizes of Rs. 500.00 each to writers of literature for adults. The government also gives awards to writers producing books for mass education.

The percentage of literacy very low in India. The success of democracy depends upon well educated citizens. The leaders of the country have realised this fact and they have made schemes for educating adults. Only literacy was not their aim. They aimed at social education which means educating the entire personality of the adult. For this purpose, adult education centres, libraries, reading rooms and Janta colleges have been opened. Suitable literature of various types has been produced for educating the adults. Education camps were also organised on the UNESCO method. Independent departments for social education were opened in various States. However, more efforts are needed in this direction.

## QUESTIONS

1. Write a short essay on social education in India.
2. What is the importance of social education for democracy?
3. Write short notes on Janta Colleges, Social Centres and UNESCO education plan for adults.

# 29

# University Education

During the British rule in India, there were about eighteen universities in the country. All taken together by 1947 at the end of the British rule, there were only 1,80,000 students receiving university education. During the Post independent period education was expanded at all levels-primary, secondary and university. The government opened many new universities and co-operated in the opening of new degree colleges. Education development schemes were also given a place in the various Five Year Plans. Scholarships and stipends were instituted for students and by 1957 the number of students in universities rose upto 6,00,000. The public was also attracted towards university education. So gradually the universities and degree colleges began to be overcrowded. In due course the Government had to face the difficult problems of giving admission to all the desirous ones.

Since the universities were limited in number, it was not possible to admit all the desirous ones in universities. Therefore, the Government encouraged the opening of many new degree colleges under the affiliation of nearby universities. For this purpose, a new affiliating universities were opened in all the States in the country.

**Different Universities**

Besides affiliating universities, a number of unitary universities have also been established. These universities do not affiliate have also been established. These universities do not affiliate colleges. There are some single faculty universities which are devoted to the study of subjects under one area, *e.g.*, Sanskrit University, Varanasi; Agricultural University, Pantnagar; Acharya Narendra Dev Agricultural University, Faizabad; a number of I. I. Ts teaching subjects under Engineering only. Our Government is thinking of opening some rural universities affiliating some degree colleges and secondary schools of the neighbouring areas. But so far this idea has been only in Government files. There are some federal universities as well like those of Bombay and Delhi. These universities do mostly post-graduate work and undergraduate teaching is done by the nearby affiliated colleges. Thus, there are the following five types of universities in our country:

1. Residential and Teaching or Unitary Universities affiliating some colleges as well, *e.g.*, Gorakhpur.
2. Unitary university which does not affiliate any college *e.g.*, Varanasi and Aligarh.
3. Federal university, *e.g.*, Delhi.
4. Affiliating university, *e.g.*, Bundelkhand.
5. Single Faculty University, Roorkee.

**Major Difficulties**

Now we shall understand some of the main problems relating to university education.

***University and the Government.*** All the universities in the country are dependent on government grants. On the recommendations of the University Grants Commission, the Central Government gives grants to the State and Central Universities. Hence both Central and State Governments are responsible for financing universities. This arrangement gives a scope to both the Centre and State to interfere in university affairs. The government controls the university in the following manner:

1. The Governor of the State is the Chancellor of the University. For the Central Universities, the president is the visitor. This feature is a hindrance in the autonomy of the university. The Regulations passed by the Executive Council or the Senate are finally approved by the Chancellor. If the Chancellor does not agree, the same may be cancelled.

2. The Vice-chancellor's appointment is also controlled by the Governor. Hence it is just possible that due to political pressure of the ruling party, the Chancellor appoints a Vice-chancellor. In fact, this generally happens. Consequently, the Vice-chancellor is always afraid of the Chancellor and he cannot displease him. Thus, the Vice-chancellor becomes responsible to the ruling party indirectly. So the autonomy of the university is infringed.

3. There are certain members of the Executive Council as representatives of the government; These members do not co-operate with the Executive Council if it wants to frame some rules and regulations within the jurisdiction of its autonomy.

4. When the atmosphere of the university becomes tense because of students' problems, the government interferes through its P. A. C. who terrorise the teachers and students. As a result, sometimes the university is closed for months.

5. Since the university has to function within the direct or indirect control of the government many small and big

matters become pending because the government instructions are awaited for the same. These instructions are strictly according to the government rules even when they are to affect the university functioning adversely.

6. According to the Indian Constitution university education is a responsibility of the State. As already stated earlier, our universities depend upon government grants for their existance. Hence their powers and regulations are determined by the government. The legislature of the States decide about the powers and jurisdiction of the universities. Not only this even the opening of a University depend upon the resolution passed by the State legislature.

7. The State Government is responsible also for the development of primary and secondary education. A major portion of the funds allocated for education by the State Government is spent over primary and secondary education. So the State government is not able to spend much on university education. Hence it, has to depend mainly upon the Central Government for financial support.

The Central Government is wholly responsible for running Central universities in the country but it has also to help the State Governments. Many of the university schemes in the State are not started unless sufficient grant is sanctioned by the Centre for the same. Under the circumstances the universities are practically under the control of the government.

**The Interaction**

In view of the above situation it is necessary to think over the question of relationship between the government and universities and also about the nature of autonomy that the university should be free to enjoy. In fact the government must not interfere in the internal affairs of the university. The university should be made free to do anything in the interest of raising of the academic standards and they should always be given the necessary grants without any string attached. Their files must not remain pending in the government secretariat. The Chancellor should give his approval to any plan or scheme or regulation submitted by the university, provided the same are sure to fulfil the objectives for which the university is established. Ministers and members of the legislature must not bring any undue pressure on the university for getting anything done. Party politics nepotism and casteism should be discouraged. The Vice-chancellor should he selected on merits and not on the basis of party politics. These days a tendency is seen to appoint retired government officers as Vice-chancellors These retired persons are generally tools in the hands of the government. The person appointed as a Vice-chancellor should be an educationist a good administrator and a person who has always been above the board. He should be a person who can think for the university and who can initiate and execute with out any fear of anyone, no matter how much that "anyone" is influential.

The university must be getting financial help timely, but the government should also see that this help is properly utilized. The financial resources must not be misused. Unworthy persons must not be appointed anywhere for any university work. It must be seen that the university is developing the spirit of democratic attitudes and behaviour and is strengthening the bonds of national integrity. If this spirit is violated, the government may interfere in the best Interests of higher education but never under pressure of party politics.

Universities and degree colleges have to function under a free environment in order that the main work of teaching, study, guidance and research does not suffer. In the absence of freedom of speech and thought, the purpose of this main work will be defeated. The universities and colleges must not be made centres of casteism, groupism, regionalism conspiracy and party politics, otherwise their very purpose will be defeated.

***Financial Problem of Universities.*** Universities and degree colleges have many items demanding heavy expenditure, but their source of income is quite poor. Students' fees and donations are the chief sources of income, but these taken together do not meet even half of the expenses. Hence they always depend upon government grants. Due to the increase in the number of private candidates the number of regular students has gone down resulting into loss of revenue to the university.

The University Commission of 1948-49 has suggested that the government through the University Grants Commission should give financial aid to universities and degree colleges for implementing the U. G. C. grades for teachers, for study leave, Provident fund, libraries laboratories, buildings, construction of hostels and teachers' residences, pension, development of means for teaching and research, technological and vocational education. Some special grants were given for implementing the scheme of three year degree courses.

The concerned institutions should be informed at the beginning of the session about the kind and amount of grant to be given. This timely information will help the institution a great deal in planning their schemes and programmes. There should be some permanent recurring grant and some grant to meet contingencies. It is very happy feature in the State of Uttar Pradesh that the government has taken the full responsibility for paying salaries to teachers and for this 80 per cent of students' fees are deposited in the government treasuries.

***Problem of Students Admission.*** With the increase in number of universities and colleges the number of students seeking admission has increased so much that all of them cannot be admitted. Hence new regulations have been made for permitting to sit at examinations as private candidates. Now the question arises if everyone should get higher education or should only a selected few having the necessary aptitudes and capabilities? After obtaining university education the graduate wanders here and there seeking some employment, but only a few get some service. The rest remain unemployed because the university education has not created in them a spirit of self-dependence and they have also not acquired any vocational skill for earning a living. So our universities and degree colleges are increasing the number of unemployed persons. This is not in national interest. In fact, only the persons having that aptitude and ability to benefit from university education should be permitted to go in for this. The rest should be encouraged to take some other worthwhile pursuits or diverted to obtaining some vocational skills for becoming economically self-dependent ultimately. This may be possible if vocational education is made compulsory at the secondary stage. This will solve the problem of unemployment in a way.

There should be some national policy regarding admission of students to universities and colleges. It is often seen that a suitable student is refused admission to the university and an unfit one is easily admitted. In fact, the admission policy should be objective and scientific. Those who cannot benefit from university education should be diverted to take up some such fruitful pursuits which may add to the national prosperity. It will be a national waste of time, energy and money if without due selection all are given admission to universities.

***Problem of Duration of Degree Courses.*** Since there are individual differences in terms of capacity, it is not good to make the duration of courses the same for all. Some can complete the courses earlier and some will naturally take more time. In our country somewhere the degree course is of three year duration and somewhere of two year. Wherever the system of intermediate education exists the degree course is of two years after the intermediate education. The poor students need to earn a living also along with their studies. Hence they should get the facility of part-time courses.

***The Problem of University Curriculum.*** After achievement of independence an attempt has been made to infuse the spirit of nationalism, internationalism and national integration in our students at all levels-primary, secondary and university. Accordingly, many necessary improvements have been made in the courses at all these stages. However, the courses still suffer from certain inadequacies at all the levels of education. The following are the inadequacies at the university level:

(1) Only a few subjects of study are available in the degree colleges. Hence the students do not get subjects corresponding to their interests and abilities.

(2) There is no provision to measure the relative merits of the students in order to guide them to more suitable pursuits. For this guidance bureaus should be instituted in each degree college and university for helping the students to choose subjects according to their interests and abilities.

(3) Vocational subjects should also be given due place in the curriculum in order that the desirous students may acquire some vocational skill by the end of university education. This will help them to stand upon their own legs after receiving university education and they will not run only after seeking some office jobs.

(4) Social sciences and natural sciences should be given a wider place in the university curriculum. This is necessary to acquaint the students with the latest development in the field of arts and sciences. This will broaden their outlook.

(5) The various subjects in the curriculum should be integrated and correlated as far as possible. In other words, interdisciplinary approach is necessary for liberalising the students.

(6) Even in specialised courses, an attempt should be made to acquaint the students with the rudiments of some other subject which are generally related with the common day human affairs.

***The Problem of Medium of Instruction.*** Upto 1960 or so the medium of university education has been generally English. But afterwards the situation changed and a demand came from the student community to make the regional language as the medium of university education. This demand has been met fully at the under-graduate level and partially at the post-graduate level. However, in many universities at the post-graduate as well, the regional language has been accepted as the medium. But the spirit of English is still living and the students using regional language as the medium are frowned upon within the minds of most of the teachers. This position is not happy, as it is not helpful to the growth of our Indian languages in the various parts of the country. In institutions of higher learning where vocational and technological and medical courses are taught, English still remains the chief medium of instruction. Perhaps, it will take at least 25 years more to switch over to Indian languages as the medium of instruction at the university stage. Ofcourse, undue hurry must not be made. First of all suitable text books of high standard should be produced in our Indian languages before the same are fully accepted as the media of instruction. In this sphere, our government has to playa special role. It should invite suitable subject-persons to write good text books on various subjects or to produce good translations of standard works. Unhappily in this connection as well, nepotism and favourtism play the major role in the selection of prospective writers. In fact, the chosen writers should know the subject as well as the language in which they have to produce the standard original or translation works.

Instances are too many to be quoted here. In each and every discipline of study translations of standard works have been made by persons who though having the command over the language in which translation has been made, have never got a chance to learn the subject for which they take the responsibility to prepare the translation works. The remedy to eradicate this evil practice is obvious.

***Problem of Teaching.*** It is often said that the standard of teaching in universities and degree colleges has fallen down to a deplorable degree and this fall is persistently continuing. Some people say that in each and every department in a university or degree college, there are some teachers who seldom teach. Such teachers even do not go to visit the department except when they have to collect their mails or sometimes they come to show their faces to the peons or office clerks who mark them present in their minds in order to speak to the immediate boss that they had been in the department. Some other people are of the view that there are some teachers who usually go late to the class by 15 or 20 minutes and leave the class usually before the period is over. Whereas, so they say, there are some other teachers who talk in the class about everything else except the subject which they are supposed to teach. Some contend that there are some teachers who are, in fact, politician teachers, busy in mustering votes or consent in their favour or in favour of their candidates or proposals in some meetings. There are some teachers in their opinion, who take much pleasure in back-biting and in black-mailing other teachers. Many teachers appear to be more interested in gaining favours from the Heads or the Vice-chancellor. Such teachers are hovering around the authorities in order that they may favour them in some way or other. There is much tussle in some teachers over obtaining examinership fetching greater amount of remuneration. In all these tragic situations, the sacred task of teaching and research which is the main duty of the university and degree college teacher is thrown to winds. To capture whole thing, there are some heads of departments who take some special pleasure in tyrannising some and in distributing favours to a few only. It is true that there are some heads of departments who take real interest in teaching and doing high order of research, but their number is very few. There are some heads of departments who try to add feathers to their clumsy caps all the basis of research works done by their junior colleagues and research scholars who have always to depend upon their whimsical mercies.

Since 1973 the pay-scales of university and degree college teachers have been made even better than many first class officers of the State and Central Governments. Then, there is no reason why the concerned teachers in universities and degree colleges cannot give up their low mentality and be dutiful towards the work they are handsomely paid for.

***Problem of Examination System.*** The current system of examination is critical in various ways. The main purpose of examination, today, has become to obtain good divisions in examinations. For his purpose, many students resort to unfair means so much so that they regard that using unfair means is their birth right. Unhappily, the teaching is also subordinated to examination. If some teachers happen to set the examination papers they choose to teach only that portions which they have included in the questions-paper. In the examination halls the teachers are terrorised and sometimes even assaulted. Such is the examination system. Now it is a general practice that examination is now conducted with the help of P. A. C.

For doing away with the evils of examination system the University Commission (1948-49) had suggested that internal assessment, from time to time should be given due weightage in finalising the final division for a candidate. For this the Commission has recommended that there should be fortnightly, monthly, third-monthly and six-monthly examinations also and the marks of all these examinations should be added to the division to be finally awarded on the basis of an annual examination. The students' day to day work should also be evaluated towards deciding the fito be givenn to be given to a student. The Commission has further recommended that the question-papers should be framed under the supervision of an examination committee which should be constituted by responsible teachers of great repute. The question-paper should have some objective items also. Accordingly, some efforts have been made to improve the examination system in our university, hut much more efforts are needed, otherwise the unfair and criminal practices resorted to by some students in the examination hall will not be curbed.

***The Problem of Social Service.*** One of the aims of university education is to fulfil some social purposes. So one of the duties of the university is to give such a training to students that they may be able to render some social service. In U. S. A. every student at the graduate level is required to do some social service. This compulsion creates a spirit of rendering some social service in the students and develops traits of healthy citizenship. So some opportunities should be created in the University in the form of social service. Under these opportunities, we may mention recreational programmes, extension lectures, dramas, exhibitions, cleaning and health programme etc. Now through the government initiative National Social Service programmes have been started in the universities. In affiliated colleges as well these programmes are instituted. The government allocates crores of rupees in every Five Year Plan for National Social Service programmes. In fact, this (N. S. S.) should be made compulsory for each university and degree college student.

***University Education Getting Expensive.*** The university education in our country is getting very expensive. The poor students inspite of their suitability for higher education are deprived of higher education because of its being too expensive. In U. S. A. part-time courses and adult education schemes have been instituted for helping poor students who can earn a part of their expenses while getting higher education. There the State universities and colleges charge nominal fees from the resident students of their own State. Thus higher education is brought within the reach of many students. The university also tries to give part-time employment to the students, if they, themselves, cannot find some. Some such kind of arrangement is necessary in our country also in order that the poor students may not be deprived of the opportunity to get higher education.

***Problem of Affiliation of Colleges.*** Universities alone cannot fulfil the needs of higher education. So some degree colleges are opened and they are affiliated to a university on fulfilment of certain prescribed conditions. These degree colleges teach courses prescribed by the university and teachers of these colleges are also appointed by the experts appointed by the university. Their examination is also conducted by the university. In U. P. now the Government has constituted a commission for appointment of degree college teachers. It should be noted that degree colleges are not so equipped as the universities are. So the standard of work there is generally lower than that in the university. There are very few degree colleges where independent research works are done. For many academic matters the degree colleges have to look towards the universities for guidance. Since the degree colleges have to be run parallel to the universities within the specified area of work, they are, just busy in duplicating in a poorer manner the work that the universities are doing. Under the circumstances, the degree colleges are not able to meet the local requirements. Moreover, many degree colleges are running on commercial lines. Such colleges offer illegal gratification to some persons in power for getting their work done in the university. Many bogus and false papers are submitted at the time of submitting application for affiliation. Certain unscrupulous persons help these delinquent colleges to spring up just to lower the standard of higher education. The university authorities must see that such proposed colleges are not granted affiliation and the delinquent ones are diaffinated.

***Problem of Research Work.*** To do research work of high standard is one of the prime duties of a university. Its function is not only to teach, conduct examination and confer degrees. Before independence satisfactory facilities were not available in universities for research. But not our State and Central Government are keen about higher order of research in various areas of study. So they are giving crores of rupees to various universities for this purpose. However, it will have to be admitted thin there are very few research works done by universities which have won international recognition. So much more efforts are needed in this direction. Most of teachers and students in universities do not appear to be very enthusiastic for high order of research. In this respect their main aim to help getting the doctorate degree any how. The result is that the degree is awarded but the thesis which fetches the degree is seldom an original piece of research of a high standard. Consequently, the same never comes before others and ever remains in the bound thesis itself. The need of the hour in this respect is to establish good laboratories, workshops and libraries where all needed research facilities are available to worthy researchers. The supervisors should be appointed with great care. They should have a missionary zeal to help the students and they must not require the research scholars to attend to their (supervisors) dometic affairs. It is an open secret that many research scholars are being misused by their supervisors in this manner.

They unnecessarily take 4 to 5 years to complete their so-called research work. Chapters embodying the results of certain investigations lie for months or years with the supervisors who are busy in many other mundane affairs-but not in actual research which they falsely profess to conduct. Such supervisors who are dishonest to their research scholars must give up their bad habits in the best interests of high order of research.

***The Problem of the Registrar.*** The Registrar occupies a special position in the administration of a university in our country. He is one of those officers of the university who are most overworked. He goes to his office early and comes back home late. His major job is to sign documents and various types of papers. He answers a number of telephones and studies files. He has to be so busy that he has , more than full time work. He enjoys a good salary and occupies a good position in the community. It is he who moves the whole administrative machinery of the university. He has to record, observe and listen. He has to make arrangements for admission, examination and convocation under the regulations specified by the Executive Council. If there are a number of affiliated colleges under the university, the job of the registrar becomes all the more difficult. He has to receive a number of Principals and teachers and students of degree colleges affiliated to the university and these persons think that the registrar has some remedy for all the problems of their own creation. The registrar, at times, is generally *gheraoed* by student-leaders for change of dates of examination and other things about which he is helpless. Under the circumstances, the job of the registrar becomes extremely difficult. It is true that he is assisted by a number of Dy. Registrars, Assistant Registrars and host of office superintendents and other assistants, but each one of these officials, high or low, have their own strong points over which the registrar has little control. Because of his onerous duties, the registrar occupies a pivotal position in the university administration in our country. Hence in any reform of university education, his position and office has to be seriously considered.

If the registrar happens to be a good, strong, honest and sincere person, everything will go on well with the university. If he is otherwise, becomes a centre of all sorts of politics cliques, groupism, nepotism, favouritism, casteism and other evils that go in train with these undesirable and unhealthy traits. Sometimes it is seen that the registrar controls the appointment of teachers in many ways. Some people think that he tries to manipulate the creation or abolition of teaching posts if his fancy or group so goads him. Some others are of the view that if circumstances have become such that he is to fail to get persons of his own group or caste appointed, then he indirectly sees that the outside experts who have to serve on Selection Committee are wrongly advised telegraphically about the postponement of the selection. Some other persons are of the view that a vicious registrar deliberately puts in some flaw or inadequacies in the wordings of the advertisement which is challanged in courts later. Certain registrars had become so vicious and malicious in their approach and method of work that U. P. Govt., has made the post of the registrar transferable within the State since 1976. Many people related to university education have taken a sigh of relief at this new order of the U.P. Government, because they believe that with the transfer of registrars from one university to another many of the evils usually associated with his office will automatically vanish. In fact, whether the evils associated with his office will go away or not depends upon the particular personality that occupies the office. Hence it is necessary that a registrar should be selected after great care and scrutiny. He should be a person of high academic merits and experienced in university work and administration and above all he should be a person ahove the hoard. His integrity must not be questionable. It is a common knowledge that there have been many registrars who have openly defied the orders of their Vice-chancellors and the weak Vice-chancellors have not been able to do anything against them. On this score there have been many Vice-chancellors who have resigned in disgust. Evidently, the registrar has become a problem for the university. So ways and means must be found out to solve this problem in a constructive manner before it is too late.

***University Education.*** Inadequate in view of the large number of students. Many new universities and degree colleges are established. Residential, Unitary and affiliation universities.

***University Education and the Government.*** Autonomy necessary in the university. Too much governmental control. For the development of democracy good regulations should be framed. The university to be free from party politics. The government to give adequate finance and be no undue interference in its internal matters.

***The Economic Problem of Universities.*** The university dependent upon government help. Many of its plans and schemes bagged down due to red-tapism. The financial grant to be given should he announced in the beginning of the session.

***The Problem of Admission of Students.*** All cannot be admitted otherwise the educated unemployed will increase in number. The suitable ones alone to be admitted. Vocational education necessary at the secondary stage.

***Problem of Duration of Courses.*** Individual differences. Hence the same duration for all is not suitable. Two year and three year degree courses. Students should be made free to seek part-time employment.

***The Problem of Curriculum.*** Too many courses should be instituted in order to cater to the varying needs of the different students. Educational and vocational guidance necessary. Integrated courses. Inter-disciplinary approach.

***The Problem of Medium of Study.*** Regional language as the medium of instruction, English to be considered as important.

***The Problem of Teaching.*** Teachers to do research also. Good teachers should be appointed.

***The Problem of Examination.*** The current system defective. Objective tests should also be introduced. Internal assessment to be given due weightage. Weekly, fortnightly, monthly, third-monthly and six-monthly internal examinations should be arranged.

***The Problem of Social Service.*** Compulsory at the graduate level. The National Social Service scheme good.

***Too much Expensive and Adult Education.*** Part-time courses and adult education scheme.

***The Problem of Affiliation.*** Affiliation keeping in view the local needs.

***The Problem of Research.*** Facilities should be increased.

***The Problem of the Registrar.*** Pivotal position. Overworked. Must be a man of integrity and above party politics. Appointment with great care.

## QUESTIONS

1. Suggest any three measures for reforms of university education.
2. Discuss any two problems of university education.
3. Should the university enjoy full autonomy? Give reasons.
4. Discuss the internal problems of the university. How can they be resolved?
5. How does a registrar of a university occupy a pivotal position in the university administration? Suggest measures for making his functioning smooth.

# 30

# School Education

Secondary education is that kind of education which is given after primary education and before university education *i.e.,* it includes all the classes after the primary school and before the university. Before Independence secondary education was classified in different manners, such as-vernacular middle school, matriculation, entrance, high school and intermediate etc. Education has been grouped into primary, secondary and university stages in different countries, but the duration of secondary education may differ in one country from that in other. At some places secondary classes begin from the sixth class and go up to twelfth. Somewhere upper primary classes go up to the eighth class and secondary classes start from the ninth and go upto eleventh or twelfth.

### Different Levels

Before independence the form of secondary education in India was prescribed by foreign educationists. Foremerly primary classes were designed upto fifth class but they generally stopped at the fourth class. Middle classes were run from fifth to seventh and high school and intermediate classes were run from eighth to twelfth. After independence the form of secondary education changed. Now the seven year secondary education is generally current. But somewhere this seven year curriculum is known as high school system. With some modification secondary education has been divided into three groups-from sixth to eighth junior high school, from ninth to tenth high school and eleventh and twelfth have been regarded as higher secondary or intermediate classes. The Mudaliar Commission (1952-53) has termed secondary education as higher secondary education and ninth to eleventh classes were included in it and the twelfth class was termed as pre-university class. Thus in India, the following two types of secondary education is current:

1. Intermediate

2. Higher Secondary

The Kothari Commision (1964-66) has recommended the intermediate system and has emphasised the three year degree course. All the States in the country have not accepted this revised pattern.

**The Infrastructure**

On the Basic education pattern, secondary education has been divided into basic and non-basic groups. Basic education, too was divided into pre-basic and post-basic. Within the basic scheme it was planned to teach the curriculum of the seven or eight year secondary school in six years. In this system the three year Higher Basic Course was considered to be equivalent to the three year higher secondary school course. In order to implement this scheme it was planned to establish a model Higher Secondary schools in rural and urban areas. In this educational organisation the introduction of three year degree course was also planned.

Mudaliar Commission had emphasised the need of reorganisation of secondary education. It recommended the introduction of three year degree course by changing the prevailing intermediate system into Higher Secondary. As already observed earlier, it has not been possible of introduce the basic system. The General Government accepted the recommendation of the Mudaliar Commission and advised the various States to introduce the three year degree course. The Commission also emphasised the need of establishing multi-purpose schools for introducing a vocational approach. The Government of India gave financial help to the States for establishing multipurpose schools. But this adventure has not been successful as expected. In partial acceptance of recommendations of the Mudaliar Commission classes 6, 7 and 8 were grouped under junior high school and 9, 10 and 11 were placed under the Higher Secondary. Kothari Commission has also emphasised the introduction of three year degree course. Below we shall understand the current organisation of the secondary education.

**High Schools**

The following types of secondary schools are generally found in India:

1. Intermediate Colleges.

2. High School and Junior High School.

3. Higher Secondary Schools.

4. Multi-purpose Schools.

5. Special Schools.

**10 + 2 Schools**

In U. P. intermediate education system has been accepted. Under this system classes 6, 7 and 8 are grouped under lower secondary, classes 9 and 10 are termed as High School and classes

11 and 12 are known as Higher Secondary. In Intermediate Colleges, there are two public examinations one at the end of class X and the other at the end of class XII. The college itself conducts the examination at the end of the Junior High School stage, *i.e.*, at class VIII, but the two public examinations are conducted by the U. P. Board.

High Schools are those secondary schools where the final examination of class X is conducted by the U. P. Board of High School and Intermediate Education. The examination of Junior High School is conducted by the institution itself. In these, schools classes 6, 7 and 8 are grouped under junior high school and classes IX and X are known as High School. The junior high schools were formerly known as middle schools or vernacular middle schools.

According to the recommendations of the Mudaliar Commission the Government of India has advised the States to run three year Higher Secondary Schools and three year degree courses. But many State Governments have expressed their inability on financial grounds to introduce this scheme. In the States where this new scheme has been accepted in principle, the progress of changing of high schools into higher secondary schools is very slow. Many universities have not accepted the three year degree course. Although the Central Government has agreed to shoulder the 60 per cent expenditure of this changeover, but the State Governments have not been able to manage for the remaining 40 per cent. The Central Government has tried to encourage the opening of multipurpose schools, but the success in this area has not been satisfactory.

The State Governments are not taking interest in opening Higher Secondary Schools, because they cannot appoint the necessary number of teachers. Another difficulty in this process is that they will have to make corresponding changes in the university system as well by way of running three year degree courses. The State Governments do not feel equal to the extra financial burden involved. The three year degree courses have been organised at places where three year secondary courses are in operation. There the Secondary Education Board conducts the public examination at the end of class XI. The candidates passing this examination are admitted to the three year degree courses.

**Model Institutions**

Mudaliar Commission recommended the opening of multi-purpose schools for giving a more meaningful vocational and pragmatic bias to education at the secondary stage. This system is regarded as very expensive, because a multi-purpose school requires a special school building, various types of tools, implements, laboratories, spacious land for farming, workshops, reading rooms and other reasonable facilities. Naturally, these things will involve heavy expenditure. Moreover, arranging for at least two or more types of vocations in the school becomes all the more expensive.

Because of the various types of curriculum in these schools, many subject-groups will have to be organised. In these schools such teachers will have to be appointed who can forge a co-relation between the teaching of various subjects. In other words, they should be trained in vocationally oriented courses. So far no arrangement has been made by university or any other State organisation to produce such trained teachers.

Multi-purpose schools may be opened as models in government institutions only. The private institutions cannot run such schools for obvious reasons. Some courses of the multipurpose schools may be taught in some vocational and industrial institutions. A harmony may be created between the general and vocational courses if the two are taught together in some industrial institutions.

There might be numerous difficulties in opening multi-purpose schools, but there is no denying of the fact that they are very useful and hence important. The multipurpose schools create self-independence and some vocational skill and develop both general intelligence and some vocational aptitude. In these schools, a student is more likely to get subjects of his special bent of mind. When students of various subjects and trade study together, they naturally acquire better social sense. Then they may also develop the spirit of mutual co-operation and brotherhood.

We shall have to change the form of the prevailing schools in order to introduce the Basic System of Education. According to the reçommendations of the Secondary Education Commission (1952-53), the Government of India planned to change the prevailing secondary schools into single purpose schools and new higher secondary schools. It was also thought to correlate the high schools in the rural area with the life of the villagers.

In U. K. the single-purpose schools are quite important. So the policy of establishing single-purpose school in India was also accepted. In the single purpose School the inadequacies of the multi-purpose schools may be avoided. Hence it was considered as more practicable to establish single purpose schools of literature, commerce, science, engineering, fine arts and agriculture etc.

Since about 70 per cent of the population of India resides in villages, opening of agricultural higher secondary schools in rural areas should be emphasised. Untill now during the periods of various Five Year Plans, educational development of villages has not been done. By the end of the Fifth Five Year Plan only in about 500 secondary schools teaching of agriculture, cottage industries, gardening and animal husbandry could be organised in the country. More attention is needed towards this development during the Sixth Five Year Plan period.

**Major Difficulties**

Now it is necessary to know the problems that are obstructing the growth of secondary education. Needless to say that growth of secondary education will not be satisfactory unless these problems are solved. In short, the main problems of secondary education may be enumerated as follows:

1. The problem of organisation and form of secondary schools.
2. The problem of determination of aims of secondary education.
3. The problem of constructing the curriculum.
4. The problem of examination.
5. The problem of management and administration.
6. The problem of lack of finance.
7. The problem of lack of necessary teachers.
8. The problem of supervision.

We shall understand each of these problems below:

***The Problem of Organisation and Form of Secondary Schools.*** There is no similarity in the forms of various secondary schools existing in our country. We have already hinted at this above under the 'organisation' section. We have also pointed towards the solution of this problem. It is not necessary to state the same here again. However, it may be said that if the forms of secondary schools of the various States of the country were the same, the students will not feel much difficulty in going for education from one State to another.

***The Problem of Determination of aims of Secondary Education.*** The Indian Constitution has provided for free and compulsory primary education. So our government has done important work in this direction. This feature has an impact on secondary education. Consequently, the number of students at the secondary stage has increased enormously. So the Government has tried to make provision for secondary education for the students coming after passing primary schools. Several new secondary schools have been opened during the various Five Year Plans. The number of students at the secondary stage has increased, but we have not been able to give them education which may enable them to stand on their own legs. Hence education imparted to them has been merely theoretical. Today the student has only two following options after having received secondary education:

1. To enter some university for further education,

2. To roam about here and there in search of some service.

The above situation is an impediment in the progress of our country. In many western countries secondary education has been so organised that after obtaining it the student is able to stand on his own legs in some vocational area. But in our country the current secondary education is accentuating the unemployment problem. Therefore, we have to make our secondary education, so useful that the students having passed this stage do not run only for admission to universities and unemployment does not increase and they become economically independent by having acquired some vocational skill of productive nature. We need able citizens for making our democracy a success. Therefore, the ultimate aim of secondary education should be to prepare such self dependent and dutiful citizens who are imbued with the spirit of intelligent patriotism contributing to the prosperity of the country.

In secondary education we have to pay special attention to the programme which contributes to the formation of characters. The purpose of our education is not only to offer opportunities for acquiring certificates but to produce youths of character. Our education has not only to impart bookish knowledge but to give such a knowledge which may contribute to personal, social and national prosperity. We want all-round development of our children. We want to make them physically, mentally, economically, morally and for think themselves and who may acquire such experiences which they may fruitfully utilise. Secondary education should be diverted to the fulfilment of all these noble objectives.

***The Problem of Constructing the Curriculum.*** In order to achieve the above objectives of secondary education, we shall have to make its curriculum more practical and useful. It is true that due to geographical variations, the needs of one State differ from those of another. However, for the whole country, we may prepare such a curriculum in outline that it is helpful in meeting the national goals. The Government of India is conscious of this necessity. The All India Board of Secondary Education has suggested that some subjects should be compulsorily taught in all the secondary schools in the country. It is trying to forge out such a curriculum which may achieve the national goals and also meet the regional needs of all classes and groups.

The problem of language teaching is a difficult issue in the curriculum construction. Hindi has been accepted as the national language of the country. Hence some people contend that each student should be taught Hindi. But some open-Hindi speaking States are opposing Hindi on the plea that it is being imposed on minorities. Many groups in South India favour English in place of Hindi. There are many people in our country who are still supporters of English. Ours is a religious country. Our basic scriptures are in Sanskrit. Hence there are many who still love Sanskrit. Keeping all these factors in view it has been proposed that at least three language should be taught at the secondary level. This is known as the Three Language Formula which may be understood as below:

(1) National language or regional language for non-Hindi speaking people.

(2) If Hindi has not been taken as a national language then Hindi or any other Indian language or Sanskrit.

(3) Sanskrit or any Indian language if not taken then a Western language (English, French or German).

In this arrangement the student will study the national language along with a regional language and as a third language he will either study Sanskrit or any foreign language.

It has been considered necessary to understand the problem relating to the aptitude and interests of students, regional needs, mother-tongue as the medium of instruction, arragement for counselling and guidance and the appropriate method for implementing the curriculum in order that some uniformity may be forged in the curriculum at the secondary stage. General science and social studies were included as the compulsory subjects keeping in view the understanding capacity of the students at the secondary level. For the other subjects students have been made free to choose their optionals according to their needs; interests, age and capacity. Keeping in view the present needs of the nation industrial, vocational and technical subjects were also included in the curriculum.

*At the Junior Secondary Level*-The above mentioned three languages, three compulsory subjects, general science, social studies, mathematics agriculture or any fine art or some commercial subject or music or physical exercises for physical development have been accepted as the main aspects of the curriculums.

*At the Higher Secondary Level*-According to recommendations of the Secondary Education Commission (1952-53) various groups have been formed for the compulsory languages and for interests of students. An attempt has been made to make curriculum multi-purpose by emphasising the inclusion of industrial and vocational subjects and crafts.

***The Problem of Examination.*** The prevailing essay type of examination has developed so many defects now that it is now no more a good measure of academic achievements and development of the students. But we cannot abolish it altogether. But we may introduce some changes and reforms into it.

External examination alone should not be accepted as a tool for measuring the success of the students. Internal examinations and tests should be used for examining the students. On the basis of all these the success or failure of a student should be determined. The sessional work of the whole year should be scrutinised. Monthly and third monthly records of the students should be prepared. Instead of marks their abilities should be measured in grades. Along with subjective type of essay questions at least 40 per cent of the marks should be assigned to objective tests. Thus the current examination system may be reformed.

***The Problem of Management and Administration.*** Three types of secondary schools are current in India-(1) Government Schools (2) Private or non-government Schools and (3) Schools run by local bodies. All the Government Schools are fully controlled by the governmental machinery. Priavate schools are managed by private managing committees under the supervision of District Inspector of Schools or some other government officer. The government gives sufficient financial aid to all the schools. The school teachers in most of the States in the country are now paid by government treasuries. The local bodies have not been very much successful in running secondary schools. The Government itself controls the education of girls and technical education at the secondary level in many states. There are many voluntary organizations also running schools for girls and technical schools. But many of them are in bad shape. Their financial, educational, building and teacher problems are acute. At some places there are too many of such institutions and at other places there are none. Some schools do not fulfil all the conditions of recognition. But now the government has started interfering in the management of these weak institutions. It has also started appointing teachers of these schools and paying their salaries from the government treasuries.

The administration of the secondary schools does not appear to be efficient. There are such administrative units as-central, regional and district to carryon the work of educational administration. There is a Board of Secondary Education in each State for determination of the nature of the curriculum, text books and for conducting examination. Thus, there is a dual administration over the secondary schools-one by the board of secondary education and the other by the governmental education department consisting of Director, Deputy Director and inspectorate staff or by private managements. Because of this dual control the secondary schools are not achieving their purpose, beacause of lack of harmony and co-ordination between the officers of these two controlling units. In fact there should be a mutual co-operation between the two for achieving the objectives of secondary education. Only then the administration of secondary schools may be useful.

***The Problem of Lack of Finance.*** So far there have been many private and voluntary efforts for the expansion of education. The government has tried to establish only one of two model higher secondary school in each district. The schools run by voluntary organisations have always to face the problem of inadequate funds. Their financial resources are not good and they have to look for the government grants. Neither they have good school buildings nor good teachers and suitable teaching materials. These schools are not in a position to teach industrial and vocational subjects because they entail heavier expenditure. In the United States every citizen has to pay an educational cess in proportion to his income. Thus adequate finances are organised there for educational purposes. Similarly, in our country as well some educational tax may be levied. Gifts from wealthy persons in favour of schools may be encouraged by exempting the gifted amount from income tax. Huge amount of money is required for the school building, laboratories, reading rooms, libraries, sports materials, workshop, teachers' salaries and teaching materials. Both the government and the public should co-operate with each other for organising the necessary funds of the schools.

***The Problem of Sufficient Number of Teachers.*** Teachers are like the signal chord of the school. The school cannot function well if the teachers are not in adequate number. Today the schools have few able teachers. In many schools, at the time of appointment, caste and group considerations play the major role and the question of suitability is thrown to winds. Consequently, unsuitable teachers are appointed in some schools. Many of the managing committees are generally vindictive against teachers. Strikes and Dharnas by teachers have become a common feature in some of the schools. Now we need vocationally trained teachers for our multi-purpose schools. Our universities and Teachers' Training Colleges are not producing such teachers. Hence in the absence of suitable teachers, the multi-purpose school and vocationalisation of education are not succeeding. For the full implementation of Basic Education we need specially trained teachers. Hence the basic education has not succeeded, though there have been other reasons also for its failure. The government should take some positive steps to solve this problem.

***The Problem of Supervision.*** Supervision arrangement of the secondary schools is not adequate in view of their large number. The inspectors are so busy with their files in their office that they get little for supervision and inspection of schools under their charge. Moreover, the behaviour of inspectors with the teachers is below the norm. Their attitude appears to be that of a master. They do not consider themselves as co-partners of the teachers in the interes of the all round development of the students. In fact, their approaches should be constructive and helpful in the sacred task of teaching children. Their attitude should be democratic and they should try to solve the difficulties of the teachers in class room situations and elsewhere in a relevant manner. Some refresher course should also be organised for acquainting the inspectors with the latest development in the field of education.

***The Form of Secondary Education.*** A connecting chain between primary and university education. It three levels—Junior, High and Higher. Somewhere high school and intermediate and somewhere higher secondary schools. The Kothari Commission has recommended three year degree course after intermediate education.

***Organisation of Secondary Education.*** Basic, Non-basic, Multi-purpose, Vocational and Industrial. Higher Secondary and the three year degree course. In the intermediate system after the twelfth class two year degree course.

Secondary School.: 1. Intermediate, 2. High School, 3. Higher Secondary School, 4. Multi-purpose Schools. Special School.

***Main Problems of Secondary Education.*** (1) *The Problem of Organisation and Form*-No similar form of secondary education in the country. It should be made uniform as far as possible keeping in view the local and regional needs. *(2) The Problem of Aims*-Secondary education should be useful. It should not accentuate unemployment. To produce able, self-dependent, dutiful and patriotic citizens. *(3) The Problem of Constructing the Curriculum*-Various types of curriuclum in view of national goals and interests of different students. The local needs should also be considered. The curriculm should be flexible. It should be vocationally useful also. New subjects should be included. Three languages, compulsory subjects-mathematics, general science, social studies and optional subjects. *(4) The Problem of Examination System*-The current examination system is defective. The teaching is examination oriented Objective tests necessary. Internal assessments should also be considered in promotion. (5) *The Problem of Management and Administration*-The government should reasonably interfere for effecting reforms. Administration should not be dual. Co-operation between various departments. *(6) The Problem of Inadequate Finance*-The private schools in a bad shape. Conditions of recognitions should be met before giving grants. Both the public and the government should co-operate. *(7) The Problem of Inadequate, Number of Teachers*-Able and suitable teachers not, available every where. Teachers should be trained in basic and vocational curriculum also. *(8) The Problem of Supervision*-Inspectors should be trained. The approach should be democratic reformative and constructive. They are co-partners in the task of teachers. They should function as guides of teachers.

## QUESTIONS

1. Describe the nature of organisation and form of secondary education in India. What reforms will you suggest in the same and why?
2. What are the main problems of secondary education? How can be the problems of aims and useful curriculum be tackled?
3. How can the administration and finances of secondary education be improved?
4. What is the utility and problem of Multi-purpose schools?
5. What reforms will you suggest in the current examination system and why?
6. How can the supervision system of secondary education be improved?

# 31

# Elementary Education

Literacy percentage is very low in India, although the position has improved much after independence. Under the Indian Constitution a provision has been made for compulsory and free education upto the age of 14 years. But we have not yet achieved this target because of many difficulties. We are hinting at some of these below.

**Fundamental Problems**

The geographical factor has a great impact on man's life. His way of living, food habits, profession and means of transport and communications are greatly influenced by this factor. plateaus enjoyed by the people in the plains are not available for these in hilly areas and deserts. The geographical conditions of hilly areas and deserts demand new set-ups of life. Hills, plateaus, deserts, rivers, lakes dense forests separate people of one area with those of another. Means of transport are difficult in these areas. Hence people in these areas are separated from each other and are scattered here and there. In these areas, there is no dense population.

Hence it is not economically feasible to open a primary school for a few people. If it is done, a number of primary schools with very few children in each area will have to be opened and this will be impracticable in view of the meagre funds at the disposal of the authority responsible for providing education. Moreover, because of difficult and inadequate means of transport, children from one area cannot go to school founded in another area. As a result, children in unfavourable geographical localities do not get primary education. India is a land of villages. More than 70 per cent of the population reside in villages. People in villages have not yet been provided with educational facilities. Teachers do not like to work in schools of difficult geographical surroundings. Hence natural obstruction has come in the way of expansion of primary education.

## Hindering Factors

The British Government before independence was indifferent to primary education in our country. So it did not try to remove illiteracy prevailing in the land. But after independence, the India Government became keen to spread primary education throughout the whole country. As we have said earlier, it has provided in the Constitution to make primary education free and compulsory. Consequently, primary education was very much encouraged throughout the whole country. But still due to some political difficulty, the efforts in this direction have been faulty.

The policy followed by the Government for the expansion of primary education has been impracticable in view of the laid down purposes. Hence those concerned do not take much interest in the expansion. There is no mutual co-operation in the various Government departments. Another difficulty is that the work of primary education has been entrusted to local bodies, *i.e.* to municipal boards, district and town areas. These local bodies do not co-operate with the Government officers appointed for looking after primary education. Many of the schemes pertaining to primary education remain incomplete either due to want of money or carelessness. Moreover, it has not yet been surveyed as to how many primary schools are necessary in our, country. If through private enterprises some primary schools are established, the government does not give the necessary financial aid or through redtapism the same is blocked. The literacy expansion schemes are closely related to free and compulsory education. If the two are run together, primary education will expand. The public in the villages also does not feel very much enthusiastic about it. It opposes any move for taxation that the Village Panchayats are not fulfilling their objectives. All the local bodies are suffering under paucity of funds and they are not able to execute any educational scheme. The educational policies are not free from local and regional politics. The need of the hour is that the public and the government should co-operate with the efforts of the local bodies and education should be freed from all sorts of politics. Only then, primary education will expand.

There are many social evils in our country. Untouchability, class and caste differences, narrow religious beliefs, conservatism, illiteracy, communalism, nepotism and jealousy are some of the black spots of our society. People of different castes, religions and communities want to open schools just to educate their own children. At some places children of Harijans and the downtrodden are not admitted to schools. Children of caste Hindus do not like to mix up with the children of Harijans studying in the same schools. Language-problem also obstructs some children from going to schools. Due to Purdah system separate schools are demanded for girls. Some conservative parents do not sent their girls to school. Staunch social workers and efficient government officers are necessary to establish personal contacts with parents for removing their wrong notions which hamper the growth of education.

The national income is the index of the income of the common man. Our national income is not satisfactory. Hence the common man is spending difficult days. The distribution of wealth is very uneven in our country. Some people are having so much wealth that they do not know how to spend it, whereas there are many who do not know how to manage for the two square meals a day. Such poor people do not send their children to school, simply because they cannot meet the involved expenses. Moreover, these poor people persuade their grown up children for earning something in order to supplement the family income. The Government, too, has not been able to spend as much money on primary education as needful. Thus economic difficulties have come in the way of expansion of primary education.

**Methods of Teaching**

The atmosphere of the school should be so attractive and natural that the children may like to spend much of their time there. Such an atmosphere may be made available only when the teaching methods, devices and materials are organised on psychological lines. For our primary schools, we do not have suitable teachers. We lack appropriate teaching materials. Consequently, we have failed to give a suitable atmosphere to the school for attracting young children. The cruel and unpsychological behaviour of teachers and harsh corporal punishment force children to leave the school in the middle of the session. Due to paucity of funds and ignorance, suitable teaching materials are not organised. The teaching methods emphasise memorisation. The students are seldom encouraged to participate in educative activities. The Basic Education Scheme has not been implemented in its real sense. The children do not get any vocational orientation. Consequently, many guardians regard primary education as useless and unprofitable. So they employ their young children in their own professions.

**The Stalemate**

There is too much of wastage and stagnation at the primary stage of education. Many children leave school or fail due to the difficulties as pointed out above. Thus money, labour and time are wasted. Stagnation is also there when children due to failure repeat classes. Hence only the mention of this problem is enough here.

Suitable teachers for primary schools are not available in adequate number. Most of the teachers are intolerant and behave very harshly with children. Hence children are very much afraid of them and they do not like to go to school. It is a pity that even after obtaining training, there is found no change in the behaviour of teachers. Their ability to teach young children is doubtful. It appears that training has not produced any impact on them. Many primary schools are single-teacher schools. One single teacher is not able to teach five classes of the primary school. Thus lack of teachers vitiates the atmosphere of the school.

**Betterment Schemes**

We have already stated earlier that in our Indian Constitution a provision has been made for free and compulsory education for all children between 6 and 11 years of age. This has also been laid down that this may be extended upto 14 years of age. So some States implemented it for the children upto 14 years of age. It was planned that this scheme of free and compulsory education should be implemented upto the junior high school stage by 1960-61. But because of many difficulties, later on it was decided that free and compulsory education should be made available for children between 6 and 11 years of age. But when this objective could not be achieved by the end of the second Five Year Plan, this programme was extended in the third Five Year Plan. And for the fourth Five Year Plan, the scheme was revised for children between 6 to 14 years of age. But even by the end of the fourth five year plan this could not be achieved. For the implementation of this educational scheme many difficulties would have to be overcome. We are mentioning below these difficulties and also their solution.

**School Organisation**

For expansion of primary education new schools should be opened. These new schools be within the easy approach of children in order that they may not have to face the problem of transport. India is a land of villages. It will not be possible to open a school for each village. It is estimated that there are about six lac villages in the Country. In order to cater to the educational needs of children of these villages thousands of schools will have to be opened. These schools should be so placed as to within the easy reach of most of the children. Moreover, each of these schools should have a number of teachers. The ideal will be that there is a teacher for each class. Hence there should be five teachers for five classes of each primary school. These teachers should be well qualified and should be willing to serve in the area concerned otherwise after the appointment they will be trying for ; transfer. The school building should also be suitable. A new school may be established in the locality inhabited by at least 500 people. On the basis of survery, it has been found out 65% of the villages have less than 500 inhabitants. So a school may be established at such central place that it may serve a number of villages.

There is not much interest for education in villages. Many do not understand the importance of education because of being illiterate. Some do not sent their girls to school because of the Purdah system. Some keep their children at home in order that they may help them in earning their bread. Some are not able to educate their children because of pauciy of funds. Some want to train their children in their hereditary trade and do not send them to school. Keeping all these difficulties in view, the school system for villages should be so organised as to help the villagers to get solution of their problems in the school some how of other. This means that the curriculum of the school should be vocationally oriented according to the needs of the locality which the schools is supposed to serve. This will help the people to understand the utility of the school and as a result they will start taking interest in the education of their children. The school should function as a community development centre also. The school should try to develop all those skills in children the villagers want them to pick up in view of their particular profession, *i.e.*, agriculture and allied professional occupations.

The school should be organised for a particular area keeping in view its religious, cultural and social traditions. Then the public will feel a belongingness with the schools. If the public desires, separate schools should be run for girls. But it will be better if upto the primary stages co-education is encouraged. The primary schools should be established for educating the children of scheduled castes, tribes and backward classes according to their particular social and cultural traditions. If private enterprises are forthcoming in this direction, they should be fully encouraged.

Suitable buildings for primary schools are very necessary. So far, few of our primary schools have buildings worth the name. The building should be in open, healthy and clean place. There should be a big playground adjoining it in order to permit adequate physical activities of the school children. There should be some separate fields for agricultural workshops and practices in cottage industries.

Till suitable school buildings are provided, free and compulsory primary education may be imparted at such public places which may accommodate the teachers and students for the purpose. Village Panchayat building, Dharmashalas, Parks etc. may be temporarily used for this purpose, in other words, for free compulsory education, we have to make all efforts.

**Role of Teachers**

For free and compulsory education, it is necessary that only those suitable teachers are appointed who are willing to work in rural areas. These teachers may be of the adjoining areas or local persons. These teachers should be conversant with the local, cultural, religious and social traditions and should be willing to honour the same. They should be fully familiar with language of the area. They should have the capacity to make the school environment healthy, attractive and useful in all respects. Teachers in a school should be of various subjects in order that the teaching of various subjects may be done satisfactorily.

If teachers for primary schools in the rural area are appointed from distant places, due arrangement should be made for their residence near the schools. Then they are likely to be less disturbed. It is estimated that there are about 8 lakhs of teachers for primary schools today, when we actually need more than 35 lakhs of them. This necessity cannot be met by local teachers. Hence we should have to recruit teachers from distant places. For the time being, the Higher Secondary Examination passed persons may be given preliminary training to work as teachers in rural primary schools. In the absence of training facilities, even untrained hands may be appointed as teachers and then they may be given in-service training later.

If the students are too many to be managed in one shift, the school may be run in two shifts. This will not necessitate appointment of additional teachers. The one-teacher school may be permitted at only those places where the students are very few and the number of teachers is inadequate.

**The Syllabi**

The purpose of primary education is to equip children in fundamental processes in order that they may be able to receive profitably further education. With changes in society, the social needs have naturally changed. Hence the curriculum of the primary education should also be modified accordingly. The Basic education curriculum should be implemented at the primary stage. The local needs should be the basis of organising the curriculum on the basic pattern in such a way that students acquire some vocational bent while receiving training in the principles of citizenship and healthy living along with the acquisition of commands over the fundamental process, *i.e.,* reading, writing and arithemtic. The primary schools of the rural area should have a different curriculum from that in the urban, because the needs of the two differ.

**Role of State**

For the development of primary education, the co-operation of the government and of the public is very necessary. Now both the Central and State governments are trying for the expansion of primary education. But success has not yet been achieved in this area because of the defective policy and the lack of necessary co-operation from the government officials made responsible for running the primary education scheme. The public, too does not give much co-operation. If some voluntary organisations extend their helping hands, the government is not able to utilise the extended help. Now there is a need of change in the government policy. The government departments should stop those bad policies which obstruct the growth of primary education. The co-operation of the public should be enlisted and the government officials should invite its co-operation. The inspectors of schools should contact the primary school teachers and the public. They have to guide the teachers and create an awakening in the public for primary education. They should study the local needs and arrange for primary education accordingly.

In the expansion of primary education, the co-operation of the public is very necessary. In fact, the public understands its needs. So it should co-operate with the government by giving financial aids, land and buildings for expansion of primary education. The school should also be made gradually a centre of community work in the context of the needs of the locally concerned.

We have hinted above at some of the major problems of primary education. The expansion and development of primary education depends upon the satisfactory solution of all these problems. For finding out solutions there is a need of research in primary education. This research should be organised in universities, teachers' training colleges and in Government research institutes. The State Governments' should encourage research in primary education in their various relevant education departments. The research scholars in this area should be given stipends for carrying out their research projects successfully.

***Natural Hindrances.*** Inconvenient transport due to unfavourable geographical conditions, such as hills, rivers, deserts and forests.

***Political Difficulties.*** Defective government policies, non-co-operation in the government departments, co-operation from the public not forthcoming. Local bodies not functioning well for primary education.

***Social Difficulties.*** Caste, class, religion and regional differences.

***Financial difficulties.*** Lack of adequate financial aid due to fall in the national income.

***Teaching Methods.*** Unpsychological teaching method. Unattractive environment.

***Wastage and Stagnation.*** Many children leave school due to difficulties. Children due to failure repeat classes.

***No Suitable Teachers in Sufficient Number.*** Teachers not available in adequate number. They behave harshly with children. Many schools are one teacher school. Lack of teachers vitiate the atmosphere of the schools.

***Reform in Primary Education.*** New schools should be established. Good school building, well trained teachers, suitable curriculum suiting the local needs, help from the government and the public.

## QUESTIONS

1. What are the problems of primary education which obstruct the expansion of free and compulsory primary education ?
2. Suggest measures for the reform of primary education. How can the same be implemented ?

# 32

# Initial Education

Formerly pre-primary education in India was almost a concern of the family. The parents used to impart instructions to their children in the rudiments of their mother tongue and general good behaviour. The family is now incapable of shouldering the responsibility. So today all these things are taught to children at the school. Consequently, the responsibility of the school has increased.

Froebel is regarded as the founder of this system of education. He founded a Kindergarten school at Blackenbery in 1837. This was the beginning of pre-primary education.

Formerly, the system of pre-primary education was not so organised as it is today. In the Mahabharata we find the example of Abhimanyu who was taught the art of demolishing the circular fort (*Chakra-Vyuha*) while he was still in mother's womb. But with the advent of modern period, in India, too, the formal pre-primary system began. For the pre-primary education, we have Froebel's Kinergarten system, Nursery system and Montessori system.

### Different Institutions

Froebel's system is called the play-way method in education. In this system, the children of four years of age are admitted. Through various plays, they are taught many things pertaining to good behaviour. Through a psychological method the children are also taught 3 Rs. The first six years of the child's life are so vital that during this period the child is able to develop many such sentiments which become almost permanent with him. Froebel studied child psychology and made it as the basis of education for young children.

### Nursery Level

Mrs. Margret Macmillan founded a Nursery school for physical and mental development of young children. in these schools qualified lady teachers are appointed for giving the necessary protection and guidance to young children. Ordinarily children between two to four years of age are admitted here. The children are provided healthy environment for their development.

The third type of nursery schools are Montessori schools. Maria Montessori started these schools. Children from two to six years of age are educated here. The children get education on their own through didactic materials and toys.

The above types of nursery schools provide good opportunities to young children for their sensory training and education in good conduct and behaviour. The physical and mental development of children is ensured through psychological methods in these schools. The impressions and habits acquired during this period of nursery schools last life-long.

These schools provide medical care, healthy food and healthy environment for good character development. The children acquire many good social traits through plays. Language, art, music, dance and rudimentary mathematics are taught to children in these schools on psychological lines.

**Current Position**

Pre-primary education in India was started by the third decade of the current century. By 1952, there were about 330 nursery schools in the country. By 1957 their number rose to about 800. Now their number is increasing approximately by 150 every year. Nursery schools are getting popular in the public. Hence its expansion is ever on increase. These schools are run on nursery, Montessori and Kindergarten lines. All these schools are individual and voluntary. The government does not give any financial aid to these schools. Therefore, these schools suffer from want of necessary material equipments, good buildings and other facilities. Trained teachers for infant education are also very few in number.

**Evolution and Development**

Now people have begun to realise the importance and utility of pre-primary schools. Sargent Report of 1944 recognised the merits of nursery schools in our country. This encouraged the people to adopt this for young children. Consequently, the government has also become interested in its development.

**Latest Trends**

As a result of some experiments and investigations, pre-primary education has been divided into the following four stages. Formerly, it used to be for children between three to six years of age.

1. From conception to the birth.

2. From birth to 2½ years of age.

3. From 2½ to 4 years of age.

4. From 4 to 6 years of age.

From conception to birth, the baby is influenced by the mental and physical dispositions of the expectant mother. In order to educate the mother in the right direction affecting would be baby in the desired manner, mother welfare centres have been established. In these centres the expectant mothers are given good environment inclusive to healthy impact on the would-be baby.

From birth to 2½ years of age the child learns something under the guidance of the mother. If the mother is of good nature and culture, the child will also be influenced by the same. Afterwards from 2½ to 6 years of age, he may receive education in some pre-primary school. As we have already observed earlier, this type of school provides the necessary environment for healthy development of children on psychological lines. Through plays, they are taught language, music, dance, art, arithmetic and general science along with manners of good behaviour.

## Methods of Teaching

In our country, the pre-primary education is run on western lines. But we should devise new techniques suited to our Indian conditions. So far we have adopted the Kindergarten, Montessori and nursery systems in our pre-primary schools. Now the children should be taught manners and social etiquettes according to our Indian traditions. We shall have to write new stories with Indian themes for our young children. So far our young children are told stories with themes imbued with European cultures. We are not yet free from copying blindly the European methods in this context.

So far we have started some pre-basic schools on the Montessori lines. The Child Education Society of Bhavanagar had done something in this direction. It has adopted a new system of nursery education by drawing the best from the Basic and Montessori systems. Some educationists of Sarvodaya Society have expressed many good ideas about nursery education. The same may be thoughtfully considered and incorporated as far as practical and desirable.

***Pre-primary Education.*** It started from Froebel's Kindergarten method. In India the family played the role of giving nursery education to young children in an informal manner.

***Pre-primary Schools.*** Nursery system, Froebel's Kindergarten and Montessori systems. In Kindergarten children of 4 to 6 years of age, in nursery schools children between 2 to 4 years of age, in Montessori schools children between 2 to 6 years of age. Sensory training and physical, mental and social development of psychological lines. Education through plays. Language, arithmetic, art and music are taught through didactic materials devised on psychological principles.

***Pre-primary Education in India.*** Started by the third decade of current century. By 1952 about 330 schools. By 1957 the number rose to *800.*

***Development Efforts.*** Sargent Report.

***New Experiments.*** Four groups-1. From conception to birth. 2. from birth to 2½, 3. from 2½ to 4 and 4. from 4 to 6. Mixed method.

***Teaching Method.*** Indianisation necessary. Education in Indian etiquette.

## QUESTIONS

1. What is pre-primary education? What are the various types of schools imparting this education?

2. Discuss the position of pre-primary education in India. How should it be Indianised ?

# 33

# Technical Education

Through vocational education one acquires a capacity to earn his living. By having this capacity, he starts production of some kind. Technical education is only a part of vocational education. For technical education, the trainee has to acquire some specific techniques on the basis of which he may convert raw materials into finished products.

### Objectives and Purposes

There are plenty of natural resources in our country. But because of lack of adequate technical education, we yet been not able to explore and exploit them fully. With the development of technical education, we may be able to explore and exploit them to our best advantage. In short, we may mention the following aims of technical education:

1. Technical and vocational education should give to the trainee fundamental scientific knowledge and skill pertaining to the latest technology. With this type of knowledge and skill, we shall be able to equip ourselves

with the latest technology in various areas. This position will add to the growth of our national prosperity.

2. Technical and vocational education should give to the trainee a correlated knowledge of general scientific and special subjects. It must not aim to make him a specialist prematurely.

3. Technical and vocational education should be so planned as to train even the handicapped individuals in the society in order that they may also usefully adjust themselves in society and may also produce something, if they can.

4. Technical and vocational education should be continual. It should be available till one becomes expert in a particular field. It should be available to even those who have entered a vocation since long and want to equip themselves further in their line or in some allied areas.

5. Technical and vocational education should create in the trainee a sense of respect for manual work.

Thus technical and vocational education should be available to all those who need it and it should be of the latest nature, comprehensive and useful to life.

**The Significance**

Good development of any nation depends upon natural resources, physical energies and skilled man power. If there is lack of any of these three fundamental necessities, no nation can progress well. For all these three fundamentals, technical and vocational education is necessary. Evidently, its importance cannot be overemphasised.

Some countries in the world lacking in many natural resources are able to organise good man power on the basis of technical and vocational education. This skilled man power converts the raw materials bought from other countries into finished products and has thus made its country very prosperous. Needless to say that good technical and vocational education may be very helpful in making a country prosperous even when it lacks in natural resources.

India does not lack in natural resources. However, it lacks in facilities for technical and vocational education. We have a huge man power which is not in a position to contribute adequately to the growth of national prosperity in absence of good and comprehensive technical and vocational education. Ours is an agricultural country. Hence comprehensive facilities in agricultural education are necessary for modernising the agricultural occupation. It is true that we have made some provision for technical and vocational education in our country after the achievement of independence, but better facilities are still necessary.

## Growth and Progress

The issue of technical and vocational education has not come before us all of a sudden. It has already been there, since ancient days. With the changes in time, ideas, circumstances and needs of life, its shape has been changing. We may understand the techincal and vocational education in our country in the following two parts:

1. Ancient period and,
2. Modern period.

The development of technical and vocational education of the ancient period may be understood in the following parts:

1. Vedic period.
2. Post-Vedic period.
3. Buddhist period.
4. Muslim period.
5. British period.

***Vedic Period***-Vedas are the oldest literature of the world. We find reference to technical and vocational education in the Rigveda and Atharvaveda. In the Rigveda we find vivid description of construction of canals, bunds and bridges, vehicles incorporating fast speed and beautiful palaces. Aryurveda is a branch of Atharvaveda. Therein we find elaborate discussion of medical science. In the Vedic literature we find ample discussion of manufacture of cotton, silken and woollen clothes, agricultural implements and arms and ammunitions.

***Post Vedic Period***-During this period the technical and vocational education as prevalent in the Vedic age continued. This is the epic (Ramayana and Mahabharat) period. In the Ramayana (*i.e.,* the epic written by Valmiki) we find frequent references of Rama's journey by Pushpak Viman (*i.e.,* Aeroplane) and construction of bridge for going across the sea *i.e.,* to Lanka (Ceylon) for conquering Ravana. In the Mahabharat, we find mention of houses made of wax and houses parts of which appear to be having water and other portions dry. The ruins of Mohanjodaro and Harappa remind us of the technical and vocational skill of that period. Of the period we find description of means of fast transport for going from one place to another. We also find description of various types of weapons and fire-arms used in wars.

***Buddhist Period***-During the Buddhist period the Vedic literature was also studied along with the Buddhist religious scriptures. The vocational study of Ayurveda (science of medicine), Dhanurveda (science of war) and Gandarbhaveda (art of music) developed much during this period. The science of medicine, architecture, painting, sculpture, veterinary and chemistry are some of the chief contrubutions of this period. Inspite of the period being religiously predominat, vocational education was not neglected.

***The Muslim Period***-During this period, the art of making various types of silken, woollen and cotton clothes, wood work, architecture, drawing and ornaments developed remarkably. Imperial palaces, mosques, carpets, utensils and embroidaries of this period have been of world fame vocational education during this period was not organised. The trainees' used to learn the art under the strict personal control and supervision of the artisans concerned.

***The British Period***-After establishment of the British rule in India, the Britishers engaged them sieves in consolidating it. For this purpose, they needed various types of workers. Amongst these they felt the need of technicians in various areas. It was very costly to borrow these expert workers from abroad. So they decided to open some technical and vocational colleges. In 1847 three Engineering Colleges were opened at Calcutta, Madras and Poona. The Wood's Despatch of 1854 emphasised the importance of making Indian education useful to life. By 1902, about 80 technical and vocational schools were established in the country. The credit goes to Lord Curzon for taking keen interest in expansion of technical and vocational education. He established an agriculture department in each province and emphasised the need of establishing agricultural colleges. Agriculture was included as a subject for classes VI to X.

According to the recommendations of the Calcutta University Commission of 1917, technical and vocational subjects were included in the university courses of studies. This Commission recommended the establishment of medical, engineering, law, agriculture and teachers' training colleges. In 1921, Lord Lyton appointed an Education Committee for considering the problem of technical and vocational education. According to recommendations of the Committee, technical institutions were opened at New Delhi, Kanpur, Dhanbad, Banglore and Madras. In 1929, the Hunter Committee recommended for imparting technical and vocational education at the university stage. In 1937 Mahatma Gandhi advocated the Basic Education scheme with a view to vocationalise education. At the primary stage some work was started in this direction according to the Basic Education plan. Abbot-Wood Committee of 1937 recommended for technical and vocational education but the outbreak of the World War II in 1939 put a stop to the scheme. In 1945 it was decided to open at least four technical college in four regions—east, west, south and north- of the country. In 1946, the All India Council of Technical Education was established for furthering the cause of technical education in the country.

**In Free India**

After independence our leaders began to pay more attention to the need of technical education in the country. In 1947 the Government of India established the Scientifc Man Power Committee for estimating the training needs in the various technical spheres. After independence, the following three commissions on education were appointed in the country:

1. University Commission (1948-49).
2. Secondary Education Commission (1952-53).
3. The Kothari Commission (1964-66).

Each of these commissions made a study of the problem of technical education in the country and made certain suggestions for the same. We are hinting at some of the more important recommendations with regard to technical education as offered by these three commissions.

**Various Commissions**

This Commission under the chairmanship of Dr. Radhay Krishnan gave the following suggestions for promotion of technical and vocational education in the country:

1. Agriculture should he taught at each level of education.
2. The engineering students should be given practical training at the concerned industrial centres.
3. Provision for higher education and research should be made in the field of engineering.

4. Rural Universities should be established in rural areas.
5. Necessary changes should be introduced in the technical and engineering courses according to the needs of the country.

This commission gave the following suggestions for the improvement of technical and vocational education:

1. The current secondary schools should be converted into multipurpose schools.
2. A close relationship should be established between the industries and technical schools.
3. Various types of technical and vocational courses should be taught.

***Kothari Commission***-This commission gave the following suggestions for reform of technical and vocational education in the country :

1. We need four times more technicians than engineers. So more technical schools (I. T. Is) and polytechnical institutes should be opened.
2. The trainees should get sandwich curriculum. They should also be given practical experience at relevant industries.
3. Brilliant B. Sc. graduates should be given training in electronics.
4. Chemical, aeronautics and technology should be taught upto a high standard.
5. Education should be production oriented. The technical students should get workshop experiences.
6. Refresher courses in-service training, summer courses and comprehensive colleges should be organised for reforms in teacher education.

**The Remedies**

Below we are hinting at some of the main problems of technical and vocational education along with their solutions:

***The Problem of Qualitative Improvement.*** Education should be both quantitative and qualitative. It is true that we have made quantitative improvement in bur technical and vocational education, but we have not yet paid adequate attention to its qualitative side. Consequently, many of our technical and vocational institutions are being run in a very bad condition. There are no good workshops, laboratories libraries and buildings. Well trained teachers are also very few.

*Solution*-The technical and vocational institutions which do not fulfil the minimum conditions should be closed. Those which are well managed and organised should be given adequate financial assistance for organising good workshops, laboratories and libraries. These good institutions should have close relationship with the relevant local industries. At these industries the trainees should be sent to obtain some practical experience.

***The Problem of Creating Favourable Attitude Toward Manual Work.*** In our country, the person engaged in manual work is looked down. Therefore, a labourer does not enjoy that respect in our society which a teacher, advocates or doctor does. Because of this situation, our trainees in technical and vocational institutions do not like to engage themselves in those operations which require manual work. As a result, they do not get adequate practical experience and our technical and vocational institutions are not producing good skilled workers. Unless this situation is changed, no reform in technical and vocational education will yield the expected result.

*Solution*-Opportunities should be given to students and teachers in schools, colleges and universities for doing various types of creative manual work. Workshops should be very well organised in order to give enough practical experience to each trainee. More time should be all owed in the time-table for practical work. The practical work assigned to a trainee should be corresponding to his capacity and interest.

***The Problem of Defective Curriculum.*** The following defects are found in he curriculum meant for technical and vocational institutions:

1. The curriculum does not fulfill the local needs, *e.g.*, in the agricultural predominant area agriculture is not given a prominent place in the curriculum.

2. There is a lack of productivity in the curriculum.

3. The curriculum does not develop in the student a love for manual work.

4. The curriculum lacks in variety. It does not have many purposes which should be a special feature of a technical institution.

*Solution*-It should be estimated as to how many teachers and guides have to be appointed for a particular stage of technical and vocational education. It is on the basis of this estimate that arrangement for the equipment should be made. The teachers and guides should be given attractive salaries and other facilities. The four regional committees established in the country should take the responsibility of doing the needful in this matter.

***The Problem of Medium in the Technical and Vocational Education.*** The mother-tongue has been accepted as the medium of instruction in the country upto the secondary stage. After passing this stage, when the student takes admission in some technical institution, he is given the training through English, because good books are not available on the subject in his mother tongue. This creates a great difficulty for the trainee. Consequently, many capable students are left behind. He has to devote much time to the study of English at the neglect of the technical subjects.

*Solution*-In the technical and vocational institutions the regional languages should be accepted as the medium of instruction. The trainee should not be compelled to acquire proficiency in English, unless he himself insists for the same. For making regional languages is the medium of instruction, it is necessary to produce standard books in regional languages in the various areas of technical and vocational education. The teachers and guides for technical and vocational institutions should be so trained that they may be able to impart the training through the medium of the regional languages concerned.

***The Problem of Administration and Control.*** The Education Ministry of Government of India is not responsible for technical and vocational education in the States of the Union. Various separate departments of the State concerned look after this type of education. At some places two departments together carry the responsibility for this education. At certain places labour department, industry, or agriculture department is made responsible for this education. At some other place a university is entrusted with its responsibility. This situation has created the problem of administration and control.

*Solution*-Many problems of technical and vocational education will be automatically solved by solving the problem of its administration and control. The Education Ministry of the Government of India should take up the responsibility of technical and vocational education in the same way as it looks after general education. A council of technical and vocational education may also be organised for looking after the various implied issues. Suitable persons from various relevant departments may be requested to serve on this council. The setting up of such a council should be done both at the Central and State levels. This will bring in a uniformity in administration and control of technical and vocational education.

***The Problem Relating to Research.*** In the various five year plans the Government of India has emphasised the problem of research in technical and vocational education but we have not yet become self-dependent in this respect and we have still to copy the Western pattern. It is true that there is no harm in adopting certain process and research styles, but the same should be according to our needs in the country. The foreign styles cannot meet our Indian needs. We have not yet succeeded in making such researches on the basis of which we may profitably use our full man power. We are still manufacturing such machines which may be used as substitutes for man power. Consequently, a major portion of our man power lies idle and unemployed. In many European countries and in the United States of America there is a lack of adequate man-power because of the population being thinner. So in place of man power, they use machines as substitutes. But our Indian condition is entirely different from the condition prevailing in the above foreign lands.

*Solution*-The research work in the field of technical and vocational education should be carried out according to the needs and conditions in the country. We should make such technical researches with the help of which we may employ our man power to the maximum extent. For this the Government should set up various types of experimental laboratories and research centres. The researchers should be given handsome stipends in order that capable persons may be attracted towards the same.

***The Problem of Post Technical Education and Training.*** This problem has not yet been attended to in our country. After getting the training, if the trainee remains unemployed for some time, he forgets all that he has learned in the technical field concerned. And those who are lucky enough to get some employment continue working for years according to the old method that they learnt several years ago. They hardly get any chance for acquainting themselves with the latest devices and techniques. Needless to add that they forget also the theoretical aspect of the training that they obtained. In foreign countries an attempt is made to familiarise the old workers with the latest researches, techniques and inventions in their relevant areas. This develops their skill and accelerates the rate of production as well.

*Solution*-The problem of post-education and training may be solved through any of the following measures:

1. Correspondence courses.
2. Part-time training.
3. Close contact with the technical institutions and industries.
4. Short term courses.
5. Refresher courses.

The correspondence courses may be organised for those workers who need enough orientation in latest theoretical principles. For in-service workers, this is a good device. They already continue their workshop practice. So for 15 or 20 days they may be invited at a certain centre for reorientation.

The part-time courses develop the theoretical knowledge and skill of the in-service workers. But the pan-time courses may be possible only at some technical institution. Morning or evening classes may be arranged for this purpose.

According to the recommendations of the Kothari Commission (1964-66) the training for in-service may be arranged by establishing a close, relationship between the technical institution and the concerned industries. This arrangement is likely to benefit both the in-service-workers and the trainees.

In short term courses the in-service workers are invited to attend certain courses for two or three weeks at some technical institution. This programme may be conveniently arranged during the holidays of some relevant industries.

Through refresher courses also the in-service workers may be trained in latest techniques and devices. This may be arranged at some technical education centre.

***The Problems of Modernisation of Technology.*** The current progress has modernised the technology in U.S.S.R. and many western countries. We in India are blindly following their method. This situation has created the following problems:

1. By modernisation we have begun to understand Westernisation. As a result, our Indian needs are not met. Our needs are different from the Western ones. So we have to modernise the technology according to our Indian needs. No one is giving attention to this pressing needs.

2. The technology dependent upon the invested capital in creating a misunderstanding between the labourers and the owner. So a gap is being created between the two. The one is the exploiter and the other is the exploited.

3. Under the influence of modernisation we forget our Indian social values and circumstances. This has an adverse impact on the society.

*Solution*-No doubt, we should modernise our technologies, but we have to Indianise them as well according to our own condition and needs. We have to modernise the technologies in such way as to obtain the maximum production by using the minimum man power, capital and raw materials. In this process the man power should be properly utilised and the maximum number of people should get employment. The strata of rich and poor, owner and labourer and the exploiter and the exploited should be eliminated. We have to modernise our technologies through such eliminations.

***The Problem of Co-ordination Between Training Facilities and Job Opportunities.*** Through our Five Year Plans we have developed opportunities for technical and vocational education. But the development of these opportunities has created the problem of unemployment of technical hands. The statistics indicate that by 1982 there were about for lac teachers, engineers, scientists and medical doctors unemployed. At the same time, we have also faced the situation that in some technical areas there were no trained hands. This situation was particularly perceptible in the State of Maharashtra.

*Solution*-For obtaining a balance and co-ordination between the technical facilities and job opportunities we should make an estimate of the man-power needed for the various areas. According to this estimate, we should give technical and vocational education to a few selected persons. The technical and vocational institutions should be closely related to the relevant industries, because it is in these industries that the trained hands are to be employed. This programme should be prepared by the various States according to their own specific needs.

***The Meaning of Technical and Vocational Education.*** Technical and vocational education is that education which enables one to earn his living.

***Aims.*** 1. To give scientific education in the latest technologies. 2. To effect a co-ordination and harmony between general, specific and scientific knowledge. 3. To give relevant vocational education even to the handicapped. 4. To make the training continual. 5. To create respect for manual labour.

***The Importance.*** Technical education necessary for exploitation of natural resources. Development of poor country possible through this education. It is a means of developing skilled man-power.

***The Development of Technical and Vocational Education in India.*** 1. Vedic Period, 2. Bauddha Period, 3. Muslim Period.

***Modern Period***-The development under the British Rule. The development after independence. 1. University Education Commission (1948-49); 2. Secondary Education Commission (1952-53); 3. Kothari Commission (1964-65)

***The Problem of Technical and Vocational Education.*** 1. The problem of qualitative improvement. 2. The problem of creating the right attitude for manual work. 3. The problem of improving the technical and vocational education curriculum. 4. The problem of establishing a co-ordination with the industries. 5. The problem of lack of teachers and guides. 6. The problem of medium of technical education. 7. The problem of administration and control. 8. The problem of research. 9. The problem of post-education and training. 10. The problem of modernisation of technologies. 11. The problem of co-ordination between training facilities and job opportunities.

## QUESTIONS

1. Give a brief critical account of development of technical and vocational education in India.
2. Describe the development of technical and vocational education in India after independence.